Research Methods in Education

Published by
Saurabh Publishing House

RESEARCH METHODS IN EDUCATION

A.K. Ahuja

Publishing House
4735/22, Prakash Deep Building,
Ansari Road, Daryaganj,
New Delhi-110002

Published by :
SAURABH PUBLISHING HOUSE

Distributed by :
LOTUS PRESS PUBLISHERS & DISTRIBUTORS
Unit No. 220, Second Floor, 4735/22, Prakash Deep Building,
Ansari Road, Daryaganj, New Delhi - 110002
Ph : 011-23280047, 32903912, 098118-38000
E-mail : lotus_press@sify.com

Saurabh Publishing is an imprint of
Lotus Press Publishers & Distributors

Research Methods in Education

ISBN : 978-93-83045-00-6 (H/B)

Printed at : Bharat Offset Works, Delhi

Preface

Educational research, as it is known today, is a relatively new branch of knowledge. In the educational world, it is only the last sixty years or so that are characterized by increasing readiness to apply methods of research to the solution of educational problems. The rise of democracy and a continuous expansion of education in various countries have been invariably accompanied by more and more research in education. Great Britain and the United States of America can very safely be termed as pioneer countries in educational research, where the beginnings of the research in education can be traced back to much further than the beginnings of the present century. Impelled by their own educational needs and problems and inspired by the pioneer Western countries, almost all countries of the world are engaged in some sort of education of research or the other by this time.

Everywhere educational research has passed through several stages in its manner of solving educational problems. The earliest efforts aimed at improvement in the field of education may be labelled as the *personal experience method,* whereby changes of some kind were introduced in educational practices as a result of the experience of certain experienced educators. This was generally followed by what may be called the *deliberative approach* consisting in a discussion of problems leading towards committee action, which system continues even during the present time. The era of *objective measurement* and *Systematic Research in Education,* destined to revolutionize appraisal and research techniques the world over, is the latest: Stage.

This book deals with the topics of—*Educational Research and Nature; Educational Research in India; Relevance of Research Sampling; Problems of Educational Research; Research Methods; Hypothesis; Sampling; Normative Survey Method; Experimental Method; Historical and Schedule Method; Research Design; Data Collection Processing and Presentation; Data Analysis of Central Tendency; Chi-Square Test;* etc.

I hope that students and those in the education field will find it useful for academic and competitive examinations. I owe a deep sense of gratitude to my publisher for materializing my present endeavour.

A.K. Ahuja

Contents

1

Educational Research and Nature

The term 'research' and 'scientific method of inquiry' are used as synonymous in educational discussions, but there are minute differences in both. Research is considered to be more formal, systematic and intensive process of carrying on the scientific method of analysis while it is possible to employ the scientific spirit without research but opposite to it is not possible. Research is a more specialized phase of scientific methòdology in which researcher wants to fill up the gaps left in a system, to discover new facts, establish new theories, generalizations and laws. Research is systematic, logical, objective and endeavours to organise data in quantitative terms. It is carefully recorded and reported. In research every term is carefully defined, all procedures are described in detail, all limiting-factors are recognised, all references are carefully documented and all results are objectively recorded. All conclusions and generalisations are cautiously arrived at, with due consideration.

Education

Education is a discipline based upon scientific research. In the study of education, a student has to be familiar with the allied fields of psychology, sociology, anthropology, history and philosophy. As a matter of fact all the social sciences are to be found in an integrated form in the field of education. In educational research therefore, the general methodology is that of social sciences.

As stated earlier, educational research is mainly scientific in nature though there are other types of educational research. These types care related to the nature of problems under investigation. *For example,* if a problem is of philosophical study. Nonetheless in research one has to be objective and scientific so that the findings are reliable and applicable to a representative areas.

NATURE OF EDUCATIONAL RESEARCH

There is a lot of confusion as regards the nature of educational research, for different researches have different approaches. This is due perhaps to the relationship of educational with social and biological sciences and other related fields.

According to Brar, "The term educational research means different things to different people. This is what one might aspect, however, in an area like education which finds its foundations distributed so generally among various fields such as history, philosophy, mathematics, sociology, psychology and the biological sciences. The diversity of meanings attached to the term educational research may also be inferred from the diversity of methods, materials and processes employed in research."

Thus, it is apparent that the nature of educational research depends upon the nature of the problem being studied and also the methodology being used. In education we have historical, philosophical, experimental, normative-survey, comparative, diagnostic and other types of researches. These types of researches in educationals provide great variety in the nature of educational research.

But the main thing is the common concern expressed by these researches, which is the education of man. Education is meant for the child so that he develops into a healthy and useful adult. Educational research is devoted to discovering new insights and understandings so that educational problems are solved satisfactorily.

According to Watts, an educational research worker has to be fully trained in theoretical and experimental psychology and then he should endeavour to do the following three things:

(a) He will aim at providing us with outline charts of formula development in various directions in the intellectual, social and aesthetic spheres by specifying the natural stages of growth particular to each and the order in which these must pass through if mental development is to be vigorous and healthy.

(b) He will help us to discover methods of learning and of teaching which are most likely to be effective for given purposes.

(c) "He will succeed in working out reliable standards of achievement in the acquisition of various forms of skill, so that we may be able to gauge with some approach to accuracy by how much the performance of any child in any direction exceeds or falls short of the average."

As is evident from the above, these aims are mainly from the mental development point of view. Watts has been concerned with the study of language of mental development of the children. Therefore, he has studied these aims from the mental development angle.

STRUCTURE OF EDUCATIONAL RESEARCH

The structure of educational research has a number of important components. One of them is the problem to be investigated. It has been observed that without a clear conception of the problem to be investigated, research is shoddy. In order to determine the nature of the problem to be studied, it is desirable to discover the difficulties felt by educational workers in that area. It has to be noted that a worthwhile and useful research is not concerned with personal problems but with such problems as are widely felt by a large number of people.

Thus, to start with, one must familiarize himself with the difficulties being faced by teachers and others in the area of education. When a particular difficulty has been spotted, the next thing is to formulate the problem in clear and concise language. Sometimes some researchers use vague words and it becomes extremely difficult to understand the exact nature of the problem being investigated. Thus, the problem has to be formulated in clear and concrete terms.

The first step in the research process is the choice of a suitable problem for research. This is a difficult but an important phase of the entire research process. Problem awareness is not ordinarily a characteristic of the beginner. Even the more experienced researcher approaches this step with considerable care. The researcher has to spend a great deal of time, energy and money at the stage of problem selection. He finds the task of identifying and selecting the problem a difficult one due to his limited knowledge of the research process and unpreparedness for identifying the problem. He may also be unfamiliar with the fields to follow for selecting a suitable field for research.

For selecting a problem for research, it is first necessary for a researcher to choose a broad field within which he will conduct the study. A thorough understanding of the known facts and ideas in the field in which he is interested constitutes the important step in the problem selection. The researcher should be familiar with his field and should know what studies have already been conducted in it. He should also know about the problems which have remained untackled. A survey of suggestions for further research given at the end of research reports and reviews of research is helpful to the researcher. Periodicals and annual bibliographies which appear in most fields of educational research are helpful in keeping the researcher informed about the developments in the field in which he is interested and wished to develop competence.

After selecting the broad field the researcher identifies and selects the specific problem. For this he must state the specific questions whose answer he seeks through the application of scientific method. There are some important sources which are helpful to the researcher for selecting a problem.

(A) The researcher should take advantage of the knowledge which has accumulated in the past in the field he has chosen for selecting his problem. The review of this knowledge will acquaint him with the current knowledge in the field of his study. It will help the researcher to avoid unfruitful and useless problems. He can also know about the recommendations of previous researchers for further research, which they have listed in their studies. The researcher can avoid unintentional duplication of well established findings.

The first step in reviewing the literature is concerned with the identification of the material in the library. It can be made through the use of primary and secondary sources available in the library. However, the use of such sources is time consuming in comparison to secondary sources. The decision concerning the use of primary or secondary sources depends largely on the nature of the research study proposed by the researcher.

To locate the source materials, a researcher should be familiar with the library and its many facilities and services. He should also be acquainted with the regulations governing the use and circulation of materials: Many libraries use a printed guide that contains helpful information. Before using a library, the researcher should learn how to use the microfilm readers, photocopies and other mechanical aids. He should schedule his work session in the library it such a manner so that he will encounter least competition for resources and services. Before initiating search for materials in a library, the researcher should write down questions that pinpoint precisely what information he wishes to locate and group the questions in accordance with the areas in the library where the answers may be found. He should keep a list of the best reference books, indexes, handbooks and other materiels in his field of study:

(1) Reference Books

1. Albert J. Walford Guide to Reference Material.
2. Arvid Burke and Mory Burdey, Documentation in Education.
3. Constance M.Winchelled, A Guide to Reference Book. 8th ed. Chicago: American Library Association, 1967
4. Mar N. Borton and Marion V. Bell (1962) Reference Books: A Brief Guide for Students.
5. International Guide to Educational Documentation (1955—1960) UNESCO, 1963.
6. The Standard Periodical Directory, New York: Oxbridge Publishing Co. 1964, date.
7. Christinc L. Wyner Guide to Reference Books for School Media Centres.
8. Encyclopedias.
   (i) Encyclopedia of Modem Education, Henry D. Revlin and H. Schueller, eds [New York: Philosophical Library (1943)].
   (ii) Encyclopedia of Educational Research, Water Scott Monroe. ed. rev. ed. (New York: Macmillan, 1950).
   (iii) Encyclopedia of Educational Research, Chester Harris, ed. 3rd ed. (New York: Macmillan, 1960).
   (iv) Encyclopedia of Education Research, Robert L. Ebel, Ed., 4th ed. (New York: Macmillan, 1969).
9. Dictionaries:
   (i) Dictionary of Education (New York: MacGraw Hill Book Co., 1973).

(*ii*) Dictionary of Sociology (Totowa, N.J. Little field, Adams and Co.).

(*iii*) Comprehensive Dictionary of Psychological and Psycho-analytical Terms (New York: David Mickay Company).

10. Year-books and Handbooks.

(*i*) The Handbook of Research on Teaching, N.L. Gage, ed. (Chicago: Rand McNally. Handbook of Education).

Arthur W. Foshay, Ed. (Chicago: Rand McNally and Co., 1963).

(*ii*) Mental Measurements Year Book (Highland Park, New Jersey: Gryphon Press, 1938 date).

(*iii*) Education Yearbook (New York: Macmillan Co., 1972 date).

11. Directories and Bibliographies.

(*i*) Guide to American Directories.

(*ii*) The Education Directory (Washington: U.S. Office of Education, 1912 date).

(*iii*) Education Index. *Index* (New York: H.W. Wilson Co. 1929, date).

(*iv*) Bibliography of Doctorate—Thesis in Science and Arts accepted by the Indian Universities for 1946–48 and 1948–50, published by Inter University Board of India.

(*v*) Kelle.Thoms, ed. Select Bibliographies of Adult Education in Great Britain. London, National Institute of Education, (1952).

(*vi*) Index to Select British Educational Periodicals (Leeds: Librarians of Institutes of Education, 1954, date).

(*vii*) British Education Index (August, 1954 to November, 1958).

(viii) Directory of Exceptional Children (perter Sargent Publishing Co., 1962 date).

(ix) Mental Health Directory (Washington: National Institute of Mental Health, 1964 date).

(x) Canadian Education Index. *Index* (Ottawa, Ontario: Canadian Council for Educational Research, stet 1965 date).

(ix) Educator's World (Englewood Cliffs: Fosjer Publishing Co. 1972-date).

12. Research Periodicals and Journals.

Information about new ideas and development often appear in periodicals long before it appears in books. There are periodicals and journals in education and other related fields that are the best source for reports on recent research studies. These provide much more upto-date treatment to current questions in education. They also publish articles of temporary, local or limited interest that never appear in book form.

13. Abstracts.

Abstracts include brief summaries of the contents of the research study or article.

(i) *Psychological Abstracts:* It is published by the American Psychological Association since.

(ii) *Education Abstracts:* It is a publication of UNESCO and is being published since 1949.

14. Thesis and Dissertation:

Thesis and dissertations also provide research material to researcher. Some countries publish annually the list of all thesis and dissertations submitted to their universities.

(i) Dissertation Abstracts International.

(ii) Buch, (M.B.) Ed., A Survey of Research in Education. (Baroda: Centre of Advanced Studies in Education, 1973).

(iii) Buch, (M.B.) ed. Section on Survey of Research in Education (1972–78). (Baroda: Society for Educational Research and Development, 1979).

15. Newspapers, pamphlets, government documents and monographs also publish research articles of particular interest to a researcher. These also include statistical data research studies, official' reports, laws and other materials that are not available elsewhere.

(B) Many of the problems confronted in the classroom or the school lend themselves to investigation. In the classroom there is a dynamic interaction between teacher and pupil, between pupil and pupil and between pupil and materials. This interaction provides a rich source of problems to be solved through action research. The teacher may be confronted with a number of behavioural problems in the classroom or school. He may seek answers to a number of questions. What organizational or management procedures are employed? How is learning material presented? To what extent does one method yield more effective results than another? How do teachers feel about these procedures? How do pupils and parents feel about them? What out of school activities and influences seem to affect students and the teaching learning process? Best is of the opinion that, "Teacher' will discover 'acres of diamonds' in their own backards and an inquisitive and imaginative mind may discover in one of these problem areas an interesting worthwhile research project'"

(C) Another source of research problem lies in the inferences that can be drawn from various educational and psychological theories known to the researcher. The application of, general principles involved in various theories to specific classroom situations suggest important problems for research.

(D) Contacts and discussions with research oriented people, attending conferences, seminars and listening to the learned speakers are helpful in locating research problems. Active membership in organizations, which are concerned. With the improvement of educational system, usually brings one into close contact with crucial problems and issues concerning education.

(E) Technological and social changes constantly bring forth new problems and new opportunities for research. The use of hardware and software in classroom instruction, the training of teachers in the methodology of teaching through 'team teaching', 'micro-teaching' etc., are being advocated by the educationists all over the country. All such innovations need to be carefully evaluated through research process.

(F) Replication or extension of completed research studies is also a profitable and worthwhile activity for a beginning researcher. Repeating a study at different times on different groups and in different places, increases the extent to which the research finding can be generalized and provides additional evidence of the validity of the findings.

Definition of the Problem

The next task after the selection of the problem area is to define it in a form amenable to research. According to Whitney (1920), 'To define a problem means to put a fence round it, to separate it by careful distinctions from like questions found in related situations on need.'

While defining the problems the researcher must adhere to the following rules:

1. He should be sure that the topic chosen is neither too vague nor too broad in scope.
2. He should make the problem clearer and more understandable.
3. He should state it in a question form which requires a definite answer.

4. He should identify the variables involved in the problem *viz.*, independent, dependent, moderator, control and intervening variables.
5. He should carefully state the limits of the problem, eliminating all aspects and factors which will not be considered in the study.
6. He should define any special terms in describing the variables indicated in the statement of the problem.

Statement of the Problem

The scope of the problem is limited here only to the extent that the statement of the problem does not become unwieldy. Sometimes the beginners try to delimit the topic completely. The statement should neither leave the scope of the problem altogether vague nor try to delight it completely at this stage only. The language of the statement should be straight forward and may omit some of the articles (a, an, the). A good statement of problem must clarify exactly what is to be determined or solved. It must restrict the scope of the study 10 the specific research question. The most important step in this direction is to specify the variables in the questions and define them in operational terms.

To illustrate, a researcher states that he is interested in studying the differences in creativity of boys and girls in relation to intelligence. This statement is broad and it communicates in a general way what the researcher wants to do. However, he can state the problem more specifically as follows:

"Sex differences in creativity at different levels of intelligence."

Operational Definition of Terms

Here, the terms used in the topic are defined by specifying what they will mean in the investigation. In the above problem, *for example*:

(a) ***Set Differences.*** May mean the difference between boys and girls of age level 12-13 years, studying in schools of Himachal Pradesh.

(b) ***Creativity.*** As measured in its different aspects of fluency, flexibility, originality and elaboration by Torrance Test of Creativeity.

(c) ***Different Levels of Intelligence.*** Three levels high (above 115 I.Q.) middle (between 90-115 I.Q.) and low (below 90 I.Q.) as measured by Raven's Progressive Matrices.

Some researchers make a distinction between' definition' and 'delimitation' by restricting the use of latter only to the defineation of the geographical boundary of the population. *For example,* in the above problem after giving the operational definition of the terms, it will be mentioned under a separate head 'Definitation' that the study will be restricted to Himachal Pradesh instead of being mentioned with "Sex difference."

Evaluation of the Problem

Before undertaking a problem for research, the researcher is to be answered before the study is undertaken. Best has mentioned the list of these questions as under:

1. Is this the type of problem that can be effectively solved through the process of research? Can relevant data be gathered to test the theory or find the answer to the problem under consideration?
2. Is the problem a new one? Is the answer already available?
3. Is the problem significant? Is an important principle involved? Would the solution make any difference as far as educational theory or practice is concerned?
4. Is research on the problem feasible? After a research problem 'has been evaluated, there remains the problem of suitability for a particular researcher.

Some of the questions that should be raised are the following:

(*a*) Am I competent to plan and carry out a study of this type? Do I know enough about this field to understand its significant aspects and to interpret my findings? Am I skilful enough to develop, administer, an? interpret the necessary data gathering devices and procedures? Am I well grounded in the necessary knowledge of research, design and statistical procedures?

(*b*) Will I have the necessary financial resources to carry on this study in What will be the expense involved in data gathering, equipment, printing, test materials, travel and clerical help. If the project is an expensive one, what is the' possibility of getting a grant from the agencies like NCERT, UGC, Ministry of Education and Social Welfare, ICSR and other organizations.

(*c*) Are pertinent data accessible? Are valid and reliable data-gathering devices and procedures available? Will school authorities permit me to contact the students, conduct necessary experiments or administer necessary tests, interview teachers, or have process to important cumulative records? Will I be able to get the sponsorship necessary to open the door that otherwise would be closed to me?

(*d*) Will I have enough time to complete the project? Will there be time to devise the procedures, select data gathering devices, collect and analyse the data and complete the research report?

(*e*) Will I have the courage and determination to pursue the study inspite of the difficulties and social hazards that may be involved? Will I be willing to work aggressively when data are difficult to gather and when others are reluctant to co-operate?

From the foregoing questions it is evident that the problems which involve some value questions cannot be answered by scientific investigations. Research cannot provide answer to ethical questions. A researchable problem is always concerned with the relationship existing between two or more variables that can be defined or measured. There is no purpose in studying a problem which has already been adequately investigated by other researchers. However, this does not mean that a problem which has been investigated in the past is no longer worthy of research. A researcher may repeat a study when he wants to verify its conclusions or to extend the validity of its findings in a situation entirely different from the previous one. The researcher should know that the problem which he has undertaken is likely to fill in the existing knowledge, to help resolve some of the inconsistencies in previous research, or to help in the reinterpretation of the known facts. In short, his findings should become the basis for theory and formulation of principles and should lead to new problems for further research. The research competencies of the researcher, his financial resources, the time at his disposal and administrative considerations are important criteria to determine the feasibility of research problem.

METHODS OF EDUCATIONAL RESEARCH

Methods of educational research can be classified on the basis of fields of research, purpose, place, application, tools of research, nature of the data, etc. Generally the historical method, the normative-survey method, the experimental method, the correlation method, the case study method and the genetic method are used in educational research.

Research is an intellectual activity which focuses on establishing new knowledge and discovering new truths concerning the basis of a certain event or events with the purpose of furthering or verifying the existing knowledge in order to enable the researcher to understand, predict, or control the events of the world. Knowledge gained by research is of the highest order. If is not merely a knowledge of facts, but of underlying principles that explain the how and why of the facts and events. Besides that, Research has two other characteristics. *First,* its results are verifiable, that is, the conclusions arrived at by one person can be verified by another and this is possible only when the collection of the data is objective and methods of analysis and interpretation of the results are overtly stated and repeatable. *Second,* Research follows what is called the 'Scientific method or procedure', which is akin to what Dewey calls the 'thinking process' and which according to him has the following steps:

1. Felt Difficulty. Research starts with a felt need. The difficultly may be of overcoming an impediment in the way or of understanding a phenomeon, for which a thorough enquiry is needed. These felt difficulties are called 'Research Problems.'

2. Formulation of Hypothesis. On the basis of previous studies or experiences the researcher guesses a solution and states it. This tentative solution is called the' 'hypothesis' and is arrived at by an 'inductive' process, that is, on the basis of a number of instances.

3. Identification and Definition of the Problem. The problem is clearly and definitely grasped and put in unambiguous terms and within well defined operational limits.

4. Generalization. The hypothesis is stated as a general principle when it holds good.

5. Evidence of Hypothesis. By 'deductive' reasoning the consequences that should follow if the hypothesis is true are thought of and then such data are collected that might corroborate or refute these consequences and thus, uphold or refute the hypothesis.

6. Testing of Hypothesis. The data collected are analysed and critically examined to decide whether the hypothesis holds good or not.

It may be pointed out that the above sequence is only theoretical: In actual practice all the steps or more than one may go together or the researcher may have to go back many a time. Moreover, if during the collection of the data another hypothesis appear to the merit it may be developed in place of the original one. In case one hypothesis fails on testing, it may be modified or another one may be thought of afresh and tested. Truly speaking, the main characteristic feature of the scientific method is the inductive-deductive sequence. In ultimate analysis research is systematically arrived at answer to meaningful questions.

Educational Research

Educational research also follows the same scientific method of investigation, but its scope is restricted to educational issues. The goal of educational research is to discover laws or generalizations concerning educational issues in order to make predictions and control of educational events and improve the quality of teaching and learning.

Need of Educational Research

The need for educational research may be seen from the following angles:

1. Education has two aspects :
   - *(a)* The, corpus of theory or knowledge, which provides the basis for.
   - *(b)* The conduct and improvement of the skill or art of instruction.

   The former may be called the 'science' and the latter the 'art' of education. As a science, education has a corpus of knowledge concerning the nature of individuals and their growth and development, the laws of learning, educational policies and planning theories of administration, etc. As an art, it seeks to impart knowledge effectively. Through careful research effort is made to enhance teacher effectiveness, extend the frontiers of educational knowledge and improve the instructional skills.

2. The implementation of new policies and practices which can be achieved through research need careful empirical testing.
3. Besides the general theories and practices of education, the effect of different environmental settings on students of different age, sex, intelligence, socio-economic and other groups have to be investigated.
4. The corpus of knowledge in the different subjects taught in our schools and colleges is increasing at a rapid pace and new methods will have to be evolved by researchers to impart this new knowledge as needed.
5. Participation in research, whatever level it may be, keeps the mind of the teacher alert and fresh and gives him an objective outlook. It prevents the teacher from becoming stale and subjective.
6. Education is a means to achieve certain goals through purposely organized programmes. Since objectives need revision, time and again, due to changing socio-economic and political conditions, there is always a need to modify educational theories and practices which would need active research.

Levels of Educational Research

Research is conducted at different levels for different purposes. Broadly speaking we may distinguish the following three levels of research in education:

1. Pure/Basic/Fundamental/Complete Research. The purpose of this type of research is to add to the theory of education. In its conduct, sophisticated procedures, tools and techniques are employed and greater controls are exercised and the generalizations arrived at have a wide application. It is concerned with the formulation of a theory and is not hampered by considerations of immediate utility.

2. Action Research. Action research is undertaken to solve an immediate practical problem. The goal of research in terms of adding to scientific knowledge by arriving at sound generalizations, takes a back seat. This research places importance on a specific problem which is present here and now. As its methodology is not as rigorous as that of pure research, the person facing the problem, that is, the teacher or the administrator can undertake it himself.

3. Applied Research. In this type of research the knowledge produced, the concepts discovered, the theory constructed and the law established are put to application in specific educational situations. The researcher in such a frame of reference works out the strategy for applying the already discovered facts, principles and truths. In educational research there is considerable scope for pursuing applications of scientific methods. This type of research is concrete by its very nature and requires understanding of the practical situation encountered by the practitioner.

The steps of Action Research are:

(a) Statement of the problem.

(b) Enlisting the probable causes of the situation to be set right.

(c) Chalking out the remedial measures.

(d) Implementing the measures.

(e) Evaluating the outcome.

Since the purpose of action-research is limited to the solution of the immediate problem at hand and no sophisticated technique is needed for conducting it, we can see the following features which distinguish this type of research from fundamental and applied research:

1. It does not need a trained and specialized researcher. The practitioner in the field becomes the researcher?
2. No sampling is needed, since it has to do with all the people concerned who form the limited and accessible population.
3. A knowledge of 'descriptive statistics' is enough. As no inferences have to be drawn about the population from the study of a sample, the 'inferential' Statistics do not come in.
4. No special tools for collection of data are needed as the efficacy of the remedial measures taken has to be assessed with the same instruments that had recorded the deficiencies.

Some people distinguish between Action and Applied research, *i.e.,* as much as the former has relevance only to view restricted situations like the classroom, while the latter probes into practical problems of greater complexity and wider applicability.

❋❋❋

2

Educational Research in India

Educational research is a relatively new branch of knowledge. Only the last fifty years or so are characterized by increasing readiness to apply methods of research to the solution of educational problems. Establishment of democracy and continuous expansion of education in various countries have been accompanied by more and more research in education. The pioneer countries in educational research are Great Britain and the United States of America. Here, the beginnings of research in education may be traced back to much further than the beginnings of the present century. Inspired by the pioneer Western countries, almost all countries of the world are engaged in some sort of educational research or the other by this time to ameliorate their own educational needs and problems.

Stages of Educational Research

Educational research has everywhere passed through several stages in order to solve educational problems.

1. Personal Experience Method. Earliest efforts aimed at improvement in the field of education, may be labelled as the personal experience method. Changes of some kind were introduced by these in educational practices as a result of the experience of certain, experienced educators.

2. Objective Measurement and Systematic Research in Education. This was destined to revolutionize appraisal and research techniques the world over. Research in education also passes through the following four steps:

(*a*) Trial and error.

(*b*) Authority and tradition.

(*c*) Speculation and argumentation.

(*d*) Hypothesis and experimentation.

3. Deliberative Approach. This consisted in a discussion of problems leading towards committee action. This system continues even during the present time.

Major Research Organizations

The major types of research organizations functioning today at the local and national levels, on the basis of the institutions maintaining them are as follows:

1. Universities. Faculties, Schools or Departments of Education, Bureau or Department of Educational Research, Institutes of Education and Child Study.

2. Autonomous Public Agencies. Organizations independent of direct government control, deriving their funds from a variety of sources; these imitate and co-ordinate research and train research workers.

3. Government Agencies. Administrative bodies at all levels of Government, *e.g.*, municipal school boards, state and provincial departments or ministries of education, federal and national offices, departments or ministries.

4. Private Concerns. Consulting organizations, textbook publishers, 'test' publishers.

5. Voluntary Professional Associations. Teachers' associations, school board associations, advisory councils or committees.

Organization of Research at International Level

Educational research have now developed to a stage where the findings of one country in this field have their impact on the educational systems of other countries. International cooperation, communication and organization have now become problems of real importance. The First International Conference on Educational Research was held at Atlanta City, New Jersey, U.S.A. in 1956. It discussed the problems of developing international collaboration in educational research. Eleven countries were represented in this conference. This was followed by another International Conference held at Tokyo in 1959. More than forty delegates from various countries participated in it. They surveyed and discussed the status and problems of educational research in their respective countries. These conferences indicated the quick development of ideas and practices in educational research in various countries. They emphasized the great need for and the many problems and issues involved in, a systematic organization and development of research on a worldwide basis. They attributed the failure of educational research in playing a major role in the establishment and development of educational systems to three likely causes. These are lack of awareness of the need for educational research, lack of faith in its results and lack of funds to support educational projects. On all local, National and International levels, these causes have resulted in much educational research being of a fragmentary character. This fact was greatly deplored by the delegates to the International Conference at Tokyo. However, attempts are being made on National and International levels to do away with the causes that stand in the way of the progress and development of educational research.

The following conditions are essential for a satisfactory organization of research at the international level:

1. International Sponsorship. 'The stimulation, assistance and sponsorship of research by an international agency like the UNESCO must be sought under the special services section of the UNESCO Department of Education. It is planned to assist recognized research organizations in promoting educational research especially in the field of teaching modern languages.

2. Need, Importance and Value. Member States must be made aware of the need, importance and mutual value of this co-operation.

3. Aid. Aid in plannmg worthwhile research and in securing technical assistance will be required.

4. Meeting etc. Meetings and other facilities for planning cooperative research must be arranged.

EDUCATIONAL RESEARCH IN INDIA

1. Report of Indian Education Commission. In its report in 1964–66, the Indian Education Commission said the following about educational research: "Educational Research is still in its infancy. Its quantity is small and its quality, mediocre or poor. This is due to several reasons. Most of the research is confined to training colleges which have very inadequate facilities for research and few competent people to guide it. In the absence of specialized institutions doing research on their own, the bulk of research comes to be done by students for the university degrees M.Ed. and Ph.D. The M.Ed. dissertations hardly deserve to be called research, although they have a useful place as an exercise in training the students in research techniques. At the Ph.D. level, the programme has been weak in methodology and has suffered further because only those students who have done the BT. or the M.E.D. can be admitted to it. There are very few scholarships available for research students in education. Again, a good deal of the research done so far has been in the field of mental testing and other fields have received but little attention. Ancillary services like documentation, computation, consultation, etc., have not been developed. The country does not have a single journal devoted to educational research. No central clearing house has been created and there has been considerable duplication of work. Even the little research that has been done has largely remained in the archives and administration has not used its findings for formulation of policies. The total expenditure on educational research—estimated as less than half a million rupees a year—has been negligible.

2. View of D.T. Chitranjivi. In the words of D.T. Chitranjivi, "We have recognized rather late in our scheme of education the importance of research." Giving an outline of the Historical background of educational reform in the country D.T. Chitranjivi points out:

> "One may trace back the earliest beginnings of educational research in India to the first decade of this century when Baroda introduced compulsory elementary education throughout the State in 1906 and Hyderabad experimented in University Education through Urdu. At the close of World War I many Universities began to organize programmes for rapid development of Indian education. Tagore was the forerunner of the new spirit of synthesis in the East and West in Vishwa Bharati. The Jamia Millia, the Banaras Hindu University and the Muslim University at Aligarh followed suit. The Callcutta University Commission of 1916 changed a good deal of both the content and organization of Secondary and University Education. The Montford Reform of 1919, aided the new features. In the sphere of Elementary Education Mahatma Gandhi introduced the Basic Scheme—formerly known as the) Wardha Scheme. Immediately after the Declaration of Independence, two Commissions were appointed by the Government of India—one for University Education and the other for Secondary Education. Both the Commissions have recommended research—intensive as well as extensive—with regard to important educational issues."

3. The Report of the University Education Commission. Published in 1949, it pointed out that till then not much systematic research in education was being carried on in India: It classified the three main agencies of educational research in the country as below:

(i) ***Universities.*** Some Universities provided courses. They required a piece of original work in educational research which was found "small and scrappy" and of not much value in the strict sense, yet good enough to start with.

(ii) ***Centres.*** Some centres for advanced work in Education and educational psychology like the Central Pedagogical Institute, Allahabad, Education Department, University of Patna and the Central Institute of Education, Delhi.

(iii) ***The Staff.*** The Staff of some Training Colleges or Departments who were engaged seriously in original work—sometimes of high quality—but isolated due to the lack of inter-university planning.

PROGRESS IN EDUCATIONAL RESEARCH

1. This is clear by the following reports: P.S. Naidu. In his paper on Research in Education presented at the First Conference of Training Colleges in India held at Baroda in 1950, Pro. P.S. Naidu remarked: "As I glance at the excellent summary of educational research in our country published in the *Indian Journal of Educational Research,* I find evidence of a very great enthusiasm for adventure in education, which, of course, s welcome, but there is little or no planning. There is discernible in these research endeavours a certain restlessness and a training after an undefined goal"

2. T.K.N. Menon. Writing in 1955 about research in education in Indian Universities T.K.N. Menon reported as follows:

> "A good number of the Universities in India have in recent years approved of courses leading to the Master's Degree in Education. One of the retirements for the award of the degree is that the candidate for the degree should do a certain amount of research In education. This research may be of two types *viz., (a)* research on a topic leading to a thesis in which case the candidate is

not required to specialize in any other subject and to appear at any other examination, *(b)* research in a topic leading to a dissertation which needs to be supplemented by three or four papers in which the candidate will be examined... The difference between the research done at the thesis and dissertation levels varies in the nature of the topics chosen, the intensity and depth of research done and consequently in its quality. Provision of courses for the Masters Degree in Education by dissertation and papers is much more frequent in Indian Universities than that by thesis."

"Whether it be for preparing a thesis, or for writing a dissertation, the amount of research done by candidates in our Universities is very impressive in quantity. If only the quantity could be accompanied by some standard in quality the research would be of tremendous consequence to the solution of the large number of problems in education." Again, he added, "No one can deny that research in education done for the Master's Degree if properly organized has tremendous potentialities."

3. Theses and Dissertations. A list of theses and dissertations approved for the Doctorate and Master's Degrees in Education published by NCERT reveals that between 1939 and 1966, twelve Indian Universities approved eightyfive theses in Education at the Doctoral level. During the same period, are recorded 114 theses for the M.Ed. Degree of seven universities. As many as 2,742 dissertations in partial fulfillment of the requirement of the degree of Master of Education were submitted. Most of these universities offered these courses after 1955.

65 Ph. D., 10 M.Ed. theses and 2,149 dissertations (partial requirement) were reported during the period 1962–1965. 19 Universities granted the Ph.D. degrees. 39 granted the M.Ed., degrees. To quote Dr. S.K Maitra, "During 1962–65 the total number of investigations carried out as a part of the degree requirements in education in Indian Universities was 2,224.

As against this during the period 1939–1961, the total number of investigations was 2,941. During the 23 year period (1939–1961), on the average, 128 investigations were carried out every year, whereas during the five-year period (1962–1966) the average is 445. The increase is practically fourfold. All those who are interested in the development of educational research will be heartened to see this rapid rise in the quantum of research done either in full or part requirements of a post-graduate degree in education in our universities. One would hope that with this quantitative expansion, there is an improvement in quality also.

4. Research after Independence. After independence more and more Universities have started M.Ed. and Ph.D. courses in Education. Some years back the Institute of Education at Bombay, attempted a consolidated review of research in education in all the states of India. In its journal it published periodically a list of research topics undertaken or contemplated by Universities in India and abroad on educational problems at various levels. Since 1950, research in education has made great progress. The amount of research work carried out by student-teachers and research scholars in relation to problems of education in India is now rapidly progressing.

5. D.T. Chitranjivi of the M.Ed. Research work. Chitranjivi reported: "Most of the researches carried on by student; of the M.Ed. Degree course in various Universities are with reference to the content of the curriculum, to subject matter, child development, textbooks; the Basic Scheme of Education and even administration. In the University of Madras nearly 203 theses were submitted between 1945 and 1957 by students. From year to year progressively more research is being done at this stage in training colleges but there is no way of disseminating information on the work done by the students. At the present moment what is needed is a co-ordination of the research done at the M.Ed. stage and projects of research carried on in training colleges under the

Ministry of Education. Such a plan will result in economy and careful planning with due attention to present needs."

6. The Central Institute of English, Hyderabad. This was also set-up in 1958 for purposes of research and training in the teaching of English as a second language.

7. Research at Central Institutes Education. Dr. M.Z. Khan writing in 1959, on research in Education, reviewed the contribution of the Central and State Governments to educational research in recent years. In its Winter Issue 1960, *Indian Journal of Educational Administration and Research,* gives an account of the progress of research work done at the central institutes of education from 1947–60. To quote it, "The post-independence period has the establishment of a number of central institutions for research, training and extension in the appropriate educational fields. The oldest of these institutions is the Central Institute of Education which was set-up in 1947. The year 1954, saw the establishment of the Central Bureau of Text Book Research and that of Educational and Vocational Guidance, since merged in the Central Institute of Education. The National Institute of Basic Education and the National Fundamental Education Centre came into being in 1959."

8. Research Projects for Promotion of Research in Training Colleges. These were set-up for the specific purpose of promoting educational research in training colleges. The First Five Year Plan in 1953–54 a large sum of money to start this scheme. In the first instance the scheme gave impetus to more than twenty training colleges all over the country. The first seminar on this subject was held at Ootacamund in 1956. It reported the work of thirteen units and recorded the work of eight units which were not represented. This was followed by another seminar held at Bangalore.

9. The Departments of Extension Services. These were set-up in many training colleges by the All India Council of Secondary Education, later replaced by the Directorate of

Extension Programmes for Secondary Education. These have been instrumental in much significant work in connection with educational research in different aspects of secondary education.

10. Conferenee of Principals of Training Colleges. A Conference of the Principals of Training Colleges was held at Bangalore in June 1961. It made a number of recommendations on educational research in the Third Five Year Plan. It recognized the importance of and need for well planned and well co-ordinated research into educational problems. Following recommendations were made in this connection:

(i) To set-up a standing committee which would devote itself to the problems of research in education.

(ii) To review periodically the research work carried on by Training Colleges and Universities.

(iii) To start a journal of its own devoted to this and other related subjects.

11. During First Two Plans. Grants were given to teacher-training colleges and departments of education in universities to conduct research mainly in problems connected with secondary education during the first two plans. Occasionally, grants were given for research in problems other than those of secondary education and also to institutions other than training colleges or university departments of education.

12. Third Five Year Plan. In it the scheme was applied on a wider scale. Grants were given to any recognized educational institution which in the opinion of the Ministry of Education was competent to undertake the research project proposed. The field of research was also widened to include problems connected with pre-primary, primary, basic and secondary education.

(i) Aim. The main purpose of the scheme was to develop research mindedness in educational institutions, It assisted teachers to undertake and carry out research projects which could not be carried out for want of funds. No aid was given for the creation of new departments, or for payment of any allowances to staff, undertaking research projects.

(ii) ***Working.*** The working of the scheme was banded over by the Government of India to the National Council of Educational Research and Training. It set-up a Standing Committee for the purpose. The Council had a scheme of grant-in-aid for research and publication in the field of Social Education and libraries. Following Advisory bodies made significant contribution:

(a) *Central Research Advisory Committee.* It co-ordinates the activities of the various institutions working under the Central Government.

(b) *National Council of Educational Research and Training (NCERT).* It was established in 1961 to promote and co-ordinate educational research in India.

(c) *National Research Advisory Council for Education.* It is functioning under the Union Education Ministry.

(d) *NCERT* Standing Committee on research.

13. Scholarships and Fellowships. Substantial financial help is being given in the form of scholarships and fellowships by the Government, the Universities and the University Grants Commission to encourage students of merit to carry out research in important problems of Indian Education. Teachers and institutions have benefited, from financial aids from several foreign agencies and schemes. Important among these are the Ford Foundation, the British Council, the Institute of Education, London, the Commonwealth Student Exchange Programme, the UNESCO Exchange of Parsons Programme, Colombo Plan, United States Agency for International Development and the U.S. Department of Health, Education and Welfare. The Ford Foundation has been assisting India since 1951, in her programmes of advancement on many fronts. The Ford Foundation sent an international team of experts to study the problems of secondary education in other countries of the world with regard to the training of teachers and the *curricula* of secondary schools. It is in co-operation with the Ford Foundation that the Ministry has been able to set-up some institutions of educational research. It has also been able to support some projects in secondary and rural education.

14. Contribution of UNESCO. UNESCO has supplied experts, finances and equipment in many areas and activities of educational research in India Men, money and materials flowed into India to assist educational efforts. Because of it the aid from several educational seminars and research projects became possible in recent years. The UNESCO Coupon Scheme helped in setting-up the necessary equipment for the advancement of educational research, educational literature, instructional materials and films.

15. Contribution by the Central Government:

(i) Improvement and extension of the facilities provided by the Central Educational Library.

(ii) A Quarterly Bulletin entitled the *Indian Education Abstracts* to help educational research workers.

(iii) The starting of an Educational Abstracting Service which publishes since September 1955.

(iv) A project to compile a Union List of Educational Periodicals.

(v) Bimonthly Abstract of Foreign Educational Literature and the *Indian Education Index* a monthly started by The Documentation Services, Central Secretariat Library, Ministry of Education.

(vi) A Register of Educational Research in India published in the Literature Notes abstracts several theses on education.

(vii) Bibliographical information for about 2500 theses and dissertations submitted to various Indian Universities collected by the Ministry of Education. A list of these theses has already been published by the NCERT. Another list of 2941 theses for the period 1962–66 was brought out by NCERT in a mimeographed Form in 1968. Abstracts for about 600 of these studies are ready for publication and more are being prepared.

(viii) Bibliographies on various subjects of Education have been prepared in science education, in elementary and secondary schools, religious and moral education, research in education, etc.

16. Organizations and Depositories of Research. Following are the major organizations and depositories of Educational Research functioning in India:

(i) The Central Institute of Education, Delhi, 1947. It acts as a teacher-training institution. It is also a research center for solving problems of the country. Attached to it are in Experimental Nursery School and an Experimental Basic School. Since 1950, Psychology Wing is engaged in preparing and standardizing different types of tests like, individual and Group intelligence tests and tests in Hindi, English and Science. The Institute has experimented with various practices in preservice teacher education programme. Its rich teacher education programmes has had an impaction the training-colleges in the country. It has won appreciation from the educationists abroad. Within the last 25 years more than 483 M.Ed. dissertations have been prepared at the Institute and 18 students have been awarded Ph.D. Degree on their theses. Scores of students are at present, on the rolls of the Institute investigating various educational problems. It undertakes institutional projects, besides the projects carried out by individual staff members. It has two fulltime research fellowships.

(ii) The National Institute of Basic Education, Delhi. It undertakes a number of major projects in the area of basic education. It brings out many useful publications. Previously, it was known as the National Centre for Research in Basic Education. It has now merged with the Department of Primary Education of N.I.E.

(iii) Central Bureau of Textbook Research. It was started in 1954, as a separate Research Bureau of the Education. It was later made a department of the Central Institute of Education. Then it became a department of the National Institute of Education renamed as Department of Curriculum, Methods and Text Books. At present it is known as the Department of Text Books. It studies the existing textbooks, finds out their shortcomings, formulates criteria of evaluation and suggests reforms in textbooks, their vocabulary, content, presentation, publication and illustration, etc.

(iv) The Central Bureau of Educational and Vocational Guidance. It was set-up in 1954, as a separate agency under the Ministry of Education. It aimed at servicing, training and research in counseling and guidance. Later it became a part of the Central Institute of Education. It has been part of the Department of Psychological Foundations of the N.I.E. since 1961.

(v) The National Fundamental Education Centre, 1956. It is concerned with adult education and social education including literacy. It conduct a number of training courses. It has completed some valuable research projects.

(vi) National Council of Educational Research and Training. It was established on September, 1961 by the Government of India as an autonomous organization. It aims at promotion of systematic research and progress in education, to conduct educational research, to train educational personnel at an advanced level and to carry on related extension and field services. It gives grants-in-aid for approved educational research projects of Universities and Colleges. It also gives aid for the publication of research theses. In collaboration with foreign Governments it undertakes important research projects.

(vii) The National Institute of Audio Visual Education. It was earlier engaged in a non-native survey of the merits of certain projected aids and in some experimental work in its laboratory. It evolved some useful aids. It conducted programmes and courses in the preparation of aids. It has a separate research and evaluation unit which has enabled it to expand its research activities. It is now known as the Department of Teaching Aids.

Report of the Review Committee in 1969, summed up the contribution of NCERT in these words:

> "To discharge its responsibility for educational research, the Council undertakes research in the departments of the NIE, either on its own or in collaboration with other institutions. In 1963, nine major research projects were undertaken for which partial financial assistance was obtained from U.S. Department of Health, Education and Welfare. All these projects, except one, were completed and reports were being processed for publication. They covered diverse fields such as wastage and stagnation, in primary schools, inspection and supervision of schools, mathematics curriculum and achievement, cost of education, pupil motivation to achievement in secondary schools and construction of tests for guidance and identification of talented children. The Council also sponsored the first major research on sociology of education, carried out collaboratively by several institutions and university departments of sociology, the report of which is being processed for publication. It has taken a co-operative research with professors of psychology and education on the development of Indian children starting from the age of two and a half years. It used to conduct courses of

training in research methodology. Under the old B2 Scheme of the Ministry of Education which was transferred to it in 1961 and is since known as the GARP Scheme (Grants-in-Aid for Research Projects), the Council gives assistance to research programmes undertaken by institutions. It has been encouraging experimental projects in schools forsome years. It publishes a half-yearly research journal and is in the process of publication of research monographs. It has published a Year-book on Educational Research, the First Mental Measurement Handbook of India and Child Development: A symposium. It also assists the publication of good theses in education approved for university degrees and has published lists of investigations in the field of education as part of the requirements of the Master's and Doctor's degree covering the period from 1939 to 1961 and (mimeographed) from 1962 to 1966."

The different Departments of NIE undertook about 70 different studies, some of which are still in progress.

NCERT produces Model Textbooks in various school subjects and other educational literature. It organizes this work through Textbook Panels under the supervision of the Central Committee on Educational Literature, It has panels for textbook in Hindi, History, Mathematics, Physics, Geography, Commerce, Agriculture, Chemistry, Biology and Technology. These have been functioning for some-time are some books have already been printed. NCERT has brought out Yearbooks on important area of Education notable among which are: Education in India since 1947, Elementary Education and Educational Research in India.

The main agencies of the NCERT are as follows:

1. The National Institute of Education (NIE). It started as the amalgamation of a number of central institutions including the Central Bureau of Textbooks Research, the Central Bureau for Educational and Vocational Guidance, the National Institute of Basic Education, the National Fundamental Education Centre, the National Institute of Audio Visual Education and the Directorate of Extension programmes for Secondary Education. It had the following departments in 1966:

(*a*) Department of Curriculum, Methods and Textbooks. Formerly, it was Central Bureau of Textbook Research.

(*b*) Department of Psychological Foundations of Education including the former Bureau of Educational and Vocational Guidance, the former Psychology Wing of the Central Institute of Education, a Child Study Unit and a Psychometric Unit.

(*c*) Department of Educational Administration.

(*d*) Department of Social and Philosophical Foundations and Comparative Education.

(*e*) Department of Teacher Education. It started its work as a unit of the Central Institute of Education.

(*f*) Department of Science Education. It has programmes of Summer Institutes, Science Talent Search, of Science Clubs and of useful publications in School Science.

(*g*) Department of Basic and Elementary Education. It has nucleus in the National Institute of Basic Education.

(*h*) Department of Audio Visual Education. It is former National Institute of Audio Visual Education.

(*i*) Division of Extension and Field Services. It is also known as Directorate go Extension Programmes for Secondary Education.

(*j*) Department of Fundamental Education. It is the former National Institute of Fundamental Education.

(*k*) Department of Instruction.

These departments engage themselves in threefold tasks—research, training and extension. Research is their main function: It is at various levels—the Master's and the Doctoral, the students and staff, individual and team and departmental and inter-departmental. Two Standing Committees on Research have been appointed by the Board of Educational Studies of the Council to facilitate and co-ordinate research work. These deal with research inside and outside the National Institute of Education. These look after the overall planning, allocation of funds, co-ordination of work, encouragement of co-operatve research and provision of consultative services.

2. ***Regional Colleges of Education.*** These have been set-up at Ajmer, Bhubaneshwar, Bhopal and Mysore as an integral part of the National Council These are large scale, experiments in four-year integrated courses providing general, professional and contents education. These offer one year teacher-education courses in agriculture, commerce and science. All of them have started the four year course. They aim at preparing teachers for multipurpose schools.

On the 29th January, 1968, the Government of India appointed a Committee to review the progress of NCERT, to evaluate the impact of its programmes and to lay down broad guidelines for the future development. Submitting its report, its Chairman said, "The Council in the few years of its existence has acted as the trailblazer. It was inevitable in such a situation that mistakes would be made. This does not detract from the commendable pioneering efforts of the Council nor does it jeopardize its future effectiveness if such mistakes are recognized or corrected... Of somewhat more, serious concern to us was the demoralizing effects of status consciousness and hierarchy in the NCERT. Greater autonomy of the Institution, development of academic criteria and a policy of deliberate discouragement of hierarchy will go a long way to strengthen the institutions.

Before Review. Before the Review Committee gave its report, the NIE had the following 11 departments of: *(a)* Foundations of Education, *(b)* Psychological, *(c)* Teacher Education, *(d)* Field Services, *(e)* Educational Administration, *(f)* Curriculum and Evaluation, *(g)* Science Education, *(h)* Audio Visual Education, *(i)* Adult Education, (j) Educational Survey Unit. *(k)* Central Science Workshop.

The Review Committee recommended that all the departments should be grouped under: *(a)* Academic, *(b)* Technical and Service.

There should be only four Academic departments: *(a)* Department of Primary Education, *(b)* Science Education, *(c)* Social Sciences and Humanities, *(d)* Educational Psychology.

The technical and service departments will be: *(a)* Audio Visual Education, *(b)* Surrey and Data-Processing, *(c)* Measurement and Evaluation.

After Review. After the recommendations of the Review Committee, the position in NCERT is different. At its headquarters in Delhi, it runs the National Institute of Education. It has the following Departments/Units: *(a)* Preprimary and Primary Education, *(b)* Science Education, *(c)* Social Sciences and Humanities, *(d)* Textbooks, *(e)* Teacher Education, *(f)* Teaching Aids, *(g)* Education Psychology and Foundations of Education *(h)* Data Processing and Educational Survey Unit, *(i)* Library, Documentation and Information Services.

(viii) The Central Pedagogical Institute, Allahabad. Its English Language Teaching Department has been engaged in research on curriculum, syllabus, methods and materials in the teaching of English.

The Uttar Pradesh Bureau of Psychology located in the C.P.I. Campus has done important work in the field of test construction and standardization.

(ix) The Directorate, of Psychological Research, Research and Development Organization, Ministry of Defence. Two years ago, it was known as. Psychological Research Wing. It has done important work in personnel selection methods, in constructing and standardizing various tools of intelligence and personality assessment. The emphasis is on research in selection of tools. The directorate has taken up studies of the human operator and human engineering problems' in the Services. It has also undertaken research in developing techniques for measuring performance under different kinds of stress and effects of environment on human performance. Other studies at the Directorate include those concerning morale, motivation, utilization of manpower and psychological aspects of engineering, design and equipment and the development of auto-instructional devices.

(x) The Central Institute of English, Hyderabad. It was started by the Ministry of Education, with the help of the British Council and the Ford Foundation. It has been engaged in giving short-term and' ongtenn courses in the teaching of English as a Second Language to teacher and Lecturers and in valuable research in the field. It has conducted research in English teaching through its own staff and through Fellowships. Some Regional Institutes of English have been started recently in different states of the country.

(xi) The Indian Institute of Education, Bombay. It was founded in 1948. It is engaged in research and publications on educational research and other educational literature.

(xii) Universities and Departments of Education. University Departments of Education and Training Colleges affiliated to Universities in India, are engaged in much useful research in Education at the M.Ed. and the Ph.D. levels. A mimeographed list of Theses and Dissertations approved for the Doctorate and Master's Degree in Education between 1939 and 1961 lists twelve Universities which have awarded degrees for Ph.D. Theses, 7 for M.Ed. Theses and 24 for M.Ed. Dissertations. Considerable amount of individual and group research in Education carried out by the members of the staff of University Education Departments and many Teacher-Training Colleges in the country. The University Grants Commission has aided and encouraged research scholars to undertake and accomplish useful studies in education.

(xiii) Professional Organizations. South Indian Teachers Union and the Indian Association of Teacher Educators have undertaken useful research work.

(xiv) State Governments. State Departments of Education have research units attached to them. Textbook Bureaus, Bureaus of Psychology and Guidance and some other agencies of some State Governments have been engaged in research work related to education. Andhra Pradesh has established a State Council of Educational Research and Training on the lines of the NCERT.

(xv) Indian Council of Social Science Research (ICSSR). It was established by the Government of India in December, 1968. Its aim is to promote social science research and its utilization in the country. It reviews progress of such research. It provides technical and financial assistance for them. It indicates topics of research. It co-ordinates research activities. It develops documentation. It organizes seminars and workshops. It awards fellowships and scholarships.

The Council has established an Administrative Committee, a Research Projects Committee, a Research Survey Committee, a Committee on Documentation Services and Committees on Research into Problems of Scheduled Castes and Scheduled Tribes. It carried out a survey of research done in the various fields and social services. It started a Research Grants Scheme in 1969. It provides assistance for research projects and for publication of research findings. It grants fellowships to competent research workers. It took over 14 research projects which were originally assisted by the Planning Commission. It publishes a quarterly News-letter and a series of research abstracts and circulates Documentation News in a mimeographed form.

(xvi) Private Bodies. Following private bodies are engaged in educational research: The Bureau of Educational Research, Ewing Christian College, Allahabad; the Sadhna School of Educational Research and Training, Bombay; the Indian Institute of Education, Bombay; the Gujarat Education Society, Bombay.

Journals and Periodicals in Education

1. Indian Journal of Psychology. It is published by the Indian Psychology Association.

2. The Journal of Education and Psychology. It is published quarterly, by the Faculty of Education and Psychology M.S. University of Baroda.

3. Indian Education Review. It is published half-yearly by the NCERT:

4. The Indian Journal of Educational Research. It started in 1949. It was edited by the Institute of Education, Bombay. It was published by the Asia Published House, Bombay. It reported educational research on under way or completed in India and educational research on Indian topics in universities abroad. It certainly rendered a much needed service, Unfortunately it did not continue for very long.

5. Education and Psychology Review. It started in January 1961. It is published quarterly by the Faculty of Education and Psychology, M.S. University of Baroda. It is intended to serve as an effective and useful forum of expert opinion and to promote learning and research in Education and Psychology.

6. NIE Journal. It is a bimonthly educational journal.

7. Educational Studies and Investigations, NCERT.

8. Teacher Education. It is a quarterly published by the Indian Association of Teacher Educators.

9. Some publications issued by Departments of Education carrying on education research:

(i) *Researches and Studies.* It was earlier termed Research in Education. It is published by the Education Department, University of Allahabad.

(ii) *Research in Education.* Its venue is Prantiya Shikshan Mahavidyalaya, Jabalpur.

(iii) *Studies in Education and Psychology.* These are issued by the Central Institute of Education, Delhi.

(iv) *Vidya Bhawab Studies.* These are issued by Vidya Bhawan Teachers' College, Udaipur.

(v) *Abstracts of M.Ed. Dissertations.* These are published by Department of Education, Kurukshetra University, Kurukshetra.

(vi) *Educational Monographs.* Faculty of Education and Psychology, Centre for Advanced Study in Education, Baroda.

(vii) *Studies and Investigations in Education.* It is from Women's Training College, Dayalbagh, Agra.

(viii) *Studies in Education.* These are published by Department of Education, Muslim University, Aligarh.

Suggestions for Improvement

Regarding the steps to be taken to improve the situation in educational research in India, Indian Education Commission recommended the following :

(1) A documentation centre and a national clearing house in educational research should be developed at the NCERT. We welcome the decision of the council to start a journal devoted to educational research. In collaboration with this centre, steps should be taken to organize periodical conferences of research workers so that their isolation is broken and educational research acquired a professional status.

(2) It is desirable to set-up a National Academy of Education consisting of eminent educationists broadly on the

lines of National Institute of Science to promote educational thought and research. This should essentially be a non-official, professional body. But it should receive adequate financial support from the Government of India.

(3) Educational research has to be developed in terms of inter-disciplinary fields. While all training colleges should do some research, the restriction of educational research to training colleges has hampered its growth. We have recommended earlier that Schools of Education should be established in four or five universities. It will be the special responsibility of these schools to' develop educational research in a big way in collaboration with other departments. The other universities also can take up different projects in their own way. We find that, as a rule, the universities have shown little interest in the study of educational problems, even those relating to higher education. For instance, socio-economic studies of their student body can be done by the department of sociology; studies in wastage and stagnation in their courses can be done by the department of mathematics and statistics. But, by and large, this is not done. We recommend that universities should make it a point to conduct research in educational problems relating to their own work and wherever possible to that of the secondary and primary schools in the neighbourhood. Outside of them special organizations like the NCERT and the State Institute of Education will have to develop large programmes of research.

(4) "It would be the responsibility of the NCERT at the national level and the State Institutes of Education at the State level to bridge the serious gap between educational research and current school practices. A similar role will have to be played by the UGC in the field of higher education. It is for them to bring to the notice of the universities, State Education Departments, schools and teachers, the new developments in education and the findings of educational research and their implications for the teaching and learning and organization of education."

(5) While the NCERT should do research on its own and in collaboration with the State Institutes of Education and run a central clearing house, we do not think it advisable to make it responsible for distribution of grants for educational research to other institutions; specially because we expect the universities and other organizations to enter the field in a big way. This is essentially a responsibility of the Ministry of Education which it should assume. We recommend that strong Education Research Council should be set-up in the Ministry of Education for this purpose. It should be presided over by a professional educationist of distinction and consists of representatives of the univiersities, training colleges, NCERT, State Institutes of Education and institutes interested in educational research and some educationists and educational administrators and planners. Its main function would be to distribute funds placed at its disposal for educational research and to bring out periodical reviews of its development for the information of all concerned. It should have a secrctariat of its own in the Ministry of Education.

(6) The total expenditure on educational research has to be increased considerably, the goal being to devote about one per cent of the State expenditure on education to it. This is merely an indication and an expenditures of this magnitude will take some years to be usefully incurred. What is important to note in the immediate future is that worthwhile project of educational research should be allowed to be shelved for want of financial support.

(7) It is necessary to bring together officers of the Educational Departments working in the likelihood field with the research workers in training colleges and the Universities. For instance, the schools of Education which we have recommended, should make it a point to hold annual conferences of selected district education officers headmasters of schools all levels and teacher educators. As far as possible, these should be of inter-state character. In these conferences, a two-way process will take place. The field officers of the

Education Department can place before the staff of the school of education, the practical difficulties, which they come across and to which they can find no solution. On their part, the teachers in the school of education can acquaint the field officers of the department with the latest findings of research and can lake up their problems for future study and investigations. This fruitful combination of fieldwork with research will have to be greatly emphasized in future, if the innumerable problems that face us in educational development have to be, solved quickly and satisfactorily.

(8) As time passes, we expect that educational research will become more and more sophisticated. There is, therefore urgent need to provide good specialized training for research work and services for data-processing, statistical analysis and consultation.

***

3

Relevance of Research Sampling

The relevance of a research problem should be compared and analysed against the criteria inherent in what Mouly has said as follow: *(i)* Research must advance knowledge, *(ii)* promote progress, *(iii)* enable man to relate more effectively to his environment, to accomplish his objectives and to resolve his conflicts. While the selection of a research problem the new researcher should keep these considerations in view. In fact educational research is the process of getting dependable solutions to problems through well thought out scientific way. The scientific process includes collection of proof which is mostly in the form of information known as data, analysis of data and data interpretation. Hence, a research problem which does not stand out in the context of above salient features can not be considered useful and worthwhile. It must no be a routine type work, the result of which is already known; for instance, 'A study of effectiveness of computer-assisted instruction'. It is obvious in this case that any instruction imparted in more careful, serious and well planned way must be more effective. In fact the research means empirical attempts or any activity which is carried out to discover relationships and facts which are not known, but which is discovered and known will make the educational process more effective. The fundamental assumption underlying all educational research is that no event, no phenomenon, no activity in the field exists by itself in the vacuum. Every phenomenon has to be understood as the phenomenon-in-context. If the phenomenon is consequent it must have specific antecedents. Research has to find and explain this bond and contingency of educational phenomena. If explained so principles and laws to understand educational problems may be developed. This understanding must result in the qualitative improvement of the educational practice.

Selection of Problem for Research

The most crucial moment in the life of a researcher comes when he has to select a problem for the purpose of his research. Every researcher is faced with this problem. Finding a problem may comprises satisfying a personal curiosity about something seen, heard or wondered about or it may include developing through natural interests or felt requirements of the researcher. Other apparent methods of problems are through life situations, relationships established by related research and implications advanced by technological advancements. It is not always possible for a researcher to select and formulate his problem simply, easily, clearly and completely. Initially he has a general diffuse, even confused notion of the problem. It takes some time for him to crystallize and clarify the specific, pinpointed question which he wants to answer. Yet, one thing is specific. If he wants to answer the question he must know inevitably what the question is.

Fixed Rules

It is hard to lay down the principles which may be unavoidable in opting a research topic. There cannot be standard and fixed rules underlying the selection process of a research problem. Yet, some guiding principles, not of course sufficient but useful, may be stated as follows. An observation made by professor M.B. Buch may, however, be helpful in avoiding errors in a problem selection. He said, "The problems selected are trivial, irrelevant non-challenging and the completed researches yield finding which are generally known".

(*i*) Avoiding duplication of the research topic is a basic consideration in selection of the topic. For this the researcher should survey the literature carefully before he starts his study. He should ensure that his problem has not been already studied and solved. However, in rare cases, some studies may be repeated for the cross-validation purpose. If there is scope for bringing new proof by using improved design, then duplication may be justified. Even then, the decision should be reviewed according to the principle that it should make a contribution to the advancement of education as a science.

(*ii*) The problem should be amenable to research; *i.e.*, on which objective proof can be collected on the basis of which it may be proved or disproved. Some problems are, in fact, no problems. They can be discussed, debated philosophically reflected upon, but can not be subjected to analysis and objective testing. *For example*, should education be vocationalized? It can be a good topic of debate, not of research.

(*iii*) The problem selected should be of the interest of the researcher.

(*iv*) The problem should be of great significance. It means that it should be such as its findings must be new, original and significant either from the standpoint of their implications and applicability or from the standpoint of its contribution to advancement of knowledge and development of education as a science. One can find a number of studies in the field of education which are of utter triviality if looked at from this angle.

(*v*) The problem should be feasible. It means that it should be possible to conduct research on that. It should be feasible to define the variables included in the research operationally and objectively. It should be possible to measure those variables and gather data. If this cannot be done, the problem should be considered impracticable. The beginners in the field of research, by and large, do not know wherefrom to get problems of the research. The Ph.D. scholars and postgraduate dissertation writers, unduly, depend for this on their research supervisors. They themselves should know what the problems sources are. There are many sources from which the researchers may get hints on selecting a problem. But the most significant of all these is the voluminous accumulation of professional literature. The researcher should turn to be a scholar in the sphare in which he desires to work. By reading literature he should, by his imagination and hard thinking, try to know what the problem area can be.

A detail list of publications are in English. Unfortunately in India the researchers face difficulty in reading and understanding these sources; and in their own state languages there is dearth of such literature. If the researcher reads the literature critically and carefully, *(1)* he may find some thoughts, statements or ideas on which he does not agree with the author, *(2)* or if he goes through some research study he may feel that its results can be challenged in which case he may like to replicate the study and verify its results, *(3)* or he may feel that if the study is conducted elsewhere under more relevant situations its results may change, *(4)* or he may come across the gaps in the knowledge. All these are conditions which may be potential sources of new research problems. Certain research journals such as the Review of Educational Research, published and unpublished Ph.D. theses, *Encyclopedia of Educational* Research and different other journals in their articles give valuable suggestions for further research. These may also be helpful in locating new research problems.

Sometimes the research studies published in these journals, may suggest that the same study, rather meaningfully, may be conducted afresh on a different population or in a different field or with a different design. The personal experience of a researcher and his environment, both, can be a very good source of new problems to be subjected to research. *For example,* a teacher working in a school may be faced with several kinds of real problems. If he discovers a little he may find that same kind of problems are faced by the teachers of other schools. Then he may also think of conducting research on one of these collecting date from other schools also. *For example,* if he experiences in his school that the quality of teaching is declining reasons behind it. This may then take form of a research problem. Having studied a lot in the area of his interest the researcher tries ultimately to decide what properly should be his research problem.

While taking the decision and specifying the actual problem numerable considerations should guide the researcher. This is the stage at which he finally establishes or states he problem. He at this stage has found the problem but now he has to make it. One consideration should be that the problem which is selected finally is neither too broad nor too narrow. For instance, if the problem selected is "A Study of School-Effectiveness", it will require a team of workers and for just one researcher it may be too tedious to manage. It will have diverse aspects and will extend over a long period. Thus, the study will be too broad for a Ph. D. student.

To make it practical it will have to be limited to one or two aspects. Conversely, the problem to be selected should not be too narrow also. *For example,* "A study of intelligence of students of Class X of a school, " such a narrow study will give information which is an artifact and trivial having no meaning. Having located the problem it is not always feasible for a researcher to formulate his problem completely and clearly. He has, at this stage, only a common, diffuse, even confused notion of the problem. He is not, yet in the position onto state his problem substantially and in a precise form. A significant consideration underlying the final statement of a research problem is that it must be possible *i.e.,* it must be testable. A very common fault on the part of the research students is to state a problem in such a way that its investigation is inevitably impossible. A problem stated as "The role of the teacher in maintaining student discipline" is certainly impossible. In fact, this problem is not answerable. A good essay can be written on this. But, for the research objective it makes no sense. However, it can, be made researchable by restating as " A study of the relationship between teacher's competence and students classroom discipline". The problem stated finally is rarely the same as was originally formulated. It is precise particular and trimmed to size which can managed easily. The problem may be expressed in the form of a question or in the form of statement. Whatever be the form the objective must be to present the exact dimensions of the problem in an explicit and concrete statement. An adequate statement of the problem must comprised all the facts, explanations and relations that the analysis of the problem indicated as relevant. The problem must be explained by giving the background of the study, the theories on which it is based and the assumptions underlying the statement of the problem. This is what specification of the problem requirements and means. The terms that occur in the statement of the problem and are not understood by all in the same way or they are used in the problem in some specific sense must be explained and defined. This clarifies the phenomenon under investigation and make possible measurement of the same. Usually, the variables comprised in the problem are defined operationally, *i.e.,* they are defined in behavioural terms which form the basis of developing measuring tools and techniques. According to Van Dalen (l0, pp. 141-143) some personal considerations should also be kept in while opting a problem research. The personal considerations constitutes *(1)* the problem should be one in which the researcher has keen interest, *(2)* it should be such as the researcher has abilities, skills and background knowledge need for working on the problem, *(3)* it should be such as the tools required for data collection can be made available, *(4)* it should be such as data collection for solving the problem may be feasible. Van Dalen also lists a few social considerations which should be kept in consideration. These are: *(1)* the problem should contribute to advancement of knowledge, *(2)* findings of the problem, should be of practical value to parents, educators, social workers or others related to the field, *(3)* will the study lead to the development of further research in same field. In the deep interest of the researchers, observations made by the Fourth Survey of Research in Education about the research topics selected on are presented in this section.

It was observed that "Education is a practical activity contrived by the society in order to attain certain desirable ends. Educational research has to help in improving the effectiveness and efficiently of the means of getting these ends. Thus, a research topic in order to satisfy the above criterion has to be not only theoretically sound but also pertinent to the practical aspect of organizing the process of education. This makes it clear that selection of the topic is a crucial step in the process of research." To achieve this purpose the Survey considered two tasks more significant *(1)* to explore the already available research literature in the particular area and *(2)* to explore the socio-culture context with a view to identifying the problems of practical relevance. In the context of second task the Survey remarked that "The educational researchers appear to suffer from a sort of problem blindness". They appear to indulge in fabrication of research topics based purely on arbitrary combination of a few variables or aspects. This way of fabricating research topics without any relevance either to practice or theory has resulted in a big number of studies which are neither socially relevant nor scientifically exact.

Other Suggestions

This is only a suggested sequence of steps:

1. Experiencing a difficulty, some phenomena, required to be understood and explains, *e.g.*, alienation of teachers in some institution.

2. Gathering more facts about the problem from different sources and establishing that it is really a problem an needs solution, *e.g.*, the alienation of teachers may be a problem only in case of a few teachers of only one institution. So, to establish whether it is a wide-spread problem and requires explanation.
3. Finding out whether the problem has been studied earlier. If so, what dimensions, how, where, with what results deriving meaning from readings tentatively, deciding to make a detail study around that.
4. Finally stating the problem.
5. Opting variables that may be or related studied is perspective of the problem. This is done after a thorough reading of the literature.
6. Erecting relationship between the Chose variables and the problem after verifying the underlying assumptions in the relationship.
7. Formulating the hypotheses.

SAMPLE AND POPULATION

Population is a statistical concept which donates a group of larger number of units from which a smaller group of some units is opted and used for achieving some objective. In psychological research in general it is the finite populations about which conculation are drawn and which can be counted and listed. The populations are defined regarding of their specific characteristics. In psychological and educational research they are termed "target populations", more often defined as "all the member of a real or hypothetical set of, events people, objects, or other units". It is a large group spread over a wide geographical area or small group concentrated in a limited narrow area. Seldom, all the units of a target population are not accessible with the result that these units if involved in the sample can not be reached for accumulation of data. Thus, a distinction is made sometimes between target population and accessible population.

Population are heterogeneous as well as homogeneous with regard to characteristics. Hence, each heterogeneous population can have homogeneous sub-population. The tiniest element or part of the population is called the units. Hence, population means the total sum of these units. A select group of some elements from the totality of the population is termed as the sample. It is from the study of this sample that something is said and known about the whole population. The assumption is that what is divulged about the sample will be true about the population as a whole. But, it may not be always true as it depends on the way the sample is drawn. If the sample is a replica of the population, the forgoing assumption is correct. But, if it is biases such inferences about the population cannot be correct. A biased sample is one that is selected in such a way that it yields a sample value which is much ranged from the true or population value. For instance, in a survey of mathematics achievement of Class X of a city students drawn from schools in a posh area will make a biased sample. Biased samples are not representative of the population and the measures derived from them are said to consist fixed or constant sampling errors.

A representative sample is a which has all those characteristics present in the same intensify or amount in which they are found in the population. Bias in a sample selection can be avoided and it can be made representative of the population by selecting it randomly. A random sample comprises small error in on predicting value of population and this error can be estimated as well. Thus, the objective should always be to draw an, random unbiased and representative sample. For drawing this type of representative sample, a sample plan has to be prepared. It means a plan which, if properly executed can ensure that if we were to repeat a study on a number of sample of various nature each of a special size drawn from a given population, our findings would not very from the findings that we would obtain if the given population as a whole was studied by more than a specified samples proportion, *e.g.*, not, more than 5 points in 90% of the sampls, that is, out of 100 samples the samples value (estimate of value) will be correct within 5 points in 90 out of 100 samples. If the plan guarantees well enough that the chances are more occuring that the selected samples is representative of the popluation, it is called a representative sampling plan.

Classification

For drawing a sampling plan a sampling frames has to be made. This means a sampling system that enables the researcher to secure the optimum sampling units allocation. For this it is assumed that there is a finite population and a complete list of sampling units of the population can be made. This list is termed as the sampling frame. It is, generally, not possible to find a perfect frame of sampling a frame may have one or more of the following feasible defects, of which the investigator should be aware and he should improve or correct the same before its actual utilising :

(i) **Inaccurate Frame.** Incorrect information about units, listing of some foreign units not belonging to the target population.

(ii) **Out of Date Frame.** A sampling frame may be obsolete if it gives the list of units as existed two or three years ago.

(iii) **Duplication of Units.** Few units may be listed mistakenly more than once.

(iv) **Inadequate Frame.** Certain categories of units are missing completely in the frame.

(v) **Incomplete Frame.** All the units are not listed in it.

In some cases the sampling unit is not a single unitary element. Rather, it is an intact group or cluster of these units. Instead of calling this unit sampling, they term it cluster sampling.

Procedure

While deciding upon a strategy for sampling a research worker should keep in mind the time at his disposal for study completion the finacial difficulties and availability of trained man power for data collection. Generally, the following steps are involved in the sampling process:

(i) Indentification of target and accessible population.

(ii) Preparing a frame of sampling.

(iii) Defining a sample unite.

(iv) Fixing the size of sample.

(v) Implementing the plan and selecting properly and carefully the units.

(vi) Deciding the technique of sampling which will be used.

Sample Selection

All the methouds and techniques that are adopted for selecting a sample are classified into broad categories:

(A) Probability sampling techniques.

(B) Non-Probability sampling techniques.

In the following paragraphs, they are discussed in detail. It is rather necessary to understand the meaning of possibility first. The question of chance or probability arises when one is not sure about something, when one does not have suffier information and so when one is made only to guess. Thus, possibility is a manifest ignorance of a person. When one is not sure about something, he has only to accept what is most probable. When there is chance that a person will fail, he has to think what is the likelihood of his succeeding. If the chances are 1 in 5, the probablity will be 1/5 or 20% or 20. The questions generally asked in resesearch are: What is the probablity of a sample value being equal to or within a certain limit of the population value? In other words it can be said that It means the probability that the population value will not differ from the sample value by more than a certain amount. Sometimes, the question asked is what is the probability that a sample comes from a given population *i.e.,* is reprentative?

The chief characteristics of pobability sampling are:

(a) One can specify the probability that it will be included in the sample. In the easiest case each element has the same probability of being involved in. the sample, although it is not always necessary. What is necesary is that there must be some specifiable probability for each element that it will be involved in the sample.

(b) Probability sampling alone makes it feasible to estimate the error in the experiment. Error is the distinction between the sample estimate and the true value of population. It is also termed as the "margin of error" or "limit of accurcy" that the researcher is prepared to accept. Probability sampling makes it feasible to know how much it is.

(c) Probability sampling is the only approach that makes possible the formulation required to have a given degree of confidence meaning thereby that the finding of sample will not differ by more than a specified amount from the results obtainable on the basis of the total population.

There are two primary forms of possibility sampling: *(i)* the Simple Random Sample (SRS) and *(ii)* stratified random, sampling (St. Rs). Each of these is discused as under:

Simple Random Sampling Form

Simple random sample is the basic theme of all scientific procedures of sampling. It is the fundamental possibility sampling design. All other techniques are its variations only. Hence, its understanding is extremly significant. SRS is based on a process that not only gives each element an equal opportunity of being selected, but alos makes the selection of every possible combination of cases in the needed size equally likely. For instance, out of 15 combinations each of 2 cases out of six cases in all (A, B, C, D, E, F,) each will have equal chance of being selelcted. Similarly out of 20 combinations each of 3 cases every combination will have an equal opopurtunity. All samples have an Equal probability of being selected in case of a random sample technique.

Selecting a simple random sample there are three methods or process: *(i)* The clasical method uses drum technique or drawing lots of use of roulette wheel or use of slips, etc. This is useful and easy only in a situation in which the population and the size of the sample are very small. *(ii)* Another method is the use of random number tables. This method is very versatile. This method according to Moser and Killton (1971) is preferable on good statistical grounds, *(iii)* The third method is the systematic sampling which includes picking out required number of units with fixed intervals. The sampling interval, i = n/N where N is the population and n is the size of the sample. All the above three methods yield a simple random sample.

Stratified Random Sampling Form

This form is a variation of simple random sampling. In this case the population is dvided into sub-populations, categories or "strata" on the ground of some variable or variables known to be related to the phenomenon under study. After this n/N fraction of the population is picked up randomly from each stratum. The strata should, be internally homogeneous but heterogeneous in comparison to other strata with regard to the characteristics under study. However, if stratification is either not possible or not desirable then a larger size stratified random sampling may be selected.

There are two kind of stratified random sample : *(i)* proportionate and *(ii)* disproportionate.

In case of proportionate stratified random sampling the units in each stratum are selected in the same proportion in which the strata stand in the whole population. It makes sure adequate representation of the attribute. But, it is must and obvious in this case that the researcher should have a complete knowledge of the distribution of units in each stratum which, is not available in general. Even if it is available it may no longer be applicable since certain attributes change over time at a great space, *e.g.,* SES income etc. It is not always essential to have proportionate stratified random sampling. Sometimes it is more desirable that units are selected in a number of strata in disproportionate numbers.

Disproportionate stratified random sampling means a sampling procedure which requires unequal and dissimilar proportions of units to be selected from every stratum. The reason of doing this is that sometimes when the stratum is very small in size it needs a larger number of units to be picked up for being properly sampled *e.g.,* if there are two third English medium schools in this stratum all the schools (100%) must be selected as "they may be quite different from one another and one of them may not be representative of all the three. In the same way when further subdivisions have to be made with the result that some strata may not have enough number of cases, disproportionate stratified random sampling may be more appropriate. In common the sample units should be proportionate to their relative variabilities regarding to the characteristics under study rather than to their relatve numbers in the population. Disproportionate stratified sampling thus, means a stratified sampling thus, means a stratified sampling in which the numbers in the population.

Following guidelintes must be kept in mind while using the technique of stratified random sampling:

(a) Information about strata should be complete uptodate, accurate and applicable to population and available to population and available to the researcher.

(b) LK Strata should be big enough so thata there is no difficulty in locating kunits needed for the sample.

(*c*) Bases or the criteria of stratification should be related to the problem under study.

(*d*) Inter—herterogenity and inta-homogeneity should be ensured.

Random sampling also termed as stratified random sampling has its own advantages and disadvantages. Its benefits are:

(*i*) It make sure that no essential category or group of units is excluded from the sample. Thus, greater representativeness is obtained. Also occassional misphaps occuring in case of stratified random sampling are avoided.

(*ii*) Greater precision with fewer cases is achieved.

Its only demerit whereas is that a full knowledge of the strata is needed which is not easy to have.

A Description

The sample-size problem arises especially in case of stratified random sampling. A common rule is that the sample should be enough. But, it should not be unnecessarily large. It should be neither too large nor too small. It should have the optimum size. An optimum sample is one which fulfils the requirements of representativeness, efficiency, flexibility and reliability. It should be small enough to avoid unnecessary expenditure. It should be large enough to avoid errors of sample beyond the tolerance limit. It should yield needed information with needed level of reliability at a minimum cost.

The choice of the size is affected by many factors such as: *(i)* nature of population (heterogeneous population calling for a larger sample), *(ii)* complexity of tabulation (larger number of categories desiring a larger sample), *(iii)* data collection and resources of the researcher comprising money and time available, length of the questionnaire, collection of data individually or in groups, location and spread of units number of field workers, mortality rates, refusal rates, type of sampling method of statistical analysis, number of uncontrolled variables larger sample required if there are several uncontrolled variables), anticipated effects (large sample required when small effect is anticipated).

Kinds of Samples

In this type of sampling the sampling unit is a cluster, a natural group of elements, for instance, a class in the shcool or the school itself. It can be used both in the case of probability and non-probability sampling. It has the merit of convenience only. Its limitations, however, m are too many. These are *(i)* being less efficient *(ii)* being devoid of the qualities of the stratified random sampling, *(iii)* suffering from much greater margin of error, *(iv)* beign devoid of the probability of representation of every combination of needed number of elements, *(v)* needing a much larger sample for getting the same level of efficiency as is possible in case of stratified random sampling.

Mahalanobis (1944) used a variant of this techique which he termed overlapping grid sampling.

This is a variant or extaension of cluster sampling. When larger groups of units (clusters) are first, randomly selected cluster, again, sampling, is done, this is called multi-stage sampling. Several stages are involved in sampling the final group of units. *For example,* first selecting school, then selecting classes within schools and finally selecting children from each selecting class. It has all those drawfacts which have been described in the perspective of cluster sampling. This technic may be used also in case of non-probability sampling.

In case of this sampling designs categories the probability of the units selected is not known, nor there is equal probability of population units to be included in the sample. Hence, it does not afford any basis for calculating the level of confidence or accuracy level. Precision of research based on such samples can not be estimated. Following are the different forms of this type of sampling:

1. Accidental Sampling Method. The Researcher picks up elements from the population he wishes to study in his own way. One very common basis of choosing these elements is that they are available easily.

2. Method of Quota Sampling. In this type of sampling the population is, first, divided into strata or sub-populations. After this the proportion of the population falling in each stratum is determined. Then, a quota of units to be selected from each stratum is assigned. Each stratum has the same proportion of selected units as achieved in the total population.

Selection of units from each class depends on the researcher's own judgement. Its own is to select a sample which is a replica of the population. It ensures that diverse elements in the population are involved in the sample.

It is also a kind of accidental sampling. It does not yield a representative sample. Hence, the error is estimate is not possible.

3. Method of Purposive or Judgement Sampling. This method emphasizes picking up the units that are judged to be typical of population. In this technique those units are selected which have the weighted sample means of certain characteristics in close agreement with the population values.

The selection of units probability in this is either zero or one. It needs a considerable knowledge of the population. It saves time, but is inaccurate and hargadous. All these sampling designs are inappropriate and do not allow estimation of proability of sampling units and error variance creeping into the results. Yet they should not be considered totally useless. Apart from being economical and convenient they may afford a basis for stimulating insight and generating some hypotheses.

***

4

Problems of Educational Research

'Problem' may be defined as a question proposed for solution by research. "The problem comes out of a situation in which there is a recognition that something is the matter, that unsolved diffculties exist."

"The unsolved problems of education are so numerous and so varied that it is necessary to simplify a survey of them by using some rather arbitrary classification." We may, *for example*, classify them under various stages of education—Infant Education, Primary Education, Secondary Education and University Education; or under various kinds of education—General Education, Technical or Vocational Education, Moral Education, Physical Education, etc. It is, however, more pertinent and convenient to classify the problems on the basis of various educational aspects, under such heads as Curriculum, Text Books and Syllabuses, Organization, Administration, Equipment, Methods of Teaching, Socio-Economic Conditions, Teacher Education and the like.

"Let us confine ourselves to setting out, in order of frequency, the subjects which most often give rise to research: Language teaching (problems of bilinguism etc.); teaching of mathematics, science, history and geography, the influence of environment on school adaptation, new educational techniques, (programmed learning, television, audio-visual aids); popular education and literacy teaching; school dropouts, pupils who repeat the same class or fail in school; highly gifted and less gifted children; teaching about nutrition and the improvement of health; comparative education."

Text Book and Syllabus

Closely allied to the formulation of suitable curricula is the question of prescribing the right type of syllabuses and textbooks. Do the existing syllabuses and textbooks prescribed in a subject achieve the aims of teaching that subject? This is a question an answer to which every searching teacher would like to know before following them. Thus, not only does the suitability of the existing textbooks and syllabuses need to be verified, but there also seems to be a need for investigation into the best types of syllabuses and textbooks. With changes in the aims and methods of teaching a subject, or in the population of students, the textbooks and syllabuses need to be changed. *For example,* with the changed status of English in our schools and also because of the changes in its methods of approach as well as in its linguistic analysis, the suitability of current English textbooks and syllabuses should be verified through appropriate research. The justification for rejecting grammar and translation and for introducing a structural syllabus in the teaching of English has to be established before the change is adopted on a large scale and textbooks written accordingly. Vocabulary content, printing and illustration of textbooks are also important issues needing attention.

Curriculum

The question of what to teach at various levels of education, to various types of pupils, needs to be answered satisfactorily. It is a very important question, for it is not until a decision has been reached as to what is to be taught that we can discuss intelligently the plan of the school building, the kind of equipment necessary, the form of organization, the qualifications of the teacher and the methods to be employed.

We know that the world of matter as well as ideas, to which children have to be introduced is continually changing and the curriculum must change with it. What we select for teaching must be, therefore, constantly or periodically under review. In India, a few years ago, *for example,* the same curriculum was prescribed for all types of students. English was a subject which was compulsory for school children from the third grade on-wards and Mathematics was compulsory for all students at the High School stage. But the changing needs of society raised doubts as to the suitability of the then existing curriculum. Reform seemed to be necessary and therefore some changes were made. But the validity of such changes, as have been introduced in the primary and secondary school curricula of today needs to be verified through practical evidence and research. What subject-matter is to be taught-how much and in what form these are questions which need to be satisfactorily answered and they give rise to innumerable problems of research. The introduction and teaching of foreign languages, various concepts in mathematics, science, social studies, art and craft, are fields in which considerable research has been undertaken in advanced western countries. In our country deliberations, discussions as well as some research are on the increase and tend to develop steadily. The quest for minimum essentials for the needs of the community and the individuals comes under this field.

Organization

The organization of education presents innumerable problems. Issues such as the age of entrance to school, the most satisfactory size of a class for the teaching of different subjects, the relative efficiency of collective and individual teaching, the various aspects of examination, promotion and wastage, co-education, comprehensive or multipurpose schools lend themselves to a good deal of scepticism and therefore, to any amount of research.

Child Development

Since the central focus of educational research is the development of the pupil and particularly in so far as this is produced by the practices of the school, it is hardly surprising that developmental studies should constitute a major area of educational research. The physical, mental, moral and personality development of children offers any amount of situations which pose important questions that require satisfactory answers. What are the conditions that lead to or hamper a full and harmonious development of a child's personality? How can schools promote favourable conditions? Are interests and attitudes hereditary or conditioned by environmental influences? How can schools develop among children certain desirable traits, interests and attitudes? What provision is to be made for individual differences among children? What is the best approach to education of gifted children? How should backward children be educated? How best can we rehabilitate and educate the maladjusted or delinquent children? Such problems usually demand the attention of teachers and educationists today.

Administration

That problems calling urgently for consideration exist in educational administration is evident. There are problems both in the financial and the educational side of administration. The problems of finance the relative contribution to educational expenditure of local and national funds and the costs of administration need to be tackled intelligently. Similarly, the distribution of freedom and responsibility among students, teachers and the Head of a school and the Directorate or Department of Education is a highly controversial subject which has to be solved through appropriate research by various institutions. The problem of promoting good human relations in educational set-up is very important.

Guidance and Counselling

The need for guidance programmes has been recognized due to a study of individual differences and the educational and vocational choices one has to make. An equitable distribution of aptitudes, interests and abilities on the one hand and of educational and vocational facilities on the other needs to be maintained. Guidance services in schools seem necessary for the nation's citizens. The field of educational and vocational guidance, now as it is, poses problems of diagnostic and prognostic research. For proper guidance to be given to children, adequate tools to diagnose their abilities and aptitudes need to be prepared and their values and limitations tested. The construction of proper attitude scales, personality inventories and intelligence tests offers the possibility of worth-while research in our country.

Skills

Handwriting, reading and spelling, etc., are skills which have to be developed through proper educational means. The field of handwriting permits much scope for research in speed, legibility, fluency, in standardizing tests and scales and in diagnostic work. Similarly, reading offers scope for research in vocabulary, comprehension, speed, in basal reader and supplementary readers, in interests and habits. In spelling also much worthwhile survey as well as diagnostic and remedial work can be and has been done.

Educational Measurement

Every teacher and educator is concerned with certain educational outcomes in the form of the acquisition of certain attitudes, behaviours and skills. How much a student has gained in these respects during a particular period of time, has to be ascertained periodically and in a systematic way. We need valid and reliable tools for measuring such educational outcomes. What are the shortcomings of essay type examinations? How can they be removed? What alternative types of tests would be more appropriate for the purpose? What are the techniques of constructing such tests and how are they to be used? Hence, a critical evaluation of the existing forms of tests, the construction and standardization of more valid and reliable instruments for measuring the educational outcomes of teaching specific subjects and of various educational activities are fields for significant research. Examination reform is the need of the day and it calls for copious research work.

Methods of Teaching

There always are some old, some current and popular and certain new or original methods of teaching a subject. "Methods are legion and most of them could be tested by experimental investigation." Constructive experiment on and evaluation and criticism of a particular method of teaching or the comparative and critical evaluation of any two or more methods of teaching the same subject are necessary for improvement in class teaching. *For example,* the effectiveness of the structural approach to the teaching of a foreign language like English, can be compared, through experiment, with that of the traditional grammar-translation approach; or, the effectiveness of the discussion method of teaching a topic can be compared with that of the lecture method.

Educational Equipment and Aids

The designing and engineering of equipment for schools is a relatively new, but important field of research and development. The designing of proper buildings, chairs, desks, tables, lockers, toilets and other school furnishing is not devoid of difficulties. The new mechanical devices that may facilitate learning their construction, utilization and evaluation offer sufficient scope for research. The effectiveness of mass-media like the cinema, radio and television and of excursions and other audio-visual aids, should be ascertained before they are made popular. The value of illustrations, charts and diagrams, in teaching a subject could be experimentally measured.

Teacher Education

A comparatively new but productive field of education, teacher-education, is open to many kinds of research—research into the goals of teacher-education, the ways of teaching those goals in terms of curriculum, syllabus and activities, into the methods and sources of educating teachers and the relative merits of the one or two year professional training after general education and the concurrent general and teacher-education courses. Sufficient research has been undertaken, in the west, in relation to the analysis of the personality pattern of successful teachers and its relation to teacher-education courses. Job analysis and aptitude for teaching can be very fruitful topics for investigations.

Philosophy of Education

There are theories of education—old and new, past and present, popular and otherwise—which are subjects of endless controversy and discussion. Every aspect of education, every type of education, every method of teaching, has some theory or the other as its basis. The soundness of the theoretical bases of education, past or present, must be examined in order that future plans of education may produce sound results. An objective examination of the suitability of educational theories to the prevalent circumstances and conditions at a place would always be highly significant and fruitful.

History of Education

The value of a study of the history of different aspects of education, in so far as the planning of future education goes, is great. Any aspect or kind of education lends itself to historical research. *For example,* we may trace the beginnings and development of Basic Education in our country, or study historically the development of nursery, primary, secondary, university, or teacher education. Similarly, we may carry on historical research in the teaching of English in our country or in the use of certain audio-visual aids in teaching, or in other specific areas of academic interest.

Psychology of Education

Conditions conducive to learning, factors promoting memory or producing worthwhile responses, measures facilitating reading: And writing and the like, are subjects with which a psychologist is as much concerned as a teacher. Eminent psychologists seemed to have solved some problems in these and allied fields in their laboratories. Teachers are, however, still confronted by situations which do not always get solved by the psychologists' solutions. Why is it so? How else can they be solved? Can there be more than one solution to them? Why? These and such other problems confront an educational research worker as much as a teacher. Group Dynamics is another field in which an educational researcher can interest himself.

Comparative Education

Different geographical, cultural, socio-economic and political conditions surely influence educational systems of different countries. The comparison of the educational systems of various countries lends itself to a variety of methods of treatment all of which have to be objective and scientific to be of any worth. The emphasis may at times be on the historical development of institutions and practices of education in different countries; at others, on socio-economic or geographical or cultural forces moulding them; and at still others, on the levels of achievement reached or aimed at.

"The areas of research," says Travers, "may be likened to areas on a map that have been roughly circumscribed to indicate gross differences in terrain. Some penetration has perhaps been made within the border of these areas, but most of them remained unexplored. Explorers of the future, will provide broad knowledge of those general areas and then must come the developers who will exploit the resources that each domain has to offer. The boundaries which have been set-up are artificial, for each one of the areas of the educational research fuses into the other."

Socio-Economic Conditions

These constitute no less important a field of inquiry as they do influence educational processes and outcomes substantially. Socio-economic factors do have their impact on the educational philosophy of a school system and the population of a school and offer various subjects for research. Such research may be of local value only, but it can still be of great practical significance. Sociological studies can be of very wide and broad application also.

Problems and Fields of Educational Research in India

The students, teachers, supervisors, educationists and even laymen in India are faced with innumerable problems, *i.e.*, 'unsolved difficulties', in almost, all the fields of education referred to above. We have come to recognize the urgent need for research as the best means to solve such problems. But while the problems are numberless, our personnel and resources to tackle them scientifically are extremely limited. Naturally when planning for research, we have to arrange the problems in order of priority. Because of different viewpoints and varied ideas about education, no order of priority given to the study of these problems can be 'the order of priority'. Different educationists in the country may draw their own orders of priority. For an example, we quote below the order of priority given to educational problems for research in India, by Prof. P. S. Naidu in 1950.

1. The Philosophical Problem—Aim of Indian National Education.
2. *(i)* The Sociological Problem.
   (ii) Educational Surveys.
3. The Psychological Problems.
4. The Technological Problems.

One may or may not agree with this order of priority, but few will disagree with the necessity for research in the above fields. Various educationists have, however, mentioned even the fields in which problems exist, differently. We may benefit by taking a glance at some.

According to Principal Lahiri, the main fields in which educational research is needed are:

1. Psychology in the Classroom.
2. Empirical Child Study.

3. History of Education.
4. Philosophy of Education.
5. Secondary School Curriculum.
6. Examination System.
7. Educational Administration and Organization.
8. Methods of Teaching.

The areas of education to be undertaken for research indicated by the Sub-committee in the Seminar on Promotion of Research in Training Colleges were:

1. Experimental Work in Curriculum Construction.
2. Organization and Administration.
3. Teaching Personnel (*e.g.*, the teaching load).
4. Psychology of the Indian Child (*e.g.*, backward, gifted and delinquent).
5. Testing and Guidance.
6. Educational Sociology.

V. V. Kamat, in his article on "Can a Teacher do Research?" published in Teaching, No. XXX, No.1, September 1957, listed some educational problems for research in India, already tackled, or worth tackling.

They are:

1. Vocabulary of children of various age groups in different mother-tongues.
2. Voluntary activities of boys and girls of various age groups.
3. Heights, weights and other physical indices of boys and girls of various age groups.
4. The public schools of India.
5. Errors committed in learning languages.
6. Reading Interests of boys and girls.
7. Education of superior children.
8. Self-government in schools.

9. Methods of Teaching Geography and History.
10. Educational contribution of various educationists in India.
11. Education of backward children.
12. L.E.A's. in the State of Bombay.
13. Administrative practices.
14. Voluntary schools in primary education.
15. Educational qualifications of primary school teachers.
16. Group methods of teaching in primary schools.
17. Hobbies of boys in various age-groups in secondary schools.
18. Differential attainment of children of urban and rural areas.
19. Comparison of attainments of children who have attended nursery schools and those who have not.
20. Hobbies of girls in various age-groups in secondary schools.

At the Sixth Conference of the All India Association of Training Colleges held at Bangalore in June, 1961, Prof. M. Varma said: Stress should be laid on the development of basic tools and to direct research activity towards the solution of problems which have a fundamental and functional importance in education.

At the same conference a list of problems was suggested for research in the following areas of education.

1. Educational and Developmental Psychology.
2. Educational Evaluation and Measurement.
3. Educational and Vocational Guidance.
4. Indian Philosophy.
5. Educational Administration.
6. Methodology of Teaching Various School Subjects.
7. Syllabus, Textbooks and Teacher-training.

***

5

Research Methods

Research has threefold objectives: Theoretical, factual and application. These objectives are achieved by employing different methods and strategies of research. A research scholar should know the meaning of the term method and strategy of research.

Meaning and Definition of Method

Method is a style of conducting a research work which is determined by the nature of the problem. M. Verma has defined the term method in the following manner:

M. Verma has presented broad meaning of the term method.

According to him matter is important for determining method. The common types of matter may be three types, hence, all the methods can be classified under three heads:

1. Theoretical problem - survey, experimental method.
2. Application problem - Action Research.
3. Factual problem - Historical, case study and genetic methods.

According to Broudy (1963) "Method refers to the formal structure of the sequence of acts commonly denoted by instruction. The term method covers both strategy and tactics of teaching and involves the choice of what is to be taught and the order in which it is to be taught." Method is more general, it includes techniques also. The research techniques are ways of implementing a method. Different techniques may be employed within the same method.

According to Webster methodology is "the science of method or arrangement" which is not a particularly useful definition. Method is defined as "orderliness and regularity or habitual practice of them in action". By placing stress on "arrangement", orderliness, regularity and habitual practice, the methodologies derive their substance inevitably from the classically ideal controlled experiments which permeates rightly or otherwise, the literature of educational research. The methodology means with reference to research that it is a kind of inquiry.

Strategy

The term research strategy has been defined in the following manner:

> "Research strategy is a generalized plan for a problem which includes structure, desired solution in terms objectives of research and an outline of planned devices necessary to implement the strategy. The research strategy is a part of a larger development scheme of research approach."

The term 'strategy' has been borrowed from military science. It refers to the objectives of research. The objectives of research work determine the strategy. A generalized plan for realizing the objective is called research strategy. The research strategy is based on the objective of research, while research method is based on the nature of the research problem. The same method of research may be kind as research strategy, if it is determined by considering the objective of research. In the recent literature research strategy is now being used.

The Concept of Scientific Method

The scientific method is a general set of procedures or steps through which the systematic approach is developed.

The scientific method and systematic approach are synonymous. It is a more specific research process. A series of steps are utilised in the scientific method of research. The initial step of the scientific method that of observing some phenomenon represents an insight into some experience. The need to resolve the problem is felt and the individual prepares to do something about the requirement.

The second step is to Identify the problem more precisely. It comprises the formulation of hypotheses based on observed phenomenon. The third step of the scientific method is to develop and apply a design for the solution of the problem and testing the hypotheses. The fourth step generally identified is a continuation of the third step - that continued testing hypotheses. Results are subjected to further analyses and tests.

Scientific Method its Assumption

The following are the chief assumptions of this method:

1. It is assumed that we are living in a real world *i.e.,* there exists an objective reality, independent of whether or not. It has been discovered.
2. The assumption of the uniformity of nature is that what has been found to be true will continue to be true and that resemblance of circumstances will produce consistently similar results. The assumption relates to the three postulates: *(a)* Common kinds, *(b)* Constancy and *(c)* Determination.
    - The demand of constancy assumes that in nature there is a certain degree of consistency. The performances of students under certain conditions are expected to be the same as they have been in the past, given the same conditions.
    - The postulate of natural types is the principle that natural phenomena can be classified according to common characteristics. We can classify student behaviour or performance *e.g.,* divisions and grading system.

- The postulate of determination assumes that within the orderliness of nature, the occurrence of a phenomenon is preceded by certain antecedent events or conditions.

The Usage of Scientific Method. The use of scientific method rests upon these assumptions and demands. It is used for studying the cause-effect relationship two or more variables. It establishes the functional relationship among variables.

Classification of Research Approach

George J. Mouly has classified research methods into three fundamental types: Survey, historical and experimental methods. The meanings and their further division have been given in the following paras:

1. Survey Method. It is related to the present and attempts to condition the status of the phenomena under investigation.

This method has been further divided into four categories: *(a)* Descriptive *(b)* Analytical *(c)* School survey and *(d)* Genetic.

(a) Descriptive survey is of four kinds:

a_1 - Survey testing method.

a_2 - Questionnaire survey method.

a_3 - Interview survey method.

(b) Analytical survey is offive kinds:

b_1 - Documentary frequency.

b_2 - Observational survey.

b_3 - Rating survey.

b_4 - Critical incident.

b_5 - Factor analysis.

(c) School survey.

(d) Genetic survey.

2. Historical Approach. This method is related to the past and which endeavours to trace the past as a means for seeing the present prospective.

The historical Approach can be divided into three types: *(a)* Historical, *(b)* Legal and *(c)* Documentary.

3. Experimental Approach. It is oriented towards the discovery of basic relationship among phenomena as means of predicting and ultimately, controlling their occurrence.

The experimental method has been further divided into four kinds as given below:

(a) Simple experimental designs.

(b) Case study.

(c) Multio-variate analysis.

(d) Predictive or correlation.

Division of Methods

The objective of research work is to examine the phenomena.

It can be studied by employing either of research approach. There are two approaches of research:

1. Longitudinal Approach. Which is related to complete information of the phenomena from its genesis upto its fruit. This is the time sense approach.

This approach employs three approaches of research:

(a) Historical method.

(b) Genetic method.

(c) Case study method.

2. Cross-sectional Approach. Which is related to the information of any aspect of the phenomena in the existing situation.

This approach employs the following three methods:

(a) Survey method.

(b) Experimental method.

(c) Casual comparative method or Ex-post facts method.

Normative Survey Approach

The word 'survey' has been derived from the words 'sur' or 'sor' and 'veeir' or 'veior' which means 'over' and 'see' respectively. Normative survey deals with "what is"? Its scope is very vast. It mentions and interprets what exists at present. In a normative survey we are related with conditions or relation- ships that exist, practices that prevail, beliefs, standpoint or attitudes that are held, processes that are going on, influences that are being realised and trends that are developing.

Writers have used various terms such as 'Normative', 'descriptive', 'survey', 'status' or 'trend' to describe such type of investigations.

Objective and Usages of Survey Approach

The following are the chief purposes and uses of survey methods of research:

Although the major objective of survey method in research is to tell "what is"? *i.e.,* to describe the problem or phenomenon, but many surveys go beyond a mere description of the existing situation. For instance, the survey dealing with curriculum courses help us in obtaining information not only about the strength and weaknesses of the current curriculum but also can elicit recommendations for change. Descriptive surveys, or normative surveys are often carried out as preliminary step to be followed by researcher employing more vigorous control and more objective methods. Descriptive surveys or studies also serve as direct sources of valuable knowledge concerning human behaviour. Descriptive studies are helpful for us in planning various educational programmes, school census, in probabsly, the most universal application of the descriptive method to educational planning, school surveys are conducted to help, solve the problems of various aspects of school *i.e.,* school plants, school maintenance, teaching staff, curriculum, teaching methods, learning objectives and the like.

3. Characteristics of the Survey Method. The following are the chief features of the survey method of research:

(*a*) It involves clearly defined problem.

(*b*) It needs experts Imaginative planning.

(*c*) It is not concerned with the characteristics of individuals.

(*d*) The survey method gathers data from a relatively large number of cases at a particular time.

(*e*) It is inevitably cross-sectional.

(*f*) Surveys vary greatly in complexity.

(*g*) It Involves definite objectives.

(*h*) It suggests the course of future developments.

(*i*) It does not want to develop an organised body of scientific principles.

(*j*) It provides information useful to the solution of local problems.

(*k*) It requires logical and skilful reporting of the findings.

(*l*) It helps in fashioning many tools with which we do the research.

(*m*) It requires careful analysis and interpretation of the data collected.

(*n*) It conditions the present trends and solves current problems.

(*o*) It contributes to the advancement of knowledge because affords penetrating insight into the nature of what one is dealing with.

4. Informations Gathered by the Survey Methods Collect. The survey methods of survey studies collect the following three types of informations:

Important informations are as under:

(*a*) Of what exists.

(*b*) Of what we want.

(*c*) Of how to get there.

The information of what exists is gathered by studying and analyzing important aspects of present situation. The information of what we want, is obtained by clarifying goods, goals and objectives possibly through a study of the conditions existing else where or what experts consider to be desirable. The Information of how to get these are collected through discovering the feasible means of achieving the goals on the basis of the experiences of others or of opinions of experts.

Analytical Studies

No category of educational research is more widely utilised than the type known variously as the survey, the normative surveyor descriptive research. Analytical research is related to the present and efforts to determine the status of the phenomenon under investigation.

Inherent Nature of Analytical Research

The nature of descriptive research can be explained with reference to other type of research.

1. Analytical and Historical Research (Longitudinal or cross sectionals). A clear distinction can be drawn between survey studies and historical studies on the ground of time, the latter deals with past, the former with present.

2. Analytical and Experimental Research. Descriptive research as are oriented toward the determination of the status of a given phenomenon rather than toward the isolation of causative factors accounting for its existence. It is based on cross-sectional samples, the sample should be representative of the population. Descriptive research involves large sample and experimental research comprises small sample. Descriptive research investigates trend of characteristics of population. This is less scientific and sophisticated.

3. Descriptive and Case Study. Both kinds of research establish cause and effect of relationship.

Objective of Descriptive Research

The following are the chief objectives of descriptive research:

(*a*) To recognise present conditions and point to present needs.

(*b*) To examine the relationships of traits and characteristics (trends and patterns).

(*c*) Facts findings.

(*d*) To study immediate status of a phenomenon.

The descriptive survey is more realistic than experimental research. Descriptive researches are oriented towards the descriptive of the present status of a provided phenomenon.

Problems of Descriptive Research

1. The problem of sampling, to opt representative sample (size of the sample).
2. The validity of the measuring instruments. Validity of the tool is decisive to the validity of the findings of study.

Classification of Descriptive Research

(A) Survey Testing. Survey testing researches are concerned with academic and psychological problems in which academic and psychological tests are administered for data collection. This kind of research includes following kinds of problems:

1. Selection of Tests, since number of meaning instruments have been developed for measuring same feature trait or variable. The problem which of them should be taken up for data collection. For this purpose following considerations would be kept in view:

(*a*) How the test defines the variable and the investigator should also define the variable in the same way.

(*b*) Ease for administration, scoring and interpretation.

(*c*) Validity of the tool.

2. Construction of Tests. It may be feasible that appropriate tool is not available for measuring the same variable. Hence, the researcher has to construct the tool. He has to estimate reliability and validity of the tool, it is not inevitable that norm should be developed. He has to follow the standard steps.

3. The major difficulty is the applicability of the test norm to the particular group under study. Since every test has limitations that it can be used for some specific population.

Usage of Survey Testing Results

Survey testing, as a research activity, generally is interested in evaluating the achievement of a class, a school, relationship of variables educational and vocational guidance and standardization of test. Researches of these kinds reveal the weakness of scholar's programme. It can be used developing the criterion of admission and selection. These researches can be used as policy discussions.

Features of Survey Testing Research

The following are chief features:

1. The sample is generally of large size the error of measurement and sampling error is put to the minimum.
2. The data are subjected to parametric treatments.
3. It provides more accurate data.
4. The conclusions are realistic.
5. The findings are authentic and accurate.
6. Descriptive-survey-test research are comparatively more scientific and accurate.

It provides the deep insight to the psychometric methods of test construction.

1. Achievement Testing. Survey testing of educational attainment has become a large and well established part of school surveys. Achievements test of objective type are constructed for this purpose. Such achievements testing surveys may serve in any objectives:

They may enable the researchers to compare the performance of the present pupils, with those of previous years or of different schools.

(*a*) The principal or teachers may use the results of city or of state wide survey testing for a critical analogies their own school or class.

(*b*) They may be utilised as one of the means of rating different educational institutions.

(*c*) They may form a part of large complex studies of other kinds than survey *e.g.,* in experimental and complex casual studies.

(*d*) They may be taken as suggestive if not a very faithful proof, of the quality of teaching.

2. Survey Intelligence Testing. Although it is utilised to a much less extent than the achievement tests in school surveys, yet intelligence tests are a very important tool for educational, researches. The very purposes for which survey intelligence testing has been used are:

(*a*) An diagnosing and adjusting individual children in educational and vocational guidance.

(*b*) For studying the socially or educationally maladjusted children.

(*c*) For dividing large classes into comparatively homogeneous sections.

(*d*) For constructing and adopting the diverse intelligence tests.

(*e*) For scientific study and experimentation.

(*f*) For finding out the intellectual level of pupils who enter the college. who succeed in the school but do not enter the college and who do not succeed in school.

(*g*) For estimating the aptitude *i.e.,* for prognosis.

3. Field of Personality Testing. Though not easy to define analyze and measure they still have given rise to some instruments for survey testing in the sphere of personality, character and adjustment which embrace a wide variety of techniques. Questionnaires, interviews, observation, check-lists and rating scale as also some carefully pre-arranged social situations are frequently employed in addition to written tests.

Personality Testing Comprises : School Appraisal Studies

It is an endeavour to measure not the objective characteristics of a school, but the effect of those characteristics on human beings. Appraisal of different aspects of a school is an inevitable element in school survey. It is related to both the objective aspects of an educational institutions including its administrative provisions and practices and the educational attainments of its pupils. In other words it takes account of both static and functional data or of conditions and outcomes. To achieve this aim besides attainment tests a school case render a community and perhaps to compare these services with those that are provided by other schools.

The final aim of all school surveys in educational progress which they achieve by focussing attention on unfulfilled requirements or unrecognized evils of a school system on the one hand and on worthwhile practices on the other. Being a large and varied scope of school survey a single Comprehensive school survey may be contributed of different parts or constituent surveys. The following are some such important parts of school surveys.

1. Teasting of Survey.
    (a) Achievement Testing.
    (b) Intelligence Testing.
    (c) Personality Testing.
2. Financial Study.
3. Curriculum Study.

4. School Appraisal.
5. Status Study.
6. Building Study.

Now, we will discuss these parts which are significant for school surveys.

A. Questionnaire Survey

This kind of descriptive research utilises the questionnaire as research tool for data collection. It is most frequently used in this type of research. Researches of this type are employed for school and educational survey and also for educational administration. Though this type of research is considered the easy yet the investigator has to face the following problem:

Questionnaire Survey : Problems

(a) The first problem is faced in planning a questionnaire and its development.

(b) Another problem is to get adequate answer or information through questionnaire of questionnaire is always doubtful.

(c) The reliability and validity of the data through questionnaire is doubtful.

(d) Selection of large and representative sample.

(e) Sometimes it is not easy to analyse the data. Only descriptive statistics can be used in this type of data.

Benefits of the Questionnaire Survey

The following are the main advantages of questionnaire survey research:

1. Among the major advantages of the questionnaire is that it permits wide coverage at a minimum expense of both money and effort. It affords wider geographical coverage it makes for greater validity in the results through promoting the selection of a large and more representative sample.

2. The validity of questionnaire data also relies in a crucial way on the validity and willingness of the respondent to provide the information requested. Research has shown that respondents are as a group of superior intelligence.

Demerits

The major disadvantages of the questionnaire are the feasibility of the misinterpretation of the questions. Misinterpretations are because of the respondent's willingness or impersonality. Mailed questionnaire are usually impersonal. The reliability of the questionnaire is often ignored.

B. The School Surveys for Education Condition

A school survey generally is a wide study of existing educational conditions undertaken to determine the overall effectiveness of the school programme with a view toward improvement where indicated. In a sense it is a form of accounting or inventory. It collects information about diverse aspects of the school programme and evaluates than in the light of objectives of the school. It can be confined to one specific element or one specific department but in general it is most useful when it is designed to complete the school programme. Comprehensive type of school surveys cover the following aspects:

(*a*) Operation and maintenance of the physical plant and related factors.

(*b*) Staff and personals.

(*c*) Pupil transposition.

(*d*) Financial policies and procedures.

(*e*) Administrative problems and procedures.

(*f*) Aims, outcomes, pupil achievement, curriculum, method and instructional aids.

1. Behavioural Approach of Study. Centred round measuring such traits and self-reliance, initiative, spontaneity, judgement, co-operation, adaptability, etc., which form no mean goals of education.

2. Attitudinal Approach of Study. Centred round the attitudes of the pupils, parents or teachers towards courses of study, activities in or out of school, professions and problems, they may encounter. Check lists, rating scales, or scores cards, the researcher must make use of other lines of proofs like reputation and subsequent success of the pupils. The school appraisal surveys use in one instance or another the whole range of normative survey procedures including the following:

(a) Score card and rating scale.

(b) Case study.

(c) Analysis of available basic data.

(d) Standard tests.

(e) Interview or questionnaire.

(f) Experimental procedure.

(g) Observation.

The school survey comprises the following steps:

(a) Plan Preparation.

(b) Interpretation of data and conclusions.

(c) Preparation of adequate tools.

(d) Report Preparing.

(e) Collecting data.

In the adequate tools the following are mainly used:

(a) Scales of Rating.

(b) Questionnaire.

(c) Score cards.

(d) Tests.

3. Study of Status. To determine the status including personal and professional characteristics of various school officials and teachers may be a part of a school study or the subject for the independent study. The questionnaires are the main means employed by the investigators for such type of study. Officials records are also used for the purpose. The problem of the selection placement of the teachers, their teaching load, their status with regard to tenure, health, law supply and demand, etc., all form the subjects of such a study.

4. Curriculum Studies. As a part of school survey, the object may be only to analyse the existing curriculum in a school system and perhaps to compare it with that existing elsewhere. But if it is carried on as an independent study, it may take a more complicated shape. It may include or analyze the principles on which the curriculum is based, the needs it fulfils, the form it has taken and the shortcomings it suffers from. The relation to the community, it serves, may also be determined.

5. Survey of Building. The survey of school buildings for the purpose of planning or evaluation or just for the sake of information, is not common feature. It usually forms parts of comprehensive or wider school surveys. The questionnaire, check list, score cards, observation are the usual tools for collecting data about buildings, their right and location, the accommodation they provide, the arrangement they have for various classes, subjects activities or staffs, the conditions they are in as regards the construction and cleanliness and the improvement or the whole procedure is however purposive, not mechanical application of steps and techniques.

C. Normative Research Documentary Frequency Studies

A definitely quantitative type of normative research documentary frequency studies are undertaken to identify and count certain characteristics found in documents under consideration. They deal with a systematic examination of currents, records documents, etc., and may merely gather and classify data from such documents or may also evaluate the content according to some established criteria.

A study of this type involves the problems of following types:

1. Problems of selecting documentary specimens for investigation.
2. Problem of ascertaining the purpose of the study.
3. Problems of determining what characteristics to count and to define them.

Following purposes are served by documentary studies:

(a) They may discover the relative significance or interest in certain topics or problems.

(b) They may analyze kinds of errors in standard's work.

(c) They may describe prevailing practices or conditions.

(d) They may discover levels of difficulty of presentation in text books or other publications.

(e) They may evaluate element of bias or propaganda in text book presentation.

For documentary studies:

(a) Books, magazines, newspapers.

(b) Printed forms, textbooks and reference books.

(c) Official reports and records,

(d) Compositions, themes, or other prepared works.

(e) Letters, autobiographies and diaries.

(f) College bulletins, Catalogues, syllabi.

(g) Pictures and cartoons, etc.

Classification of Documentary Studies. The following are the main types of documentary studies:

(a) Job analysis.

(b) Textbook analysis.

(c) Analysis of longer bodies of literature.

(d) Curriculum analysis.

(*e*) Analysis of assembled specimens:

- Vocabulary analysis.
- Error studies.
- Analysis of characteristics of school records and reports.

D. Survey Appraisal Studies

Appraisal studies of particular aspects of existing educational phenomena such as schools, students, teachers, textbooks, etc., are also of the normative survey type, survey appraisal studies learn more heavily upon the human element than surveys of other type; especially because appraisal is itself an attempt to determine the effect of characteristics upon human beings. The studies that involve the direct judgement commonly use the jury technique whereby the judgement of a number of persons with regard to certain persons, features or specimens is pooled to secure a final verdict. Checklists attitude scales, scaled specimens, rating scales, score cards and index numbers are the tools commonly utilised for the purpose of appraisal. These appraisal instruments are based on two basic assumptions:

1. One assumption is that better judgement can be secured on the important aspects of an object or situation by focussing attention on one aspect at a time.
2. The other assumption is that a common value can be approximated by assumption of the value of the parts.

In so far as both these assumptions are open to doubt and criticism these instruments of appraisal fail in being perfect. Yet they are not without their use.

E. Follow-up Studies for Normative Survey

The follow-up studies form another kind of normative survey investigations which study individuals who have left an institution after a course of study or programme of work.

They concern themselves with engagements, occupations, or status of the individuals, subsequent of their study and the impact of their earlier institution and programme upon them. They examine the status of those who have passed out of an institution or seek their opinions directly as to the value of the courses, experiences or treatments received at the institution.

The follow-up study may serve the chief purposes given below:

1. They may provide the valuable information on the process of selection or recruitment of the candidates for a course.
2. They may prove the adequacy or otherwise of the institution's programme of work.
3. They may evaluate the influence of certain psychological, social educational factors found among youngsters on their after life.
4. They may lead to the improvement of the curriculum, syllabus, methods of teaching, administrative procedures. guidance and service. etc.

The diverse tools used singly or in combination in follow-up studies are:

(a) Questionnaires.

(b) Check Lists.

(c) Rating scales.

(d) Attitudes Scales.

(e) Score cards.

(f) Interview.

(g) Observation.

Method Based on Philosophical

The educational researches are designed to achieve the following four objectives:

1. To setup new truth or reality.
2. To find out new facts.
3. To advise new applications.
4. To formulate new theory, principles and laws.

These objects are achieved by conducting historical, experimental survey and philosophical researches. The philosophical researches are conducted to establish truth or reality. Education has two respects: theoretical and practical. The practical aspect is enriched by scientific researches and conducting philosophical researches can develop theoretical part of education. Our system of education is based on the western philosophy. The theoretical aspect of our education is not our own, it is borrowed from the west.

6

Hypothesis

The word hypothesis is a compound of two words 'hypo' and 'thesis' and literally hypo means under or below and thesis means a reasoned theory or rational viewpoint. Accordingly, hypothesis would mean a theory which is not fully reasoned. In other words, hypothesis is a theory entertained in order to study the facts and examine the validity of the theory.

Mill has defined hypothesis as "any supposition which we make (either without actual evidence, or an evidence avowedly insufficient) in order to endeavour to deduce conclusions in accordance with facts which are known to be real, under the idea that if the conclusions to which the hypothesis leads are known truths, hypothesis itself either must be or at least likely to be true." According to Coffey, "A hypothesis is an attempt at explanation : A provisional supposition made in order to explain scientifically some fact or phenomenon." And, according to Cohen and Nagel, "A hypothesis directs our search for the order." It is not essential for a hypothesis to be necessarily true. In fact hypothesis is a bridge in the process of inquiry or search which begins with some felt difficulty or problem and ends without the resolution of the problem. In the words of Cohen and Nagel, "The function of a hypothesis is to direct our search for the order among facts. The suggestions formulated in the hypothesis may be solution to the problem. Whether they are such is the task of the inquiry. The truth of hypothesis involves observation, imaginative thinking, anticipation and deductive verification."

According to Cottey, "A hypothesis is an attempt and explanation : A provisional supposition made in order to explain scientifically some facts or phenomena."

According to George A. Lundberg, "A hypothesis is a tentative generalization, the validity of which remains to be tested. In its most elementary stage the hypothesis may be any hunch, guess, imaginative idea, which becomes the basis for action or investigation.

According to William H. George, "Theory is elaborate hypothesis. The hypothesis actually emerges from the theory. It is generalization drawn from the theory itself and when it has been tested and found correct it becomes a part to the theory itself. Thus, theory itself in its early form is only a hypothesis and the two are interdependent upon each other."

According to Cohen and Nagel, " A hypothesis directs our research for the order."

Sources of Hypothesis

According the Goode and Hart following are the sources of a hypothesis:

1. General Culture. The general pattern of culture facilitates in formulating a hypothesis and also to guide its trend. Culture having immense influence upon the thinking process of people a hypothesis may be evolved to test one or more of these ideas. The metaphysical basis in Indian culture and these metaphysical ideas may form a suitable basis for hypothesis of a social research.

2. Scientific Theory. A theory provides the basic idea of what has been discovered to be correct. The knowledge of theory enables one to form further generalizations and such corollaries or generalization form the part of hypothesis.

3. Analogies. There are situations when a hypothesis is formed from the analogy. The step taken is to find out a similarity between two phenomena. The next step is to form a hypothesis to test whether the two phenomena or similar in any other respect.

4. Personal Experience of the Researcher. Goode and Hatt feel that not only do culture, science and analogy effect the formation of hypothesis the way in which an individual reacts to each of these is also a factor in the statement of hypothesis. Sometimes the facts are there, but a right individuals sees it in right perspective and formulates a hypothesis.

Origin of the Hypothesis

What is the origin of hypothesis is another problem connected with its study. There are various sources of the origin of hypothesis. The general culture in which a science develops furnishes many of its basic hypothesis *e.g.* America's stress upon personal happiness has had considerable effect upon social science in that country. Happiness has been correlated with income, education, occupation and even marriage, etc. In this way cultural emphasis upon happiness has been productive of an almost limitless range of hypothesis for American social scientists. In Western societies races is thought to be an important determinant of human behaviour and it will not be very difficult to think of any number of commonsense propositions which can serve as the source of hypothesis. While discussing the origin of hypothesis Goode and Hatt say that, "Thus, the doctrines of both liberalism and progressivism have played important roles in social science. The latter by embracing change, challenges to the old assumptions and the former by emphasizing the importance of the individual, insists that he not be pre-judged. In either case there is present some kind of skepticism which is productive of hypothesis." The role of new thought patterns and social changes help in the generation of new hypothesis.

The hypothesis originates in the science itself as well. As already pointed out firstly that theory gives direction to research, logical deductions of which lead to creation of new problems. Secondly, science is a social relation and that the scientist must acquire the folkways of his discipline. In actual practice there are many deviant cases which result in the origins of new hypothesis. Socialization also helps in giving birth to new hypothesis. Since before socialization, the range of thinking is very limited and there are certain assumptions which are taken for granted, after socialisation new ranges, ideas and assumptions come to light and new hypothesis are developed for research.

Analogies are often a sources of useful hypothesis. Julian Huxley makes us believe that casual observations in nature or in the framework of another science may be fertile source of hypothesis. The phyothesis that similar human types or activities may be found occupying the same territory came from the plant ecology and was an analogy. The observation that the behaviour of human groups seems of exhibit some of the same patterns as found in gravitational and electrical fields led to the basic hypothesis of what is called social physics and is again based on an analogy.

But the use of analogy as a source of hypothesis needs some care. It will be dangerous to assume that natural areas in human society are a product of symbiosis as in true biology. There is also no empirical method of applying—the concept to human beings. Goode and Hatt have rather rightly pointed out that, "In short, analogy may be very suggestive, but care must be taken not to accept models of sociology or from other disciplines without careful examination of the concepts which make up the methods."

Hypothesis are also the consequence of personal, idiosyncratic experience. The individual experience of the scientist contributes to the type and form of the question he asks. Some persons may perceive from what may merely seem a jumble of facts to another. History is a withess that many important discoveries were made because right individuals could make right observations at appropriate times. Discoveries of Newton and Darwin can safely be placed in this category and so is the work of Thorstein Veblen.

Folk wisdom can be one important source of hypothesis. Current popular beliefs and practices suggest both the problems as well as the hypothesis to be studied and developed. Thus, many a time with the help of folk wisdom it becomes possible to develop hypothesis without taking recourse to highly advanced scientific knowledge and terminology.

Types of Hypothesis

1. Explanatory or Descriptive Hypothesis. A hypothesis may be about the cause of a phenomenon or about the law of which it is an instance. A hypothesis about cause is explanatory whereas a hypothesis about law is descriptive.

2. Tentative Hypothesis. When a phenomenon cannot but fully understood because of technical difficulties we make tentative hypothesis about it and see how far this is successful in explaining. Sometimes we simultaneously test two or more hypothesis. The famous hypothesis about propagation of light, namely wave theory and corpuscular theory of light both explain the phenomenon of light but none of them is final. They are tentative.

3. Representative Fictions. According to Bain, "Some hypotheses consist of assumptions as to the minute structure and operation of bodies. From the nature of the case, these assumptions can never be proved by direct means. Their only merit is their suitability to express the phenomenon. They are "Representative Fictions." Einstein's fromula $E = MC^2$ is an instance of representative fiction.

The hypothesis is based upon imaginative reasoning and it primarily involves thinking without the help of concrete instances. This is why hypothetical reasoning is abstract.

A hypothesis which proves to be correct becomes a theory or law. The law of gravitation was a hypothesis in Newton's mind, but when it proved to be true it became a law.

Principles of Confirmation of Hypothesis

A hypothesis may be directly or indirectly conformable. It is confirmed directly if some observation or experiment can test it. The hypothesis that coffee taken at night makes a man sleepless can be tested by giving coffee at night to a number of people a number of times and observing its effect upon them. Where we cannot confirm a hypothesis directly we may test it indirectly by verifying the consequences derivable from it or we may examine the validity of its opposite consequences. This will be made clear by an example. The law of gravitation is not directly observable, but if it is true, heavy things must fall. An aeroplane does not fall. But an aeroplane uses some special device to in air; therefore, the law of gravitation is ture. Again, if we want to know what is the effect of moral education upon man and we have a hypothesis that moral education produces indecision, we will have to see how a man without moral education acts in comparison with a man with moral education when confronted with a chance of pre-marital sex adultery, taking job etc.

According to *Cohen* and *Nagel*, "A study of what is involved in making observation will enable us to offer the *coup de grace* to the utterly misleading view that knowledge can be advanced by merely collecting facts." The following difficulties or short comings in observation make it unreliable for confirmation of hypothesis:

(*a*) Observation itself requires hypothesis for interpretation of sensations and perceptions.

(*b*) The hypothesis which directs observation also determines in large measure what factors in the subject matter are noted. Therefore, the observation is unreliable and even worthless unless its conditions are known.

(*c*) The observation may be erroneous.

(d) Since scientific observations are carried on by the aid of instruments, the nature and limitations of such instruments must be known.

The function of a hypothesis is to research fact, where the term fact, "denotes those things existing in space or time, together with the relations between them, in virtue of which a proposition is true." The above limitations of observation are equally applicable to experiment though to a lesser degree. As regards the claim of what is known as crucial experiment to verify a hypothesis, Cohen and Nagel have pointed out, "Crucial experiments, we must conclude, are crucial against a hypothesis only if there is relatively stable set of assumptions which we do not wish to abandon. But no guarantee can be given, for reasons we have stated, that some portion of such assumptions will never be surrendered.

Conditions of a Valid Hypothesis

A hypothesis may be an idea, generalization or imagination, subject to further verification. The process of verifiability is an important chararcteristic. Goode and Hatt have put forth a description of different kind of hypothesis arising in the mind of the scientists. According to them, "In the privacy of the scientist's mind alone or in social gatherings, in odd moments or in the press of business many hypothesis are entertained. Most of them are left to die alone. A few survive to be exhibited at bull sessions or be tried out on sleepy undergraduates at 8 o'clock on a wintry morning. Most are not destined to play any significant role in the growth of science. It is only by imposition of firm standards that it is possible to window out the good ideas from the bad."

The main qualities (conditions) of workable (valid) hypothesis are being mentioned below:

1. It must be Specific. Then, another characteristic of a usuable hypothesis is that it must be specific. In other words, all the operations and predictions indicated in the hypothesis must be clearly spelled out. In the words of Goode and Hatt,

"After hypothesis are expressed in such general terms and with so grandiose a scope, that they are simply not testable. Because of their magnitude, such grand ideas are tempting because they seem impressive and important. It is better for the students to avoid such problems and instead develop his skills upon more tangible notions. In this regard it may be pointed out that for making the hypothesis specific it is necessary that indexes, if any being used, must be clearly described. In other words, a hypothesis to be usable must include a statement of indexes which are to be used *i.e.*, political office, occupation, effective income, education, etc. It is only then that research can become practical and significant and validity of research can then increases. It has been said that, "Scientific predictions and hypothesis must then, avoid the trap of selective evidence by being as definite and specific as possible."

2. Relevant to Available Technique. As a hypothesis must be capable of being tested or verified, thus, we have to take into consideration the available technique of study. According to Goode and Hatt, "The theorist who does not know what techniques are available to test his hypothesis is a poor way to formulate usable question." Thus, if a researcher seeks to study the degree of vertical social mobility, he cannot do so as definite technique has yet been evolved so far to prepare index numbers for measuring this kind of mobility. This makes it clear that for being really workable and valid a hypothesis must be capable of being studied, measured and tested according to techniques available. On the necessity the availability of techniques, the sociologists do not agree. It is pointed out that 'if the hypothesis poses some very important problem, it may induce the scientists to evolve some technique of verification and measurement afterwards, *for example*, socio-economic hypothesis of Mark or Durkheim's work on suicide. The techniques for the measurement of these hypothesis were fully evolved much later.' Goode and Hatt have expressed—"In many serious sociological discussions research frontiers are continuously challenged by the assertion that various problems ought to be investigated even though investigations are presently impossible."

3. Conceptually Clear. The hypothesis must be clearly defined. Often we have certain facts in mind, but when it is reduced to writing, it may not carry exactly the same idea that exists in mind. For this purpose two things are essential:

(*a*) The definition and terms used in the hypothesis should be commonly accepted terms and devoid of one's own creations.

(*b*) In case new terms are to be used their definition and meaning in terms of already existing concept must be clearly brought about.

It is suggested that to achieve this end the person formulating hypothesis should first of all study the relating concept thoroughly, know the various terms that are used and their exact meaning. Then the hypothesis should be provisionally reduced to writing and discussed with friends and scholars, to see if it carries that exact sense'. Whenever required, necessary changes should be made it is only after complete satisfaction that the hypothesis should be finally adopted for conducting further research.

4. Capable of Empirical Test. The hypothesis selected should be capable of being put to empirical test. 'It should not be a mere moral judgement'. Empirical test being the basis of objectivity is essential for any scientific method. In case a good hypothesis it must be possible to collect necessary facts and figures, so that it can be easily verified and the generalizations thus, arrived at will not differ from person to person. This leads to better uniformity.

5. In Continuation to Earlier Theory. It is considered desirable that hypothesis must be in continuation with theory already evolved, however, there is no hard and fast rule about it, but it is considered essential for the proper growth of science. Thus, if various hypothesis are selected at random and piece meal they cannot be studied in the context of broader theory. In advanced sciences the usual procedure is that different scientists are working on small but correlated problems. Their findings are ultimately consolidated and coordinated to form a broader theory. It also puts forward another ground of test for the hypothesis, as it can be viewed and tested against the background of theory as a whole.

6. Simplicity. The hypothesis should be simple, to the point and devoid of any complexities. This quality has been described as "Occam's razor", meaning that the hypothesis should be as sharp as razor's blade. William Occam an English philosopher in fourteenth century, stressed that 'informing a hypothesis neither more nor less onerous causes are to be assumed than are necessary to account for the phenomena. Insight of the phenomena is essential for simplicity'. According to P.V.Young, "The more insight the researcher has into the problem the simple will be his hypothesis about it."

Importance of Hypothesis in Scientific Research

The importance of hypothesis lies in its indispensability for any research. Hypothesis forms the basis of the scientific research. In the absence of a clear, simple and scientific hypothesis it would defeat the very purpose of research as in such a situation a lot of time and labour is wasted in fruitless research. The advantages of hypothesis in any scientific enquiry are briefly mentioned below:

1. It Gives Point to Enquiry. Hypothesis makes the research more specific and to the point and lead towards the destination. It is opined that 'in the absence of hypothesis the researcher is like a sailor on the vast unchartered sea without compass or rudder'. Hypothesis provides direction to research.

2. It Enables the Researchers to Draw Specific Conclusions. Hypothesis helps in coming to particular and well-defined conclusions. In the opinion of Goode and Hatt,

"Without hypothesis the research is unfocussed, a random empirical wandering. The results connot be stated as facts with clear meaning. Hypothesis is necessary link between theory and investigations, which lead to discovery of addition to knowledge."

3. It Helps in Selecting Required Facts. A researcher comes across a number of factors while studying and he must confine himself to the study only those factors that are relevant to our study. This necessitates the process of delimiting and singling out pertinent facts and hypothesis is essential for this purpose. P.V. Young has rightly remarked, "The use of hypothesis prevents a blind search and indiscriminate gathering of masses of data which may later prove irrelevant to the problem under study."

4. It Helps in Deciding the Direction of Research. Since research aims at discovery of new facts, it must be proceeded in a right direction to achieve the goal. Hypothesis provides that direction and thus, 'a scientist with proper hypothesis can arrive at right conclusion in the long run'.

How to Formulate Hypothesis? In research problem hypothesis, occupies an important place and position. It is the hypothesis which is to be accepted, refuted, proved or disproved. All the data is to be collected with an eye on the hypothesis. It is, therefore, essential to know how to formulate hypothesis. A hypothesis can be developed in the initial stages but as the investigations proceed the original hypo-thesis may undergo numerous changes, in some cases there may be even substantial changes. The reason for the same being not far to seek, as new accumulative evidences not anticipated at the commencement stage may come to light. In the words of Robertson and Wright, "Even in the case of most carefully planned research project, some hypothesis are not likely to be formed until the evidence, obtained to test other hypothesis is being analysed.... Sometimes hypothesis developed in the course of analysing evidence necessitates the collection of additional Data." It is always in the interest of researcher that he should keep his mind open and flexible. He should be prepared to retrace the steps and to revise his hypothesis, if need be. In some cases, after the collection of data, it may even become necessary to abandon the original hypothesis. In some other cases hypothesis may take formulative and definitive stage only after some data has been collected.

Formulation of careful hypothesis becomes necessary because that makes the investigation easy. There can be number of hypothesis and some may be discarded in the vary beginning while others in the course of investigation. Hypothesis should be such that it results in efforts to discover something not already known; that is why it is also called creative art. Important consideration for workable hypothesis have already been discussed and care should be taken to see that the hypothesis or problem of study is not only interesting but also useful both for the society as well as the research.

Hypothesis Testing

Hypothesis testing is a device to test some hypothesis about parent population, from which the sample is drawn. Hypothesis testing begins with an assumption, called a Hypothesis that we make about a population parameter. A hypothesis is a supposition made as a basis for reasoning. According to Hamburg, "A hypothesis in statistics is simply a quantitative statement about a population." There can be several types of hypothesis. *For example,* a coin may be tossed 200 times and we may get heads 80 times and tails 120 times. We may now be interested in testing the hypothesis that the coin is unbiased.

The first thing in hypothesis testing is to set-up a hypothesis about a population parameter. Then we collect sample data, produce sample statistics and the use this information to decide how likely it is our hypothesized population parameter is correct. The conventional approach to hypothesis testing is not to construct a single hypothesis about the population parameter, but rather to set-up two different hypothesis. These hypotheses must be so constructed that if one hypothesis is accepted, the other is rejected and *vice versa*. The two hypothesis is a statistical test are normally referred to as:

(A) Null Hypothesis and

(B) Alternative Hypothesis.

(A) Null Hypothesis (Ho). In its simplest form the hypothesis asserts that there is no real difference in the sample and the population in the particular matter under consideration (hence, the word "null" which means invalid, void, or amounting to nothing) and that the difference found is accidental and unimportant arising out of fluctuations of sampling. The null hypothesis is akin to the legal principle that a man is innocent until he is proved guilty. It constitutes a challenge; and the function of the experiment is to give the facts a chance to refute (or fail to refute) this challenge. *For example,* if we want to find out whether extra coaching has benefited the students or not, we shall set-up a null hypothesis that "extra coaching has not benefited the students". Similarly, if we want to find out whether a particular drug is effective in curing malaria we will take the null hypothesis that "the drug is not effective in curing malaria". The rejection of the null hypothesis indicates that the differences have statistical significance and the acceptance of the null hypothesis indicates that the differences are due to chance. Since many practical problems aim at establishment of statistical significance of differences, rejection of the null hypothesis may thus, indicate success in statistical project.

(B) Alternative Hypothesis (Ha). As against the null hypothesis, the alternative hypothesis specifies those values that the researcher believes to hold true and of course, he hopes that the sample data lead to acceptance of this hypothesis as true. The alternative hypothesis may embrace the whole range of values rather than single point. Now-a-days, it is usually accepted common practice not to associate any special meaning to the null or alternative hypothesis but merely to let these terms represent to different assumptions about the population parameter. However, for statistical convenience it will make a difference as to which hypothesis is called the null hypothesis and which is called the alternative.

General Procedure of Hypothesis Testing

The procedure of testing hypothesis is briefly described below:

1. Set-up a Hypothesis. The first thing in hypothesis testing is to set-up a hypothesis about a population parameter. Then we collect sample data, produce sample statistics and use this information to decide how likely it is that our hypothesized population parameter is correct. Say, we assume a certain value for a population mean. To test the validity of our assumption, we gather sample data and determine the difference between the hypothesized value and the actual value of the sample mean. Then we judge whether the difference is significant. The smaller the difference, the greater the likelihood that our hypothesized value for the mean is correct. The larger the difference, the smaller the likelihood.

2. Set-up a Suitable Significance Level. Having set-up the hypothesis, the next step is to test the validity of H_O against that of H_a at as certain level of significance. The confidence with which an experimeter rejects—or retains—a null hypothesis depends upon the significance level adopted. The significance level is customarily expressed as a percentage, such as 5 per cent, is the probability of rejecting the null hypothesis if it is true.

3. Setting a Test Criterion. The third step in hypothesis testing procedure is to construct a test criterion. This involves selecting an appropriate probability distribution for the particular test, that is, a probability distribution which can properly be applied. Some probability distributions that are commonly used in testing procedures are t. F and χ^2. Test criteria must employ an appropriate probability distribution; *for example,* if only small sample information is available, the use of the normal distribution would be inappropriate.

4. Making Decisions. It is the last step in the process of taking decisions. A statistical conclusion or decision is a decision either to reject or to accept the null hypothesis. If the hypothesis is being tested at 5% level and the observed set of results has probabilities less than 5%, we consider the difference between the sample statistics and the hypothetical parameter significant. We then decide to reject H_0 and state "the null hypothesis is false. On the other hand, if at 5% level of significance, the observed set of results has probabilities more than 5%, we do not reject H_0 and state that the sample observation are consistent with null hypothesis.

4. Doing Computations. Having taken the first three steps, we have completely designed a statistical test. We now proceed to the fourth step—performance of various computations—from a random sample of size n, necessary for the test. These calculations include the testing statistic and the standard error of the testing statistic.

***

7

Sampling

Sampling may be defined as the selection of some part of an aggregate or totality on the basis of which a judgement or inference about the aggregate or totality is made. In other words, it is the process of obtaining information about an entire population by examining only a part of it. In most of the research work and surveys, the usual approach happens to be to make generalisations or to draw inferences based on samples about the parameters of population from which the samples are taken. The researcher quite often selects only a few items from the universe for his study purposes. All this is done on the assumption that the sample data will enable him to estimate the population parameters. The items so selected constitute what is technically called a sample, their selection process or technique is called sample design and the survey conducted on the basis of sample is described as sample survey. Sample should be truly representative of population characteristics without any bias so that it may result in valid and reliable conclusions.

What is Sampling?

When a social researcher undertakes a research work he is to decide basically two important things namely, what will be the scope of his study and secondly, what will be his population or universe. He may decide to cover the whole population concerned with his subject, if he has time, energy, resources and capacity but that is usually not possible due to several constraints. If that is done, that is known as census method of study. On the other hand, he can pick up a small sample out of the whole study. Such a unit is expected to be representative of the whole population. It is felt that when this unit has been studied, the whole population has been studied. In other words, the conclusions drawn will be representative of the whole group When that is done it is called sampling method. Sampling is, of course, nothing new and is adpoted either in one form or the other in our day-to-day life. But before 'Sampling' is defined it is proper to understand the term, 'universe' or population.

In sampling, universe or population is not understood in the same sense in which it is commonly understood by a layman. Here, a population means only the people or documents etc., who are proposed to be covered under the scheme of study. Population can have up population as well *i.e.,* it can be made or female population, can have sub-population as well *e.g.,* poor population; below poverty line population and so on. Each sub-population is mutually exclusive segment or section. Even female population can be divided into girls and women for the purposes of study.

Today it is being increasingly felt that social researchers have neither time, nor money, nor energy, nor resources to study the entire population which is connected or proposed to be covered in a study. In other words, census method of study is proving more and more costly and time consuming. Accordingly it is felt that a representative sample should be picked up and conclusions drawn should be supposed to represent the whole population. In the words of P.V. Young, "A statistical sample is miniature picture of cross section of the entire group or aggregate from which the smaple is taken. The entire group from which sample is chosen is known as 'The population', 'Universe' or 'Supply'. In the words of Goode and Hatt, "At the present, however, sampling is so essential a part of research procedure that every sociologist, though not required to be a sampling expert, must at least be thoroughly familiar with its logic and with some of its basic techniques."

Thus, each sample has some universe behind it, because the former is the part of the latter. But what need not be forgotten is that a researcher can never give full assurance that the sample fully reflects all features of the universe or population unless there is simultaneous conduct a comparable study of complete population, which is not possible. Therefore, if it is possible to devise a sampling plan which has a good measure of confidence then the findings based on a sample of a given size drawn from a given population will give sufficiently similar results as that of the study of the whole population and that should serve the purpose. It is presumed in sampling that the sample is indicator of population and as such its findings are indicator of the characteristics of the whole population.

Some Fundamental Definitions

Before we talk about details and uses of sampling, it seems appropriate that we should be familiar with some fundamental definitions concerning sampling concepts and principles.

1. Universe Population. From a statistical point of view, the term 'Universe' refers to the total of the items or units in any field of inquiry, whereas the term 'population' refers to the total of items about which information is desired. The attributes that are the object of study are referred to as characteristics and the units possessing them are called as elementary units. The aggregate of such units is generally described as population. Thus, all units in any field of inquiry constitute universe and all elementary units (on the basis of one characteristic or more) constitute population. Quite often, we do not find any difference between population and universe and as such the two terms are taken as interchangeable.

The population or universe can be *finite* or *infinite.* The population is said to be finite if it consists of a fixed number of elements so that it is possible to enumerate it in its totality. For instance, the population of a city, the number of workers in a factory are examples of finite populations. The symbol '*N*' is generally used to indicate how many elements (or items) are there in case of a finite population. An infinite population is that population in which it is theoretically impossible to observe all the elements. Thus, in an infinite population the number of items is infinite *i.e.,* we cannot have any idea about the total number of items. The number of stars in a sky, possible rolls of a pair of dice are examples of infinite population. One should remember that no truly infinite population of physical objects does actually exist in spite of the fact that many such populations appear to be very very large. From a practical consideration, we then use the term infinite population for a population that cannot be enumerated in a reasonable period of time. This way we use the theoretical concept of infinite population as an approximation of a very large finite population.

2. Sampling Design. A sample design is a definite plan for obtaining a sample from the sampling frame. It refers to the technique or the procedure the researcher would adopt in selecting some sampling units from which inferences about the population is drawn. Smapling design is determined before any data are collected.

3. Statistic(s) and Parameter(s). A statistic is a characteristic of a sample, whereas a parameter is a characteristic of a puopulation. Thus, when we work out certain measures such as mean, median, mode or the like ones from samples, then they are called statist(s) for they describe the characteristics of a sample. But when such measures describe the characteristics of a population, they are known as parameter(s). For instance, the population mean (μ) is a parameter, whereas the sample mean ($\overline{X}$) is a statistic. To obtain the estimate of a parameter from a statistic constitutes the prime objective of sampling analysis.

4. Sampling Error. Sample surveys do imply the study of a small portion of the population and as such there would naturally be a certain amount of inaccuracy in the information collected. This inaccuracy may be termed as sampling error or error variance. In other words, sampling errors are those errors which arise on account of sampling and they generally happen to be random variations (in case of random sampling) in the sample estimates around the true population values.

Sampling errors occur randomly and are equally likely to be in either direction. The magnitude of the sampling error depends upon the nature of the universe; the more homogeneous the universe, the smaller the sampling error. Sampling error is inversely related to the size of the sample *i.e.,* sampling error decreases as the sample size inereases and *vice-versa.* A measure of the random sampling error can be calculated for a given sample design and size and this measure is often called the precision of the sampling plan. Sampling error is usually worked out as the product of the critical value at a certain level of significance and the standard error.

As opposed to sampling errors, we may have non-sampling errors which may creep in during the process of collecting actual information and such errors occur in all surveys whether census or sample. We have no way to measure non-sampling errors.

5. Sampling Frame. The elementary units or the group or cluster of such units may form the basis of sampling process in which case they are called as sampling units. A list containing all such sampling units is known as sampling frame. Thus, sampling frame consists of a list of items from which the sample is to be drawn. If the population is finite and the time frame is in the present or past, then it is possible for the frame to be identical with the population. In most cases they are not identical because it is often impossible to draw a sample directly from population. As such this frame is either constructed by a researcher for the purpose of his study or may consist of some existing list of the population.

For instance, one can use telephone directory as a frame for conducting opinion survey in a city.

6. Precision. Precision is the range within which the population average (or other parameter) will lie in accordance with the reliability specified in the confidence level as a percentage of estimate ± or as a numerical quantity. For instance, if the estimate is ₹ 4000 and the precision desired is ± 4%, then the true value will be no less than Rs. 3840 and no more than ₹ 4160. This is the range (Rs. 3840 to ₹ 4160) within which the true answer should lie. But if we desire that the estimate should not deviate from the actual value by more than ₹ 200 in either direction, in that case the range would be ₹ 3800 to ₹ 4200.

7. Sampling Distribution. We are often concerned with sampling distribution in sampling analysis. If we take certain number of samples and for each sample compute various statistical measures such as mean, standard deviation, etc., then we can find that each sapmle may give its own value for the statistic under consideration. All such values of a particular statistic, say mean, together with their relative frequencies will constitute the sampling distribution of the particular statistic, say mean. Accordingly, we can have sampling distribution of mean, or the sampling distribution of standard deviation or the sampling distribution of any other statistical measure. It may be noted that each item in a sampling distribution is a particular statistic of a sample. The sampling distribution tends quite closer to the normal distribution if the number of samples is large. The significance of sampling distribution follows from the fact that the mean of a sampling distribution is the same as the mean of the universe. Thus, the mean of the sampling distribution can be taken as the mean of the universe.

8. Confidence Level and Significance Level. The confidence level or reliability is the expected percentage of times that the actual value will fall within the stated precision limits. Thus, if we take a confidence level of 95%, then we mean that there are 95 chances in 100 (or .95 in 1) that the sample results represent the true condition of the population within a specified precision range against 5 chances in 100 (or .05 in 1) that it does not. Precision is the range within which the answer may vary and still be acceptable; confidence level indicates the likelihood that the answer will fall within that range and the significance level indicates the likelihood that the answer will fall outside that range. We can always remember that if the confidence level is 95%, then the significance level will be (100—95) *i.e.*, 5%; if the confidence level is 99%, the significance level is (100—99) *i.e.*, 1% and so on. We should also remember that the area of normal curve within precision limits for the specified confidence level constitute the acceptance region and the area of the curve outside these limits in either direction constitutes the rejection regions.

Features of Sampling Technique

The sampling technique has following good features and these bring into relief its value and singificance:

1. Reliability. If the choice of sample units is made with due care and the matter under survey is not heterogeneous, the conclusion of the sample survey can have almost the same reliability as those of census survey.

2. Economy. The sampling technique is much less expensive, much less time consuming than the census technique.

3. Detailed Study. Since the number of sample units is fairly small these can be studied intensively and elaborately. They can be examined from multiple viewpoints.

4. Scientific Base. This is a scientific technique because the conclusion derived from the study of certain units can be verified from other units. By taking random samples we can determine the amount of deviation from the norm.

5. Greater Suitability in Most Situations. Most of the surveys are made by the technique of sample survey, because wherever the matter is of a homogeneous nature, the examination of few units suffices. This is the case in the majority of situations.

Common Mistakes in Sampling Technique

1. Less Accuracy. In comparison to census technique the conclusions derived from sample are more liable to error. Therefore, sampling technique is less accurate than the census technique.

2. Misleading Conclusions. If due care is not taken in the selection of samples or if they are arbitrarily selected, the conclusions derived from them will become misleading if extended to all units. *For example,* in assessing the monthly expenditure of university students if we select for sample study only rich students, our results will be highly erroneous if extended to all students.

3. Changeability of Units. If the units in the field of survey are liable to change or if these are not harmonious the sampling technique will be very hazardous. It is not scientific to extend the conclusions derived from one set of sample to other sets which are unlike or are changeable.

4. When Sampling is not Possible. Under certain circumstances it is very difficult to use the sampling technique. If the time is very short and it is not possible to make selection of the sample, the technique cannot be used. Besides if we need 100% accuracy the sampling technique cannot be used. It can also not be used if the material is of heterogeneous nature.

5. Need for Specialized Knowledge. The sample technique can be successful only if a competent and able scientist makes the selection. If this is done by average scientist, the selection is liable to be wrong.

What is a Good Sampling? It need be realised that sampling method is really advantageous in social research, but what is to be seen is that the samaple is good and representative. In this regard what is essential is to decide how the itmes to be included in the sample should be picked up and secondly, how to measure the reliability of a sample.

In a good sample it is to be seen that it is closely representative of the universe the study. Sometimes it is believed that a good sample will be one which will be large, so that it becomes possible to incorporate all the characteristics of the universe. In the words P.V. Young, "The size of a sample is no necessary insurance of its representatives. Relatively small samples properly selected may be much more reliable than large samples poorly selected. The actual selection of the sample should be so arranged that every item in the universe under consideration must have the same chance for inclusion in the sample." But at the same time it is very essential that it must be adequate in size, so that it can become really reliable.

The selection of the sample should be unbiased. The items which are included in the sample should be based on objectivity rather then on subjectivity. A sample which is not representative is called biased sample. This bias in the sampling can come on account of various reasons, *e.g.*, the investigator may be subjective in picking up the sample. Then another reason can be that the instruments may not be perfect or it can be that the researcher may not be properly trained or equipped to use the instruments made available to him and so on. In a good sampling there will always be conformity to subject-matter and means. It is not always possible that every means should fulfil the needs of the subject-matter but as far as possible the representative units selected should be according to subject-matter and means. In the sample only such units should be included, which as far as possible, should be independent. In other words, if need be these should be inter-changeable. It is of course correct that the sample should not be too large. It is equally true that size of sample does not make it representative. But all the more it is important that the sample should not be too small because then that may not remain representative.

It is expected of good sample design that its results can be applied and in it biases, if any, can be controlled. It should be such that its results can be considered dependable and for completing study necessary funds for studying such sample are available. The units included in the sample should have some homogeneity, *i.e.,* these should have some sort of likeness with each other. It is this likeness which will make it scientific otherwise the unit will become unscientific and thus, not good for drawing proper conclusions. While drawing sample a researcher should not hesitate to draw some benefit from the experience of his predecessors who have been on the field. They have knowledge about practical difficulties which are likely to come on the way. Consultation with them are bound to benefit the study as a whole and the researcher is not likely to lose much by consultation.

Criteria for Constructing a Sampling Design

While constructing a sampling design it is important that measurable or known probability sample technique should be used. If such method is used then expected discrepancies between estimated value from the sample and the true value will decrease. Then in terms of scientific standards, sampling procedures which do not provide a sound basis for estimating sampling errors should be avoided. Then another criteria is that only simple, straightforward, workable methods which have been adopted to available facilities should be used. Availability of personnel should also not be lost sight of. As far as possible elaborate and complicated techniques should be avoided. It should always be remenbered that much work of coding and tabulating etc., is to be done by non-technical staff. As such procedures that are practicable and readily understandable should be used.

Before picking up sample is essential that universe of the study should be clearly defined, out of which sample is to be picked up. Before selecting sample clear decision should be taken about sampling units. Similarly sample frame or source list from which sample is to be picked should also be decided before hand. What is to be ensured while picking up sample size is that it is neither too large nor it is too small. It should be an optimum sample, *i.e.,* it should be representative, reliable, flexible and efficient. In the sample alongwith the interests of main group, those of sub and small-groups should also be taken due care and their representatives included in the sample. Techniques to be used for the study of sample should be decided before the sample is actually picked up and finalized.

Still another point which needs consideration is that an optional balance between expenditure and maximum reliable information should be struck.

In this regard one must remember that two costs are involved in a sampling analysis *viz.*, the cost of collecting data and the cost of an incorrect inference resulting from the data. Researcher must keep in view the two causes of incorrect inferences *viz.*, systematic bias and sampling error. A systematic bias results from errors in the sampling procedures and it cannot be reduced or eliminated by increasing the sample size. At best the causes responsible for these errors can be detected and corrected. Usually a systematic bias is the result of one or more of the following factors:

1. Inappropriate Sampling Frame. If the sampling frame is inappropriate *i.e.*, a biased representation of the universe, it will result in a systematic bais.

2. Natural Bias in the Reporting of Data. Natural bias of respondents in the reporting of data is often the cause of a systematic bias in many inquiries. There is usually a downward bias in the income data collected by government taxation department, whereas we find an upward bias in the income data collected by some social organization. People in general understate their incomes if asked about it for tax purposes, but they overstate the same if asked for social status or their affluence. Generally, in psychological surveys, people tend to give what they think is the 'correct' answer rather than revealing their true feelings.

3. Indeterminancy Principle. Sometimes we find that individuals act differently when kept under observation than what they do when kept in non-observed situations. For instance, if workers are aware that somebody is observing them in course of a work study on the basis of which the average length of time to complete a task will be determined and accordingly the quota will be set for piece work, they generally tend to work slowly in comparison to the speed with which they work if kept unobserved.

4. Defective Measuring Device. If the measuring device is constantly in error, it will result in systematic bias. In survey work, systematic bias can result if the questionnaire or the interviewer is biased. Similarly, if the physical measuring device is defective there will be systematic bias in the data collected through such a measuring device.

5. Non-respondents. If we are unable to sample all the individuals initially included in the sample, there may arise a systematic bias. The reason is that in such a situation the likelihood of establishing contact or receiving a response from an individual is often correlated with the measure of what is to be estimated.

Sampling errors are the random variations in the sample estimates around the true population parameters. Since they occur randomly and are equally likely to be in either direction, their nature happens to be of compensatory type and the expected value of such errors happens to be equal to zero. Sampling error decreases with the increase in the size of the sample and it happens to be of a smaller magnitude in case of homogeneous population.

Sampling error can be measured for a given sample design and size. The measurement of sampling error is usually called the 'precision of the sampling plan'. If we increase the sample size, the precision can be improved. But increasing the size of the sample has its own limitations *viz.*, a lager sized sample increases the cost of collecting data and also enhances the systematic bias. Thus, the effective way to increase precision is usually to select a better sampling design which has a smaller sampling error for a given sample size at a given cost. In practice, however, people prefer a less precise design because it is easier to adopt the same and also because of the fact that systematic bias can be controlled in a better way in such a design.

In brief, while selecting a sampling procedure, researcher must ensure that the procedure causes a relatively small sampling error and helps to control the systematic bias in a better way.

From what has been stated above, we can list down the characteristics of a good sample design as under:

(a) Sample design must result in a truly representative sample.

(b) Sample design must be such which results in a small sampling error.

(c) Sample design must be viable in the context of funds available for the research study.

(d) Sample design must be such so that systematic bias can be controlled in a better way.

(e) Sample should be such that the results of the sample study can be applied, in general, for the universe with a reasonable level of confidence.

METHODS OF SAMPLING

There are various methods that may be used. The choice of method will be determined by the purpose for which sampling is sought and the nature of the population. The basic fact always to be kept in mind is the representative character of the sample, which can be ensured, by various methods and not necessarily by the method of random selection alone.

While judgement sampling is non-probability sampling technique, the quota sampling combines of the aspects of probability sampling and judgement sampling.

Random Sampling

In the words of W.M. Harper, "A random sample is a sample selected in such a way that every item in the population has on equal chance of being included." According to Simpson and Kafka, "Random samples are characterised by the way in which they are selected." 'Random' is not used in the sense of haphazard or 'hit-or-miss'. A random opportunity of being selected.

The method is formally defined as follows:

Suppose we take a sample of size n from a finite population of size N. Then there are ${}^{N}C_{n}$ possible samples. A sampling technique in which each of the ${}^{N}C_{n}$ samples has an equal chance of being selected is known as random sampling and the lot obtained by this technique is termed as a random sample. It is not easy in practice to ensure true randomness in the selection of items in a sample. However, to ensure randomness of selection one may adopt either the Lottery method or consult table of random numbers.

1. Lottery Method. This is the simplest and the most popular method of obtaining a random sample. Under this method, the various units of the universe are numbered on small and identical slips of paper which are folded and mixed together in a drum thoroughly. A blindfold selection is then made of the number of slips required to constitute the desired size of sample. The method is illustrated below by means of an example:

Suppose we want to select 40 candidates out of 1000. We assign the numbers 1 to 1000, one number to each candidate and write these numbers (1 to 1000) on 1000 slips which are made as homogeneous as possible in shape, size colour, etc. These folded slips are then put in a drum and thoroughly shuffled and then 40 slips are drawn one by one. The 40 candidates corresponding to numbers on the slips drawn, will constitute a random sample.

This method of selection is quite independent of the properties of population. Generally, in place of chits cards are used. We make one card correspond to one of the units of the population by writing on it the number of the unit. A pack of cards is a kind of miniature of the population for sampling purposes. The pack is shuffled a number of times and then a card is drawn at random from it.

2. 'Mechanical Randomization' or use of 'Random Numbers'. The lottery method described above it quite time-consuming and combersome to use if the population is sufficiently large. The most practical and inexpensive method of selecting a random sample consists in the use *'Random Number Tables'*, which have been so constructed that each of the digits, 0, 1, 2, 3, 4, 5, appear with approximately the same frequency and independently of each other. If we have to select a sample from a population of size N (≤ 99) then the numbers can be combined two by the two given pairs from 00 to 99, Similarly if N ≤ 999 or N ≤ 9999 and so on, then combining the digit three by three (or four by four and on), we get numbers from 000 to 999 or (0000 to 9999 and soon. Since each of the digit 9, 1, 2, 3, ..., 9 occurs with approximately the same frequency and independently of each other, so does each of the pairs 99 to 00, triplets 000 to 999 or quadruplets 0000 to 9999 and so on.

The method of drawing a random sample comprises the following steps:

(a) Identify N units in the population with the numbers 1 to N.

(b) The population units corresponding to the numbers selected in step.

(c) Select at random, any page of the 'random number table' and pick up the numbers in any row, column or diagonal at random.

(d) Constitute the random sample.

We have given below different; sets of random-numbers commonly used in practice. The numbers in these tables have been subjected to various statistical tests for randomness of a series and there randomness has been well established for all practical purposes.

1. Tippet's (1927) Random Number Tables. Tippet number tables consist of 10,400 four digited number, giving in all 10,400×4, *i.e.,* 41,600 digits selected at random from the British census reports.

2. Fisher and Yates (1938) Tables (in Statistical Tables for Biological, Agricultural and Medical Research) comprise 15,000 digits arranged in two's. Fisher and Yates obtained these tables by drawing numbers at random from the 10th to 19th digits of A.S. Thomson's 20-figure logarithmic tables.

3. Rand Corporation (1955) random number tables consists of one million random digits consisting of 2,00,000 random numbers of 5 digits each.

4. Kendall and Babingoton Smiths random tables consist to 1,00,000 digits grouped into 25,000 sets of 4 digited random numbers.

Merits

1. **Scientific Method.** It is a more scientific method of taking about sample from universe since there is little possibility of personal bias affecting the results as the items in the sample depend entirely on chance.
2. **More Representative.** As the size of the sample increases it becomes increasingly representative of the population as per the laws of the Interia of Large Numbers and of the Statistical Regularity.
3. **More Economical.** This method provides the most reliable information at the least possible cost and thus, saves time, money and labour in investigating a problem.

Demerits

1. The sample will not be a true representative of the universe if its size is small.
2. The sampling method requires complete list of units of the universe and such uptodate list is not available in many inquiries.
3. From the point of a view of field survey is has been claimed that cases selected random sampling tend to be too widely dispersed Geographically and that the time and cost of collecting data become too large.

Stratified Random Sampling

This method of sampling is used when the population is composed of diverse segments or natural subdivisions of units. The method consists a classifying the population units into a certain number of groups called strata (plural) and then selecting random samples independently from each group or stratum singular). The division of the population into strata (termed stratification) is usually done in such a way that:

(a) There is greater homogeneity within each stratum. Lesser is the variability with each stratum of the population, greater is the efficiency;

(b) As marked are the differences as possible between the various data;

(c) There is no overlapping in various strata.

The practice geographical, sociological and economic characteristics are often used for stratification of the universe. *For example,* if it is desired to study the wage levels of workers in an industry, it would be better to classify all workers into skilled and unskilled, clerical and unclerical, sexwise categories and then select random sample from each class or group in proportion to the size of the group in population. The combined sample so obtained will represent better the characteristics of the population as a whole.

The size of the sample from each strata can either be *(i)* proportional, or *(ii)* disproportional to the size of each stratum.

1. Proportional Size. Under this a given percentage of items are elected from each stratum. *For example,* in case of 50% selection there with be a selection of 10 out of 20 units and 20 out of 40 units the strata from comprising 20 and 40 units. This selection will, however, be a random one, following any of the methods indicated earlier.

2. Disproportional Size. A disproportional selection may also be recommended if different strata reveal different levels of within strata variability. Following the normal sampling rules, a larger sample is recommended if some sub-universes (strata) reveal greater degree of variability with regard to a phenomenon relevant to the inquiry compared with the general lot. However, any estimate with regard to the total universe will be based on the weighted average of all the strata.

Merits

1. **Administrative Convenience.** As compared with simpled random sample, the stratified samples would be more concentrated geographically. Accordingly, the time and money involved in collecting the data and interviewing the individuals may be considerably reduced and the supervision of the field work could be allotted with greater case and convenience.
2. **Greater Accuracy.** Stratified sampling provides estimates with increased precision. Moreover, startified sampling enables us to obtain results of the known precision for each of the stratum.
3. **More Representative.** In an unstratified random sample some strata may be over-represented, others may be under-represented, while some may be excluded altogether. Stratified sampling ensures a

desired representation of various strata in the population. It over rules the possibility of any essential group of the population being completely excluded in the sample. Stratified sampling thus, provides a more representative cross-section of the population and is frequently regarded as the most efficient system of sampling.

4. Stratification is great advantage when the distribution of the universe is skewed.

   As W.M. Harper writes: "The reason why stratified sampling is an improvement over a pure random sampling is that it lessens the possibility of one-sidedness."

5. Sometimes the sampling problems may differ markedly in different parts of the population, *e.g.*, a population under study consisting of *(i)* literates and illiterates or *(ii)* people living in institutions, hostels, hospitals etc., and those living in ordinary homes. In such cases, we can deal with the problem through stratified sampling by regarding the different parts of the population as strata and tackle the problems of the survey within each stratum independently.

Demerits

1. It is a very difficult task to divide the populations into homogeneous strata. This may require considerable time, money and satistical expertise.
2. The supplementary information to set-up starta is not available sometimes.
3. If different strata of a population overlap such a sampling would not be representative.

Systematic Random Sampling

This method is popularly used in those cases where a complete list of the population from which samples has to be drawn is available.

Under this method the kth item is picked up from the sample frame and k is the sampling interval defined as

$$k\ N/n$$

Where, N is the total size of the population and *n* is the proposed size of the sample.

Therefore, if 2000 items are to be selected from a universe or 2,000 items the k will be 10. Now if the starting number is say 6 then the kth numbers will be 16th, 26th, 36th etc. It is therefore necessary to select the starting point carefully either by drawing a card from a well shuffled pack of cards or by throwing a dice or by taking out a number chit from a lot of 10 numbers or so.

This method although called a systematic random is not necessarily a very scientific method. It is suitable when there is no unique variation in the universe. *For example,* if in a housing colony every 10th house (10th, 20th, 30th...) is constrcuted on a corner plot which is larger than the rest taking every 10th house starting with 1 will give a biased selection in favour of the wealthier sections, who occupy these costly corner houses. Therefore, care should be taken to see that the systematic sampling does not introduce any bias for a given characteristic, keeping in view the purpose of the inquiry.

Judgement Sampling

Under judgement sampling there is a deliberate selection based on the judgement of the person entrusted with the job. It is also called "deliberate sampling" or "purposive sampling". The worth of this method will depend of the sampling design. The purpose of representativeness can also be realized be it if the selection is objective and proper judgement is exercised by an expert in the field who knows the limitations of such a selection.

Purposive sampling can ensure proper representation of a cross-section of various strata of a universe without actual stratification of the persons handling the operations have full knowledge of the composition of the universe. *For example,* the financial institutions can ensure representative character in a purposive selection of sick units financed by them. Similarly, The Steel Authority of India Ltd. (SAIL) can ensure the section of the user of steel, in say engineering, construction, transportation, etc.

Multistage Random Sampling

Under this method, the random selection is made of primary, intermediate and final (or the ultimate) units from a given population or straum. This, the area of investigation is scientifically restricted to a small number of ultimate units which are representative of the whole. This will reduce the cost compared with a simple sampling from the whole area with a number of straight random selections. *For example,* from a stratum of a climatic region of the Eastern States the two primary sampling areas may be North-Eastern and South-Eastern. From within each of these primary sampling areas a certain number of blocks may be selected at random for ultimate selection of the villages for complete enumeration or the selection of the required number of households. At each stage there is a random selection and the size of sample may be proportional or disproportional depending on the size and character of variations relevant to the purpose of inquiry.

Suppose, a socio-economic survey has to be conducted in distinct where a complete list of all households is not available but the list of villages is readily available. In such a situation, first a sample of villagers may be selected and then a sample of households may be drawn from each selected village after making a complete list of households therein. This is case of two-state sampling. It may happen that even the list of village is not available but a list of tehsils only is avaible. Then a sample of households may be selected in three selected in three stages; the tehsils will be taken as first stage and will constitute the primary units, village will be selected in the second stage pre-ultimate stage from the list prepared in the selected tehsils and households as the third or the ultimate state units from the selected villages. It is three-stage sampling and can be extended further, if necessary.

Quota Sampling

In this method the interviews select respondents in accordance with the instructions and guidelines provided to them. They try to complete the quota assigned to them by supplementing new respondents in place of those not available or are uncooperative of course from amongst the selected ones. This latitude to the interviewers, especially in rural areas, for certain marketing studies helps in the completion of the work in the allotted time. The time lost in reference to higher authorities and awaiting instructions for replacement as per original plan may consume quite a lot of time. Often the instructions are for substitution of the like units, from all angles, keeping in view the purpose of the inquiry. With properly trained field staff this should not distort the basic purpose of the study.

Cluster Sampling

This method presupposes the divison of the population in a finite number of divisions and other identifiable groups. *For example,* a human population might be regarded as composed of individual persons, families or group of persons residing in town or a village. The smallest unit into which the population can be described are the elements of the population and groups of elements are called clusters. Cluster sampling consists in forming suitable clusters of units and surveying all the units in some clusters selected according to an appropriate sampling scheme.

Sequential Sampling

In this method, a number of sample lots are drawn one after another from a universe depending on the results of the earlier samples. Such sampling is generally adopted in statistical quality control. If the first sample is clearly acceptable, no new sample is drawn. If it is completely unacceptable, the lot is rejected straight away. However, if the initial lot is of a doubtful and marginal character failling in the band lying between acceptance and rejection limits, a second and if need be a third sample of large size may be drawn to arrive at a decision on final acceptance or rejection of the lot. Such sampling can be based on any of the random or non-random methods of selection.

Convenience Sampling

It is said to have been used when selection is made from an available source like that of telephone directory, automobile registration records, industrial or exchange directories, etc. This is because it is so convenient to use these sources. But whether it will be proper to use these sources which depend on the purpose of inquiry. They do represent a certain cross-section of people sharing some common characteristics yet not alone in all respects. *For example,* the subscribers to the "Readers Digest" may represent a geographical or intellectual cross-section but not of income or literacy or rural-urban cross-section. Similarly a list of students in college may be suitable for an inquiry into matters pertaining to education in the college but not the university education as a whole.

To sum up, there is no particular sanctity in a given system. Much depends on the purpose of the inquiry, how sampling is conducted and how effective is the control during the operation. Two or more methods may be combined to suit the purpose but the procedure once adopted must be following consistently. Further, the method adopted should be self-defined so that ambiguities and inconsistencies are eliminated. This is particularly important in case of repeated experiments conducted to assess changes is a given phenomenon.

Sampling and Non-sampling Errors

Errors in statistics are classified in two categories, namely 1. Sampling errors and 2. Non-sampling errors.

1. Sampling Errors. Samplings errors have their origin in sampling and they arise on account of the fact that sample has been used to estimate parameters or population values. Such errors are not found in census enquiry where the whole universe is investigated. Sampling errors are attributed to fluctuation of sampling and that is why they are called sampling errors. Such errors would always be there is sample studies, notwithstanding the fact, that the sample has been properly chosen and it is of adequate size. Samples always give estimated figures about the universe and the difference between the actual and estimated figures would always remain and the differences are called sampling errors.

Generally, sampling errors are due to the following reasons:

(a) **Faulty Demarcation of Statistical Units.** If statistical units are not properly demarcated, the sample will become unrepresentative or give faulty conclusions. It is true, particularly in crop-cutting experiments where sample fields have to be demarcated to ensure precision. If there is a mistake in demarcation, results or the experiment would be faulty.

(b) **Substitution.** If a sample unit is absent or any information from it is not available and this unit is substituted by another unit the sample will lose its representative character and this can also introduce an element of error in the sampling.

(c) **Errors due to Variability of Population and Wrong Method of Estimation.** Sometimes a population is highly hetrogenous and in such a case a sampling result may be very much different from the actual value of the parameter. This would also be so if the parameter or population values are not properly estimated on the basis of sampling results.

(d) **Improper Selection of the Sample.** If the sample has not been properly selected, it would lead to sampling error. *For example,* if the sample has been selected on the basis of personal judgement or convenience, it

may not be representative of the universe and the sampling error in such a case can be substantial. This bias can be overcome if the selection of the sample is on the basis of random sampling.

Measurement of Sampling Error. A measure of sampling error is provided by the standard error of the estimate. Estimation of sampling error can reduce the element of uncertainty associated with interpretation of data. In most cases, the degree of precision or the opposite or error, would depend on the size of the sample. The standard error of estimate is inversely proportional to the square root of the sample size. In other words, as the sample size increases, element of error is reduced.

2. Non-Sampling Error. As distinct from sampling errors (which are due to drawing inferences about the universe on the basis of the sample studies) non-sampling errors generally arise when data are not properly observed, approximated and processed. These are not chance errors. Such errors are present in both Census as well as Sample methods of survey. In the Census method although the data are free from sampling errors yet there could be non-sampling errors in them. The data obtained from sample surveys are subject both to sampling and non-sampling errors. Non-sampling errors generally arise due to the following reasons:

(a) Improper converage and inadequate or incomplete response also results in non-sampling errors.

(b) **Incomplete Questionnaire and Defective Methods of Interviewing.** They may also give rise to non-sampling errors.

(c) **Improper or Ambiguous Definition of the Various Terms.** If the different terms used in a survey are not properly defined and cannot be easily identified, mistakes would creep in an the element of non-sampling errors would go up.

(*d*) **Personal Bias of the Investigator,** is also responsible for non-sampling errors as the data collected in such a situation would not be representative.

(*e*) **Lack of Trained and Qualified Investigators and Failure** of respondents to give correct answers also leads to such errors.

(*f*) **Errors in Compilation and Tabulation.** Very often mistakes are committed in the tabulation and classification of data which result in non-sampling errors. Such errors may also arise on account of defective printing of the tabulated results.

Measurement of Errors. Statistical errors can be measured either:

(*a*) Absolutely.

(*b*) Relatively

Absolute and Relative Errors. If the error is measured absolutely it is called an absolute error and if it is measured relatively it is called relative error. Absolute error is the difference between the true value and the estimate. If the actual figure of sales of a concern is ₹ 9,900 and the approximated figure is ₹ 10,000 there is difference of ₹ 100 in these two figures. This is an absolute error. Relative error is the ratio of the absolute error to the estimate. In the above example if the absolute error of ₹ 100 is divided by the estimated figure of ₹ 10,000 the result $\frac{100}{10,000}$ or 0.01 is the relative error. The relative error can also be expressed in terms of percentages. It is then known as percentage error. In this example percentage error would be $\frac{100}{10,000} \times 100$ or 1%.

Absolute and relative errors can be either positive or negative. If the true value exceeds the estimate, the error is said to be positive and on the other hand if the estimate exceeds the true value the error is called negative.

Sampling Distributions

Some important sampling distributions, which are commonly used, are : (1) sampling distribution of mean; (2) sampling distribution of proportion; (3) student's '*t*' distribution; (4) F-distribution; and (5) Chi-square (χ^2) distribution. A brief mention of each one of these sampling distributions will be helpful.

1. Sampling Distribution of Mean. Sampling distribution of mean refers to the probability distribution of all the possible means of random samples of a given size that we take from a population. If samples are taken from a normal population, N.(μ, σ_p), the sampling distribution of mean would also be normal with mean $\mu_{\bar{X}} = \mu$ and standard deviation = $\sigma_p \sqrt{n}$, where μ is the mean of the population, σ_p is the standard deviation of the population and *n* means the number of items in a sample. But when sampling is from a population which is not normal (may be positively or negatively skewed), even then, as per the central limit theorem, the sampling distribution of mean tends quite closer to the normal distribution, provided the number of sample items is large *i.e.,* more than 30. In case we want to reduce the sampling distribution of mean to unit normal distribution *i.e., N* (0, 1), we can write the normal variate $z = \dfrac{\bar{X} - \mu}{\sigma_p / \sqrt{n}}$ for the sampling distribution of mean. This characteristic of the sampling distribution of mean is very useful in several decision situations for accepting or rejection of hypotheses.

2. Sampling Distribution of Proportion. Like sampling distribution of mean, we can as well have a sampling distribution of proportion. This happens in case of statistics of attributes. Assume that we have worked out the proportion of defective parts in large number of samples, each with say 100 items, that have been taken from an infinite population and plot a probability distribution of the said proportions, we obtain what is known as the sampling distribution of the said proportions, we obtain what is known as the sampling distribution of propertion. Usually the statistics of attributes correspond to the conditions of a binomial distribution that tends to become normal distribution as *n* becomes larger and larger. If p *r*epresents the proportion of defectives *i.e.,* of successes and q the proportion of non-defectives *i.e.,* of failures (or q = 1 – p) and if p is treated as a random variable, then the sampling distribution of proportion of successes has a mean = p with standard deviation = $\sqrt{\frac{p.q}{n}}$, where n is the sample size. Presuming the binomial distribution approximating the normal distribution for large n, the normal variate of the sampling distribution of proportion $z = \frac{\hat{p} - p}{\sqrt{(p.q)/n}}$ where $\hat{p}$ (pronounced as p-hat) is the sample proportion of successes, can be used for testing of hypotheses.

3. Student's t-Distribution. When population standard deviation (σ_p) is not known and the sample is of a small size (*i.e.,* n $\not>$ 30), we use t distribution for the sampling distribution of mean and workout t variable as:

$$t = \left(\bar{X} - \mu\right) / \left(\sigma_x / \sqrt{n}\right)$$

where,

$$\sigma_x = \sqrt{\frac{\Sigma\left(X_i - \bar{X}\right)^2}{n} - 1}$$

i.e., the sample standard deviation. t-distribution is also symmetrical and is very close to the distribution of standard normal variate, z, except for small values of n. The variable t differs from z in the sense that we use sample standard deviation (σ_3) in the calculation of t, whereas we use standard deviation of population (σ_p) in the calculation of z. There is a different t-distribution for every possible sample size *i.e.,* for different degrees of freedom. The degrees of freedom for a sample of size n is n – 1. As the sample size gets larger, the shape of the t-distribution becomes appoximately equal to the normal distribution. In fact, for sample sizes of more than 30, the t-distribution is so close to the normal distribution that we can use normal to approximate the t-distribution. But when n is small, the t-distribution is far for normal but when $n \rightarrow \alpha$, t-distribution is identical with normal distribution. The t-distribution tables are available which give the critical values of t for different degrees of freedom at various levels of significance. The table value of t for given degrees of freedom at a certain level of significance is compared with the calculated value of t from the sample data and if the latter is either equal to or exceeds, we infer that the null hypothesis cannot be accepted.

4. F-distribution. If $(\sigma_{x1})^2$ and $(\sigma_{x2})^2$ are the variances of two independent samples of size n_1 and n_2 resepectively taken from two independent normal populations, having the same variance, $(\sigma_{p1})^2 = (\sigma_{p2})^2$, the ratio $F = (\sigma_{x1})^2/(\sigma_{x2})^2$, where $(\sigma_{x1})^2 = \Sigma(\bar{X}_{1i} - \bar{X}_1)^2 / n_1 - 1$ and $(\sigma_{x2})^2 = \Sigma(\bar{X}_{2i} - \bar{X}_2)^2 / n_2 - 1$ has an F-distribution with $n_1 - 1$ and $n_2 - 1$ degrees of freedom. *F* ratio is computed in a way that the larger variance is always in the numerator. Tables have been prepared for F-distribution that give critical values of F for various values of degrees of freedom for larger as well as smaller variances. The calculated value of F from the sample data is compared with the corresponding table value of F and if the former is equal to or exceeds the latter, then we infer that the null hypothesis of the variances being equal cannot be accepted. We shall make use of the F ratio in the context of hypothesis testing and also in the context of ANOVA technique.

5. Chi-square (χ^2) Distribution. Chi-square distribution is encountered when we deal with collections of values that involve adding up squares. Variances of samples require us to add a collection of squared quantities and thus, have distributions that are related to chi-square distribution. If we take each one of a collection of sample variances, divide them by the known population variance and multiply these quotients by $(n-1)$, where n means the number of items in the sample, we shall obtain a chi-square distribution. Thus, (σ_x^2/σ_p^2) $(n-1)$ would have the same distribution as chi-square distribution with $(n-1)$ degrees of freedom. Chi-square distribution is not symmetrical and all the values are positive. One must know the degrees of freedom for using chi-square distribution. This distribution may also be used for judging the significance of difference between observed and expected frequencies and also as a test of goodness of fit. The generalised shape of χ^2 distribution depends upon the d.f. and the χ^2 value is worked out as under :

$$\chi^2 = \sum_{i=1}^{k} \frac{(O_i - E_i)^2}{E_i}$$

Tables are there that give the value of χ^2 for given d.f. which may be used with calculated value of χ^2 for relevant d.f. at a desired level of significance for testing hypotheses.

Central Limit Theorem

When sampling is from a normal population, the means of samples drawn from such a population are themselves normally distributed. But when sampling is not from a normal population, the size of the sample plays a critical role. When n is small, the shape of the distribution will depend largely on the shape of the parent population, but as n gets large ($n > 30$), the shape of the sampling distribution will become more and more like a normal distribution, irrespective of the shape of the parent population. The theorem which explains this sort of relationship between the shape of the population distribution and the sampling distribution of the mean is known as the central limit theorem. This theorem is by far the most important theorem in statistical inference. It assures that the sampling distribution of the mean approaches normal distribution as the sample size increases. In formal terms, we may say that the central limit theorem states that "the distribution of means of random samples taken from a population having mean μ and finite variance σ^2 approches the normal distribution with mean μ and variance σ^2/n as n goes to infinity."

"The significance of the central limit theorem lies in the fact that it permits us to use sample statistics to make inferences about population parameters without knowing anything about the shape of the frequency distribution of that population other than what we can get from the sample."

Sampling Theory

Sampling theory is a study of relationships existing between a population and samples drawn from the population. Sampling theory is applicable only to random samples. For this purpose the population or a universe may be defined as an aggregate of items possessing a common trait or traits. In other words, a universe is the complete group of items about which knowledge is sought. The universe may be finite or infinite. Finite universe is one which has a definite and certain number of items, but when the number of items is uncertain and infinite, the universe is said to be an infinite universe. Similarly, the universe may by hypothetical or existent. In the former case the universe in fact does not exist and we can only imagine the items constituting it. Tossing of a coin or throwing a dics are examples of hypothetical universe. Existent universe is a universe of concrete objects *i.e.,* the universe where the items constituting it really exist. On the other hand, the term sample refers to that part of the universe which is selected for the purpose of investigation. The theory of sampling studies the relationships that exist between the universe and the sample or samples drawn from it.

The main problem of sampling theory is the problem of relationship between a parameter and a statistic. The theory of sampling is concerned with estimating the properties of the population from those of the sample and also with gauging the precision of the estimate. This sort of movement from particular (sample) towards general (universe) is what is known as statistical induction or statistical inference. In more clear terms "from the sample we attempt to draw inference concerning the universe. In order to be able to follow this inductive method, we first follow a deductive argument which as that we imagine a population or universe (finite or infinite) and investigate the behaviour of the samples drawn from this universe applying the laws of probability." The methodology dealing with all this is known as sampling theory.

Sampling theory is designed to attain one or more of the following objectives :

1. Statistical Estimation. Sampling theory helps in estimating unknown population parameters from a knowledge of statistical measures based on sample studies. In other words, to obtain an estimate of parameter from statistic is the main objective of the sampling theory. The estimate can either be a point estimate or it may be an interval estimate. Point estimate is a single estimate expressed in the form of a single figure, but interval estimate has two limits *viz.*, the upper limit and the lower limit within which the parameter value may lie. Interval estimates are often used in statistical induction.

2. Testing of Hypotheses. The second objective of sampling theory is to enable us to decide whether to accept or reject hypothesis; the sampling theory helps in determining whether observed differences are actually due to chance or whether they are really significant.

3. Statistical Inference. Sampling theory helps in making generalisation about the population/universe from the studies based on samples drawn from it. It also helps in determining the accuracy of such generalisations.

The theory of sampling can be studied under two heads *viz.*, the sampling of attributes and the sampling of variables and that too in the context of large and small samples. (By small sample is commonly understood any sample that includes 30 or fewer items, whereas large sample is one in which the number of items is more than 30). When we study some qualitative characteristic of the items in a population, we obtain statistics of attributes in the form of two classes; one class consisting of items wherein the attribute is present and the other class consisting of items wherein the attribute is absent. The presence of an attribute may be termed as a 'success' and its absence a 'failure'. Thus, if out of 600 people selected randomly for the sample, 120 are found to possess a certain attribute and 480 are such people where the attribute is absent. In such a situation we would say that sample consists of 600 items (*i.e.*, $n = 600$) out of which 120 are successes and 480 failures. The probability of success would be taken as $120/600 = 0.2$ (*i.e.*, $p = 0.2$) and the probability of failure or $q = 480/600 = 0.8$. With such data the sampling distribution generally takes the form of binomial probability distribution whose mean (μ) would be equal to $n - p$ and standard deviation (σ_p) would be equal to $\sqrt{n.p.q.}$. If n is large, the binomial distribution tends to become normal distribution which may be used for sampling analysis. We generally consider the following three types of problems in case of sampling of attributes :

(*a*) The parameter value may be given and it is only to be tested if an observed 'statistic' is its estimate.

(*b*) The parameter value is not known and we have to estimate it from the sample.

(*c*) Examination of the reliability of the estimate *i.e.*, the problem of finding out how far the estimate is expected to deviate from the true value for the population.

The theory of sampling can be applied in the context of statistics of variables (*i.e.*, data relating to some characteristic concerning population which can be measured or enumerated with the help of some well defined statistical unit) in which case the objective happens to be; *(i)* to compare the observed and expected values and to find if the difference can be ascribed to the fluctuations of sampling; *(ii)* to estimate population parameters from the sample and *(iii)* to find out the degree of reliability of the estimate.

The tests of significance used for dealing with problems relating to large samples are different from those used for small samples. This is so because the assumptions we make in case of large samples do not hold good for small samples. In case of large samples, we assume that the sampling distribution tends to be normal and the sample values are approximately close to the population values. As such we use the characteristics of normal distribution and apply what is known as *z*-test. Then *n* is large, the probability of a sample value of the statistic deviating from the parameter by more than 3 times its standard error is very small (it is 0.0027 as per the table giving area under normal curve) and as such the *z*-test is applied to find out the degree of reliability of a statistic in case of large samples. Appropriate standard errors have to be worked out which will enable us to give the limits within which the parameter values would lie or would enable us to judge whether the difference happens to be significant or not at certain confidence levels. For instance, $\overline{X} \pm 3\sigma_{\overline{X}}$ would give us the range within which the parameter mean value is expected to vary with 99.73% confidence.

The sampling theory for large samples is not applicable in small samples because when samples are small, we cannot assume that the sampling distribution is approximately normal. As such we require a new technique for handling small samples, particularly when population parameters are unknown. Sir William S. Gosset (pen name Student) developed a significance test, known as Student's *t*-test based on *t* distribution and through it made significant contribution in the theory of sampling applicable in case of small samples. Student's *t*-test is used when two conditions are fulfilled *viz.*, the sample size is 30 or less and the population variance is not known. While using *t*-test we assume that the population from which sample has been taken is normal or approximately normal, sample is a random sample, observations are independent, there is no measurement error and that in the case of two samples when equality of the two population means is to be tested, we assume that the population variances are equal. For applying *t*-test,we work out the value of test statistic (*i.e.*, '*t*') and then compare with the table value of *t* (based on '*t*' distribution) at certain level of significance for given degrees of freedom. If the calculated value of '*t*' is either equal to or exceeds the table value, we infer that the difference is significant, but if calculated value of *t* is less than the concerning table value of *t*, the difference is not treated as significant. The following formula are commonly used to calculate the *t* value :

(i) To test the significance of the mean of a random sample

$$t = \frac{(\bar{X} - \mu)}{\sigma_{\bar{X}}}$$

where, $\bar{X}$ = Mean of the sample,

μ = Mean of the universe/population,

$\sigma_{\bar{X}}$ = Standard error of mean worked out as under :

$$\sigma_{\bar{X}} = \frac{\sigma_x}{\sqrt{n}} = \sqrt{\frac{\Sigma(X_i - \bar{X})^2}{n-1}} / \sqrt{n}$$

and the degrees of freedom = (n -1).

(ii) To test the difference between the means of two samples:

$$t = \frac{\bar{X}_1 - \bar{X}_2}{\sigma_{\bar{X}_1 - \bar{X}_2}}$$

where, $\bar{X}_1$ = Mean of sample one,

$\bar{X}_2$ = Mean of sample two,

$\sigma_{\bar{X}_1-\bar{X}_2}$ = Standard error of difference between two sample means worked out as :

$$\sigma_{\bar{X}_1-\bar{X}_2} = \sqrt{\frac{\Sigma(X_{1i}-\bar{X}_1)^2+\Sigma(X_{2i}-\bar{X}_2)^2}{n_1+n_2-2}} \times \sqrt{\frac{1}{n_1}+\frac{1}{n_2}}$$

and the d.f. = $(n_1 + n_2 - 2)$.

(iii) To test the significance of the coefficient of simple correlation :

$$t = \frac{r}{\sqrt{1-r^2}} \times \sqrt{n-2} \qquad \text{or} \qquad t = r\sqrt{\frac{n-2}{1-r^2}}$$

where, r = the coefficient of simple correlation,

and the d.f. = $(n - 2)$.

(iv) To test the significance of the coefficient of partial correlation,

$$t = \frac{r_p}{\sqrt{1-r_p^{\,2}}} \times \sqrt{n-k} \qquad \text{or} \qquad t = r_p\sqrt{\frac{(n-k)}{1-r_p^{\,2}}}$$

where, r_p is any partial coefficient of correlation,

and the d.f.=$(n -k)$,

n being the number of pairs of obsevations and k being the number of variables involved.

(v) To test the difference in case of paired or correlated samples data (in which case *t* test is often described as difference test) :

$$t = \frac{\bar{D}-\mu_D}{\sigma_D}\sqrt{n} \quad \textit{i.e.,} \quad t = \frac{\bar{D}-0}{\sigma_D}\sqrt{n}$$

where,

Hypothesised mean difference (μ_D) is taken as zero (0),

$\bar{D}$ = Mean of the differences of correlated sample items,

σ_D = Standard deviation of differencer worked out as under :

$$\sigma_D = \sqrt{\frac{\Sigma D_i^2 - \bar{D}/n}{n-1}}$$

D_i = Differences {*i.e.*, $D_i = (X_i - Y_i)$},

n = number of pairs in two samples,

and the d.f. = (*n* -1).

8

Normative Survey Method

The normative survey type of research is not peculiar to education or to other social sciences, It is a significant mode of attack in any field of knowledge where geographic distribution is involved or where the objects of any class vary among themselves, *e.g.*, in studying the climatic conditions of various parts of the world, or the distribution of natural resources.

Survey research is a method for collecting and analysing data, obtained from large number of respondents representing a specific population collected through highly structured and detailed qucstionnaire, or interviews. The researcher is usually interested in describing the population he is studying.

The survey approach to educational problems is one of the most commonly used approaches. It is followed in studying local, as well as state, national and international aspects of education. It goes beyond mere gathering and tabulation of data. It involves interpretation, comparison, measurement, classification, evaluation and generalization—all directed towards a proper understanding and solution of significant educational problems. There are any number of questions that arise concerning current conditions in the educational world. *For example*, one may ask: What kind of curriculum do people really want their children to have? At what age and grade level do pupils leave school? What happens to children after they leave school? What higher institutions or vocations do they enter? What is the average achievement-level of school children in particular subjects at various grades in different schools or in different states? How do the private schools compare with government schools in their educational outcomes?—and so on. Such information is important for administrators, teachers and educational planners alike. It brings into the focus of our attention existing educational problems and also suggests ways of meeting them. Worthwhile survey studies collect three types of information:

(i) Of what exists by studying and analysing important aspects of present situation.

(ii) Of how to get there through discovering the possible means of achieving the goals on the basis of the experiences of others or the opinions of experts.

(iii) Of what we want by clarifying goals and objectives possibly through a study of the conditions existing elsewhere or what experts consider to be desirable.

Characteristics

Some characteristics of the Normative Survey Research may be listed below:

1. It gathers data from a relatively large number of cases.
2. It is essentially cross-sectional, mostly of the what exists type.
3. It is concerned not with the characteristics of individuals but with generalized statistics of the whole population or a sample thereof.
4. It is an important type of research involving clearly defined problems and definite objectives. It requires an imaginative planning, a careful analysis and interpretation of the data and a logical and skilful reporting of the findings.
5. Surveys may be qualitative or quantitative. At One level survey or status studies may consist of naming

and defining constituent elements of various phenomena, *e.g.*, the qualities of a good teacher. At another level they may involve ascertaining the amounts of constituents or characteristics.

6. It does not aspire to devdop an organized body of scientific laws but provides information useful to the solution of local problems. It may, however, provide data to form the basis of research of a more fundamental nature.
7. Descriptions may be either verbal or expressed in mathematical symbols.
8. Surveys vary greatly in complexity, some concerning themselves only with the frequency count of events, while others seek to establish relationship among events.
9. The great range of phenomena forming the subject of educational surveys may be classified as:
   - *(a)* Behavioural conditions related to learning (behaviour of pupils, teachers and parents, etc.).
   - *(b)* Physical conditions related to learning (building, furniture and libraries, etc.).
   - *(c)* The results of learning or the pupils' ability to learn (achievement or basic skills, information or attitudes).
10. It fits appropriately into the total research scheme or the stages in exploring a large field of investigation. It may *(a)* serve as a reconnaissance or getting aquainted stage of research in entering a new area, or *(b)* represent a specific interest in current conditions within a field that has long since been explored and developed by research.

Significance

Scientists do not generally regard the normative survey investigations as research of high order. But the type of information the normative survey method procures is in wide demand and is capable of rendering important service because :

1. It determines the present trends and solves current practical problems.
2. It helps fashion many of the tools with which we do research, *e.g.*, in the development of instruments for measuring many things in quantitative research as well as various data-gathering instruments like checklists, schedules, score cards and rating scales.
3. It secures historical perspective through a series of cross-sectional pictures of similar conditions at different times.
4. It suggests the course of future developments. Although it is not notably forward-looking, it does tend to focus attention on needs, to reveal practices which are well above average and to give pertinent data to persons whoare forward-looking and are engaged in planning for the future.
5. It contributes to advancement of knowledge because it affords penetrating insight into the nature of what one is dealing with. *For example,* by studying children of different ages we can differentiate our findings according to age and obtain some picture of the trend of development.
6. It provides the background ideas and data from which many more refined laboratory or controlled studies of causal relations are made.

Kinds of Normative Survey Research

Normative survey investigations may be variously classified on the basis of the fields they study, the purposes they achieve, the geographical areas they cover, or the techniques they employ. According to the fields of study, we come across social surveys, commercial surveys, community surveys and educational surveys. We are concerned here with the normative surveys in the educational field which may be classified further according to:

1. The maior aspects of the school systems they study: school plant, educational programme, educational outcomes, behaviour and attitude, etc.
2. The geographical areas they cover: local, state, regional, National or International.
3. The levels of instruction they investigate into nursery, elementary, secondary and higher.
4. The type of preparation they aim at: general, teacher-training, engineering, medicine, law or social work.
5. The data gathering techniques or procedures employed: questionnaire, interview, observation, testing, socio-metrics, rating and ranking.
6. The purpose they fulfil follow-up youth out of school, describe the membership of an educational organization, describe the characteristics of a group of institutions, poll the opinions of a group of parents, identify trends or engage in survey testing or educational appraisal.

We will now consider in some detail educational surveys of different types current in the educational world.

A. School Surveys

"It can be well said that no other unified undertaking so fully represents the normative-survey method of research in all its various phases as does the schools survey."

School surveys of the comprehensive type cover such aspects as:

1. Aims, outcomes, pupil achievement, curriculum, methods and instructional aids.
2. Operation and maintenance of the physical plant and related factors.
3. Pupil transportation.

4. Administrative problems and procedures.
5. Financial policies and procedures.
6. Staff and personnel.

Some school surveys may be concerned with the problem of school building only. They study community and school setting, estimate further school enrolment, school plant planning, pupil transportation system, available financial resources for buildings, etc. Other surveys may concern themselves with the directly educational problems of instructional programme aims and objectives, curriculum and methods, aids, activities and achievement.

A school survey is commonly conducted in order to determine the services that a school can render a community and perhaps to compare these services with those that are provided by other schools. The ultimate aim of all school surveys is educational progress which they achieve by focusing attention on unfulfilled needs or unrecognized evils of a school system on the one hand and on worthwhile practices on the other. They appraise the efficiency of a system and of the personnel and help in determining the next desirable steps. Though employing procedures and tools (score card and checklist, etc.) which are not highly objective and which involve a considerable element of subjectivity or personal reaction, school surveys yet, have real strength and value as they focus personal opinion and reactions on the important problems of a school.

School surveys have been sponsored and undertaken by a variety of groups and organizations like local or district boards of education, state or national committees of education, departments of education and the like. An individual investigator, working alone, can seldom attempt comprehensive school survey except in a very small school system. However, many researchers have worked out worthwhile functional types of theses and dissertations through participation in comprehensive, educational or school-plant surveys.

Large and varied as the scope of school survey is, a single comprehensive school survey may be constituted of various parts or constituent surveys. The following are some such important parts of school surveys:

1. Survey testing:
   (a) Achievement Testing.
   (b) Intelligence Testing.
   (c) Personality Testing.
2. School Appraisal.
3. Status Studies.
4. Financial Studies.
5. Curriculum Studies.
6. Building Survey.

1. Survey Testing

(a) Achievement Testing

Survey testing of educational attainment has become a large and well-established part of school surveys. Achievement tests of the objective type are being and have been, constructed for the purpose by various agencies. They are based upon the current courses of study adopted by the schools within the area or system under investigation and may cover any or all subjects and grades. It is not a routine administration of such tests but their use in the thorough analysis of some important problem which constitutes research of an important kind. Such achievement-testing surveys may serve many a purpose:

1. They may enable the superintendent to compare the performance of present pupils with that of the previous years, or of different schools and may in the case of unsatisfactory performance lead to an investigation of the causes of and remedies for inadequate attainment.
2. They may be taken as suggestive, if not a very reliable evidence, of the quality of teaching.

3. They may be used as one of the means of rating different educational institutions.
4. Principals and teachers may use the result of city or state-wide survey-testing for a critical analysis of their own schools and classes.
5. They may form a part of large, complex studies of other types than survey, *e.g.*, in experimental and complex-causal studies.

A number of regular achievement-testing programmes covering large areas such as states, regions or country as a whole, is an important feature of educational research carried on in the U.S.A. Several agencies conduct achievement-testing on a national scale. The European countries—England, France and Germany, etc., do not share the American attitude toward achievement-testing to any large degree, although they, too, have utilized survey-testing of achievement for some specific purposes (*e.g.*, for selection of candidates for particular courses of study). In India, we are at the beginning stage in this field. Many research institutions are constructing adequate achievement tests for the purpose of more or less wide educational surveys.

(b) Intelligence Testing

Although used to a much less extent than the achievement tests in school surveys, yet intelligence tests are a very important tool for educational researchers. For the purpose of large group studies of the survey type, the intelligence tests used are invariably group tests—verbal or non-verbal, or both. The many purposes for which survey intelligence-testing has been used are:

1. For dividing large classcs into relatively homogeneous sections.
2. For estimating aptitude, *i.e.*, for prognosis.
3. For diagnosing and adjusting individual children in educational and vocational guidance.

4. For constructing or adopting intelligence tests.
5. For scientific experimentation and study.
6. For ascertaining the intellectual level of pupils who enter college, who succeed in school but do not enter college and who do not succeed in school.
7. For studying the socially or educationally maladjusted children.

(c) Personality Testing

Among the desired educational outcomes modification of behaviour and formation of desirable attitudes are given an important place. In other words, personality traits are among the most important educational outcomes to be hoped for. Though difficult to define, analyse and measure, they still have given rise to some instruments for survey-testing in the field of personality, character and adjustment which embrace a wide variety. of techniques. Questionnaires, interviews, observations, checklists and rating scales, as also some carefully pre-arranged social situations, are frequently employed in addition to written tests. None of these tools is fool-proof and in interpreting the data collected by any of these the investigator is required to use logical analysis, imaginative interpretation and right judgement.

Personality testing includes:

(i) Behaviour studies: centred round measuring such traits as self-reliance, initiative, spontaneity, judgement, cooperation, adaptability, etc. which form no mean goals of education.

(ii) Attitude studies: centred round the attitudes of pupils, parents or teachers towards courses of study, activities in or out of school, professions and problems they may encounter.

2. School Appraisal

"Appraisal is a form of classification or scaling according to subjective values". It is undertaken for the specific purpose of including the human element in the verdict on schools, because problems of education are fundamentally different from those of physical sciences. It is an attempt to measure not the objective characteristics of a school, but the effect of those characteristics on human beings. Appraisal of different aspects of a school or school system is an essential element in school surveys. It is concerned with both the objective aspects of an educational institution including its administrative provisions and practices and the educational attainments of its pupils. In other words, it takes account of both static and functional data, or of conditions and outcomes. It aims at an evaluation of all the elements in a situation which are significant indicators of good educational influence. To achieve this aim, besides attainment tests, checklists, rating scales, or score cards, the researcher must make use of other lines of evidence such as reputation and subsequent success of the pupils. Many instruments for the purpose of school appraisal have been prepared and used in the U.S.A., *e.g.*, the checklists by Wade, N.E.A. and Frednck and Schorling; the score card by Mort and Hilleboe; and the various criteria worked out by accrediting institutions like the North Central Association and others. These emphasize a study of practices and provisions with some attention to pupil results. A series of schedules for evaluating secondary schools In such areas as agriculture, art, business education, English, foreign languages, health and safety, home economics, industrial arts, mathematics, music, physical education, science, social studies, progress of studies, pupil activity projects, library service, guidance, school plant, school staff and administration, etc., are made available.

School-appraisal surveys utilize in one instance or another the whole range of normative survey procedures including the following:

1. Analysis of available basic data.
2. Score card and rating scale.
3. Experimental procedure.

4. Interview or questionnaire.
5. Case study.
6. Standard tests.
7. Observation.

The major steps involved in a school survey include:

1. Preparation of plans.
2. Interpretation of data.
3. Gathering data.
4. Preparation of adequate tools-questionnaire, tests, rating scale and score cards.
5. Preparing the report.

The whole procedure, however, has to be definitely purposive and not a mechanical application of steps and techniques. Survey must be regarded as a research problem worked out in the field.

3. Status Studies

Determining the status, including personal and professional characteristics, of various school officials and teachers may be a part of a school study, or subject for independent study. In the U.S.A. independent status studies have been undertaken on a national basis for high school principals, city superintendents of schools, rural school teachers, etc. Similar studies have been made in various States also. Questionnaires are the main means employed by the investigators. Official records are also utilized. The problems of selection. and placement of teachers, their teaching load, their status with regard to tenure, health, law, supply and demand, etc., all form subjects of such a study.

4. Financial Studies

The financial position of a school forms an important aspect of school studies. To ascertain the sources of finance, the items of expenditure, the deficit or indebtedness, expenditure per pupil and the teachers' salaries, etc., questionnaires are used.

5. Curriculum Studies

As part of a school survey the object may be merely to analyse the existing curriculum in a school system and perhaps to compare it with that existing elsewhere. But if carried on as an independent study it may take a more complicated shape. It may include an analysis of the principles on which the curriculum is based, the needs it fulfills, the form it has taken and the shortcomings it suffers from. The relation to the community it serves may also be determined.

Study of Current Practices

A study of current practices forms another prominent part of school surveys. Practices with reference to school equipment, administration, teacher personnel, classroom teaching, extracurricular activities, etc., are studied. They may form subjects of independent investigations or comparative studies. Methods of teaching, ways of class-organization, use of audio-visual aids and other educational devices are important fields of study and provide interesting and useful data for the solution of educational problems.

6. Building Surveys

Survey of school buildings for the purpose of planning or evaluation, or just for the sake of information, is not an uncommon feature. It usually forms part of comprehensive or wider school surveys. Questionnaire, checklist, score card, or observation are the usual tools for collecting data about buildings their site and location, the accommodation they provide and the arrangement they have for various classes, subjects, activities or staff, the condition they are in as regards construction and cleanliness and the improvements or expansions they stand in need of. These studies too may be independent and complete in themselves, or comparative and part of wider school surveys. Building surveys generally deal with the community background and setting of schools, an estimate of future school enrolment, school plant planning and available financial resources for school buildings.

B. Documentary Frequency Studies

A definitely quantitative type of normative research, documentary frequency studies are undertaken to identify and count certain characteristics found in documents under consideration. They deal with a systematic examination of current records or documents and may merely gather and classify data from such documents or may also evaluate the contents according to some established criteria.

A study of this type involves problems:

1. Of ascertaining the purpose of the study.
2. Of determining what characteristics to count and of defining them.
3. Of selecting documentary specimens for investigation.

Documentary studies may serve the following purposes:

1. They may describe prevailing practices or conditions.
2. They may discover levels of difficulty of presentation in textbooks or other publications.
3. They may discover the relative importance, or interest in certain topics or problems.
4. They may analyse types of errors in students' work.
5. They may evaluate element of bias, prejudice or propaganda in textbook presentation.

The sources of data for documentary studies may be:

1. Official reports and records.
2. Printed forms, textbooks and reference books.
3. Pictures and cartoons, etc.
4. Compositions, themes or other prepared work.
5. Letters, autobiographies and diaries.
6. College bulletins, catalogues, syllabi.
7. Books, magazines, newspapers.

Types of documentary studies are:

1. Textbook analysis made to determine the extent to which certain significant objective characteristics occur in a book, or concerned with some features in the content of the book. Studies of vocabulary burden are a popular theme for such analyses. Allied to and based on textbook analysis procedure is the procedure of textbook appraisal.
2. 'Job-analysis' or 'activity analysis' in particular professions and occupations.
3. Analysis of farger bodies of literature as to the methods or techniques. It is employed with regard to certain problems or topics in an extensive body of literature on a subject.
4. Curriculum analysis in terms of frequency analysis of social activities, interests and needs.
5. Analysis of assembled specimens:
   (a) Vocabulary analysis, the studies of the writings of certain groups of individuals to ascertain common basic vccabulary or spelling achievement.
   (b) Error Studies concerned not with the frequency of use but the frequency of errors made in usage. These are also based on the analysis of informal writings of individuals. They are devoted chiefly to language in its various phases-spelling, punctuation, grammar, sentence structure, speech, etc. Arithmetic, geography and modern foreign languages lend themselves, to this kind of studies due to their 'usage' fields.
   (c) Analysis of characteristics ot school records and reports are also based on collected specimens which constitute an important phase of administration as well as instruction. They

determine the extent to which certain items or characteristics that appear in the forms of and the extent to which they are present in, various schools.

C. Follow-up Studies

Follow-up studies form another type of normative survey investigations which study individuals who have left an institution after a course of study or programme of work. They concern themselves with engagements, occupations and status of the individuals subsequent to their study and the impact of their previous institution and programme upon them. They examine the status of those who have passed out of an institution or seek their opinions directly as to the value of the courses, experiences or treatments received at the institution.

Follow-up studies may serve the following purposes:

1. They may prove the adequacy or otherwise of the institution's programme of work.
2. They may provide valuable information on the process of selection and recruitment of candidates for a course.
3. They may evaluate the influence of certain psychological, social or educational factors found among youngsters on their after life.
4. They may lead to the improvement of the curriculum, syllabus, methods of teaching, administrative procedure, guidance and service, etc.

The various tools used singly or in combination in follow-up studies are: questionnaires, checklists, rating scales, attitude scales, score-cards or interview and observation.

D. Survey-Appraisal Studies

Appraisal studies of certain aspects of existing educational phenomena like schools, students, teachers, textbooks, etc. are also of the normative survey type. Survey-appraisal studies lean more heavily upon the human element than surveys of other types, especially because appraisal is itself an attempt to determine the effect of characteristics upon human beings.

Studies that involve direct judgement commonly use the jury technique whereby the judgement (rating or ranking) of a number of persons with regard to certain persons, features or specimens, is pooled to secure a final verdict. Checklists, attitude scales, scaled specimens, rating scales, score-cards and index numbers are all tools commonly used for the purpose of appraisal. These appraisal instruments are based on two fundamental assumptions. One assumption is that better judgements can be secured on the significant aspects of an object or situation by focusing attention on one aspect at a time. The other assumption is that a general value can be approximated by assumption of the value of the parts. In so far as both these assumptions are open to doubt and criticism, these instruments of appraisal fail in being perfect. Yet, they are not without their use. "After all, appraisal schedules are normative instruments, they reflect general tendencies, tempered by the superior and by the inferior, but they represent in the main the things we are most used to."

E. Sample-Surveys

During recent years sampling has been increasingly used in education to ascertain information necessary in answering certain questions about a specific population. William G. Cochran, while discussing the advantages of the sampling method in surveys, writes:

> "In every branch of science we lack the resources to study more than a fragment of the phenomena that might advance our knowledge."

He analyses four principal advantages of sampling as compared with complete enumeration. They are:

(i) Reduced cost.

(ii) Greater speed.

(iii) Greater scope.

(iv) Greater accuracy.

In the field of education normative surveys of various types (described above) are usually sample surveys. That is, they usually define and measure the properties of an accurately defined population by means of the information obtained from a sample thereof. Until recently, relatively little attention was given to the problem of how to draw a good sample. This does not matter so long as the material from which We are sampling is uniform, so that any kind of sample gives almost the same results. But in the field of education material is usually far from ,uniform so that the method by which the sample is obtained becomes critical.

Sampling Problems. Almost all research studies in education may be termed sampling studies as data is usually collected from parts of the whole population. The obtained facts from samples should only be considered 'estimates' of the 'true' facts. Determination of sample should be based upon the purposes of the investigation, a precise description of the population to be investigated and the sources of that population, from which samples can be selected. Is the problem restricted to a particular group or are the conclusions to be generalized to a broader population?

The determination of the size of the sample is always a difficult problem for the researcher. Of course, the sample should be 'adequate' and 'representative'. But what do these terms mean with reference to a particular research project? No definite answer can be given to this problem. The researcher should be able to give conclusions based on samples with great confidence. The number should be larger in a sample from a heterogenous population as compared with the number in a sample from a homogenous population. If there are several categories of data in an educational experiment, *e.g.*, size of the school, type of school, age of pupil, sex, rural, urban etc., the number in the sample is bound to become larger.

Principal Methods of Sampling

To obtain a sample representative of its population four main techniques have been devised: Random, stratified or quota incidental and purposive.

Random Sampling

Sometimes termed as simple random sampling, sometimes as unrestricted random sampling and sometimes as just random sampling, this form of device is one in which every single unit of the population has an equal chance of being selected. A simple random sample is drawn unit by unit. The population is numbered from 1 to N and a series of random numbers is drawn either by means of a table of random numbers (*e.g.*, the FisherYates table of random numbers made up of 300 blocks, 25 numbers each printed on pages of 10 rows and 5 columns each. For using it, one can begin at any point on any page and read in any direction, in order and choose the required number of units to form 'n') or by placing the numbers (1 to N) in a bowl, mixing them thoroughly and drawing 'n' numbers in succession.

Stratified or Quota Sampling

A modified form of random sampling, stratified or quota sampling, sometimes cahed controlled sampling, is a device which ensures representativeness in selecting a sample from a population composed of subgroups or strata of different sizes. A good sample from such a population needs to contain individuals drawn from each category in accordance with the size of the sub-groups. Within each subgroup the sampling is random.

In stratified sampling, the population of N units is first divided into different strata—N_1, N_2, ... units respectively and then a sample is drawn from such stratum. The sample sizes within the strata are denoted by n_1, n_2, ... respectively.

Incidental Sampling

Incidental, or sometimes called accidental sampling, is a term which is applied when such groups are used as samples as are easily available, *e.g.*, children in a school, an orphanage or a reformatory, students enrolled in particular classes, etc. The number and conditions of these groups are not chosen specifically for the purpose.

Such groups are but poor samples of any definable population and adequate generalizations can hardly be based upon such data.

Purposive Sampling

As different from incidental sampling, purposive sampling is the device which selects a particular group or category from the population to constitute the sample because this category is considered to mirror the whole with reference to the characteristic in question. *For example*, purposive sampling is used when the selected sample is constituted of all the newspaper editors of an area to represent the public opinion of that area. In this type of selection the sample is restricted to units considered by someone to be especially typical of the population.

The Principal Steps in a Sample Survey

The steps that are usually involved in the execution of a survey of any type are:

1. Statement of the objectives of the survey.
2. Selection of the methods of data collection.
3. Choice of sampling unit.
4. Definition of the population to be sampled.
5. Determination of the data to be collected.
6. Selection of the sample.
7. Preparation of sampling survey report.
8. Summary and analysis of data.
9. Organization of the field work.

Characteristics of Good Sample

A good sample of a population is the one which, within restrictions imposed by its size, will reproduce the characteristics of the population with the greatest possible accuracy. That is to say, a good sample should be free from :

1. Error due to bias.
2. Random sampling error.

To select a good sample for any purpose, therefore, one should avoid such faulty methods as the following:

1. Deliberate selection of the unit of the sample.
2. Selection by a procedure where there is a connection between the method of selection and the characteristic under consideration.
3. Substituting one unit (included in the sample but found not available) by some other more convenient one.
4. Incomplete coverage of the units selected for study, *i.e.*, ignoring the failures in the sample in responding to the study.

However, it is found that even if the procedure of selection follows the canons of random sampling process, the sample cannot be exactly representative of the whole population. The inevitable errors resulting from the process are called random sampling errors. Probable Error formulae are the statistical devices to calculate the amount or probability limits of such errors. The amount of probable errors can be reduced by increasing the size of the sample. Thus, for increasing the accuracy of the sample, besides excluding all bias in selection, increasing the size of the sample is the simplest means. In the interpretation of the results and, in reaching conclusions the use of appropriate Probable Error formulae for particular statistic becomes essential. These formulae, however, fail to indicate anything reliable if applied to data secured from a biased sample.

***

9

Experimental Method

The experimental method in educational research is the application and adaptation of the classical method of the science laboratory. It is the most exacting and difficult of all methods and also the most important from the strictly scientific point of view. The main features of experimental method are:

1. Its basic assumption rests on J.S. Mill's law of the single variable which states that if two situations are similar in every respect and one element is added to or subtracted from one but not the other, any difference that develops is the result of the operation of that element added or subtracted. Experimentation, therefore, involves an attempt to control all essential factors save a single variable which is manipulated with a view to determining and measuring the effect of its operation. This procedure is distinctly different from the historical and the normative survey methods.

2. Most classroom experiments have attempted to eliminate one or more of the variables of age, achievement, intelligence, or reading ability, social status and race, etc. Experiments often have to be conducted using intact, existing groups, trusting that the variables not controlled are irrelevant or insignificant for the purpose of the study. The control group and the experimental group are never as identical as they ought to be for an exact experiment.

3. The concept of educational experimentation has developed since the beginning of the last decade of the 19th

century and interest in the experimental method of research in education has made rapid progress in the last fifty years or so. Wundt was the first to study experimentally the learning process and clarify and define learning patterns. Ebbinghaus invented methods of measuring association and memory in 1880's and his studies as well as of some others, in memory, puzzle-learning and in the acquisition of skills affected teaching techniques. More recently the experimental work of Thorndike, Judd and Freeman has paved the way for further experimental research in education. The beginning of strict educational experimentation may be found, however, in the work of Rice and Cornman during the last decade of the 19th century who made studies of spelling achievement among students.

4. Now a frequently used procedure in educational research, it has been applied with considerable success in the classroom where within certain limits, significant factors or conditions can be controlled.

5. Since in the field of education complex human beings are the subjects and since it is unlikely that all variables can be successfully controlled, experimentation is not a perfectly precise method. The experimental findings in education are somewhat inexact because some variables (like teacher's enthusiasm for or competence in using a particular method or material, regularity of attendance, mental or emotional state of the child determined by a number of factors) are extremely difficult or even impossible to control. The basic condition of other things being equal is difficult for fulfilment in educational research.

6. Experimentation in education has been put to various uses, main among which are:

(i) To determine and evaluate the adequacy and effectiveness of educational aims and objectives through the measurement of outcomes.

(ii) To serve as basis for the formulation, execution and modification of educational policies and programme.

(*iii*) To ascertain the effect of any change in the normal educational programme or practices.

7. Another difficulty, in principle at least, arises from the fact that educational experiments are carried through with human beings and affect mental processes and attitudes. Gestalt psychology and related research have shown that the introduction of any specific influence, howsoever well and exactly defined, intended to change one specific type of mental process or attitude will change the 'whole field' of mentality, often in aspects and ways that escape the control of the experimenter.

8. All experiments in education are ultimately experiments with children, *i.e.,* human beings, who for ethical reasons must not be subjected to conditions that may harm them. The popular slogan—"No experimenting with children"—may not be wholly justified, but there certainly are boundaries of a moral character for experimentation which must not be infringed.

9. Experimental studies in education though never strictly empirical, can yet approximate strictly empirical research in many areas. *For example,* the teaching of spelling through different methods, difference between the effect of the authoritarian and democratic set-up in education and the possibility and extent of one subject improving the achievement in another, are problems which have been handled in a scientific way through the experimental approach. But there are areas where a strictly empirical approach is impossible. *For example,* in finding out whether centralization of educational administration produces better results than local freedom, in deciding if co-education is preferable to separate school's for boys and girls and in establishing whether certain achievements of education stay when formal schooling stops, nothing more than a partly empirical approach is permissible. In such areas ana for solving such problems where we cannot experiment we look out for cases where education goes on under different conditions.

10. Major steps in experimental research are three:

(*a*) Planning the experiment.

(*b*) Conducting the experiment.

(*c*) Reporting the results.

Planning the experiment—the first step-includes the following sub-steps:

(*a*) Investigating the needs in the field of education and deciding upon a problem.

(*b*) A preliminary try-out.

(*c*) Formulating an outline or plan of procedure.

(*d*) Studying the literature related to similar problems.

(*e*) Determining the method of experimentation.

(*f*) Determining and delimiting the experimental factor.

(*g*) Selecting the subjects and groups.

(*h*) Determining the place, time, duration and materials of the experiment.

The second major step-conducting the experiment includes the following sub-steps:

(*a*) Controlling variable or non-experimental factors.

(*b*) Applying the experimental factor or factors.

(*c*) Classifying, analysing and interpreting experimental findings.

(*d*) Keeping a careful record of steps in the procedure.

(*e*) Measuring the experimental results.

(*f*) Verifying the findings.

(*g*) Drawing conclusions from the findings.

The third step involves all the main factors which the reporting of results of any research study does.

Classification of Experiments

Experimental investigations can be variously classilled on different bases. The usual bases observed for classification of experiments are:

(*a*) **Type of Control.** Scientific or practical, formal or informal, actual or inferred.

(*b*) **Place where Conducted.** Laboratory, field or classroom.

(*c*) **Means of Approach.** Analytical, comparative, quantitative or qualitative.

(*d*) **Treatment of Subjects.** In groups or individually.

(*e*) **Grouping of Subjects.** One group, equivalent group or rotation group.

(*f*) **Sponsorship or Investigation Agency.** Independently or cooperatively, by an individual or an institution.

(*g*) **Function or Purpose.** To study direct effects, indirect effects, or causes.

Among the several bases of classification listed above, the most significant, perhaps, is the one which takes into account the grouping of subjects because the design of an experiment is largely determined by this factor. We shall consider here the three major experimental designs distinguished on this basis.

1. One-group Experimentation

A one-group experiment involves the application of an experimental factor or factors to an individual or a group in such a way that certain changes in the outcome can be determined. Its main steps are:

(*a*) A group of subjects is measured with regard to certain factors under study.

(*b*) The group is measured again to determine the changes produced by the experimental factor in the dependent variable.

(*c*) All factors are kept constant except one which is the experimental factor or the independent variable.

(*d*) Other factors may be introduced, one at a time and their results determined likewise.

(e) The experimental factor is applied for some definite period of time.

For example, if 'A' denotes the group, 'X' the experimental factor and 'R' the initial result of measuring the particular factor in question, the one-group experiment could be represented graphically thus:

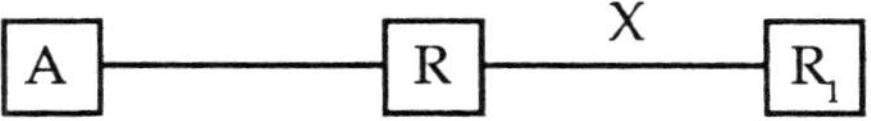

The difference between the initial result (R) and the result achieved after the introduction of the experimental factor (R_1) can be attributed to the experimental factor (X). That is, (R_1—R) can be expected to be caused by the application of X over a specified period of time. Similarly, the introduction of other experimental factors (X_1, X_2...) may be calculated to produce (R_2—R_1), (R_3—R_3)... etc.

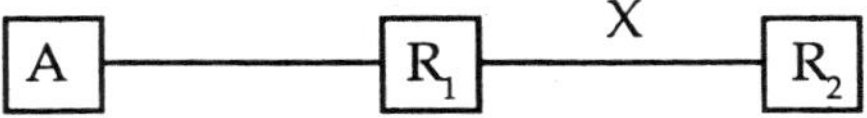

This type of simple experimental design has some advantages over other complex designs. It is simple to plan and operate. It requires no equation or rotation of groups. It is well-adapted to class room use and provides a stimulus to better class-room teaching.

One-group design has many shortcomings too. It is not always thoroughly valid because of:

(a) The carry-over effect of attitude or method from one to the other phase of the experiment.

(b) The practice-effect produced by the taking of a series of measuring devices.

(c) Errors due to maturation of children during the course of the experiment.

(d) Inequality and lack of comparable units of measurement.

(e) Variation in learning speed at various stages of the learning process.

2. Parallel or Equivalent Group-Experimentation

This is perhaps the classical experimental design, more complex than the one-group experiment, but more accurate too. In this, two or more groups of subjects equivalent in all significant respects are selected. One of these parallel groups serves as the control group and the experimental factor or factors are applied to one or more of the other groups, known as the experimental groups, one by one for a specified period of time. The difference observed at the end of the period in the particular factor under study between the control and the experimental groups is expected to be due to the introduction of experimental factor. If 'A' is the control group and 'B' the experimental group, a parallel-group experiment carried out to determine the influence of one experimental factor could be represented graphically thus:

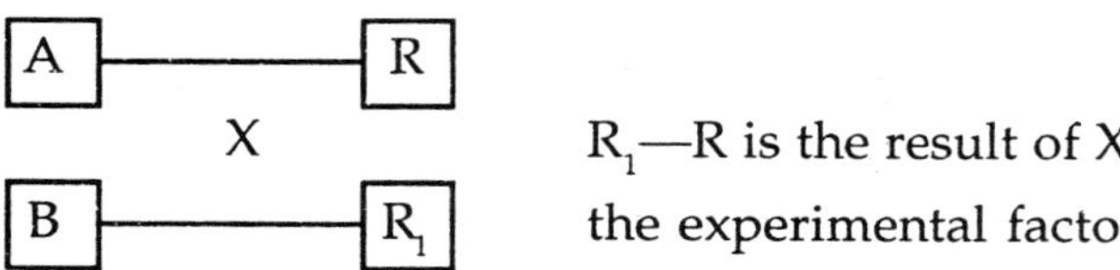

In case more than two parallel groups are used to determine the influence of more than one experimental factor, the experimental design may take the following form:

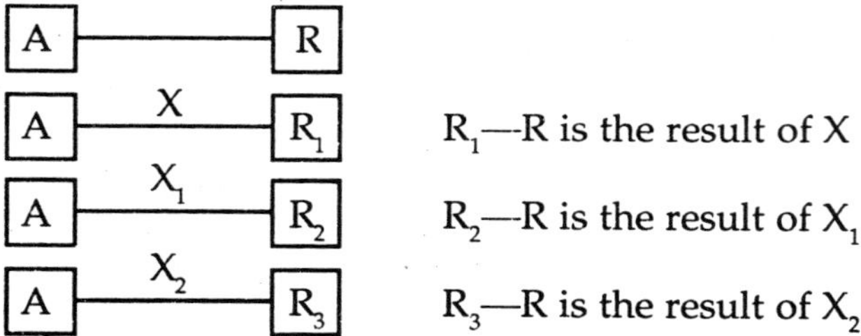

The various steps in a simple experiment of the equivalent group type can be represented thus:

Experiment Group	*Control Group*
1. Pretest	1. Pre-test

2. Application of experimental factor.	2. Application of control factor.
3. Final test.	3. Final test.
4. Measure pupil mean gain (Final test scores minus pre-test scores).	4. Measure pupil mean gain (Final test score minus pre-test scores).

5. Calculating the difference between the control pupil mean gain and the experimental pupil mean gain to get an idea of the relative superiority of the control and experimental factor under study.

Thus, the main steps in the parallel group method are the following:

(a) Applying the experimental factor.

(b) Comparing the results.

(c) Interpreting and reporting the results.

(d) Securing equivalent groups.

The initial step of securing equivalent groups is a crucial one due to the varying degrees of inherited and acquired characteristics in the members of any group. The control factors usually considered are:

(a) Chronological age.

(b) Physical condition.

(c) Intelligence.

(d) Previous achievement.

(e) Sex.

(f) Race.

(g) Personality traits.

(h) Study habits.

The last two, obviously, do not lend themselves to objective measurement and so are less reliable factors than the earlier ones, although no less important.

Among the many methods of equating groups for experimental purposes, the following devices are frequently employed:

(a) Chance or random selection.

(b) Equating by matched pairs.

(c) Equating by co-twin method.

(d) Equating on the basis of mean scores and standard deviations.

It is expected that the device of selecting groups by random selection from a large population, should lead itself to formation of groups which are more or less equal in composition. Equating groups on the basis of equal mean scores, however, is a more exact method if all the significant factors (age, intelligence, achievement, etc.) are measured. When standard deviations of groups are also taken into consideration, the groups are equated on the basis of homogeneity also. Equating by matched pairs involves the finding of pairs of pupils whose signincant characteristics (age, sex, intelligence, home back ground, race and personality traits, etc.) approximate closely. One pupil from every selected pair forms the control group and the other pupil from every pair the experimental group. The groups are expected to be parallel on the assumption that the sums of equals are equal. The co-twin method is a form of the matched-pair technique by which pairs of identical twins are placed in the control and the experimental group.

Once equivalent groups are secured, one experimental factor has to be applied on one (or more) of the groups while one group has to work under normal conditions. The two or more equivalent groups are thus, ensured identical treatment in all respects but the experimental variable or variables. Control of all significant variables and the application of the experimental variable has to be done for a particular period of time, divided into preplanned units, at previously determined intervals, under uniform conditions.

The results secured at the end of the experiment have to be compared. The differences found in achievement at this stage are supposed to be largely due to the experimental variable. But One cannot interpret the differences and come to certain conclusions on their basis so easily. The interpretation and conclusions have always to take into consideration and discount to the extent, that all variables were not equated. In the report of an experimental study not only the obvious results but also the limitations of the devices employed of equating and testing the groups have to be indicated. Appropriate statistical devices have to be applied for interpreting the differences in the results of the two or more groups and for finding out their levels of significance or reliability limits.

The main advantage of this type of experimental design is that it is free from the weaknesses of the one-group method. Both the control and the experimental factor or factors are applied simultaneously on different groups so that the difficulties due to maturation or practice effect, etc., do not arise. But this method suffers from the difficulty of equating groups and controlling significant variables and from many administrative problems of reorganizing classes.

3. Rotation Group Experimentation

This experimental design may be looked upon as a variation of either the one-group or the equivalent group method. If applied to a single-group, it involves changing the time sequence of the experimental and control units in two or more cycles.

Cycle I would apply the control factor first, then the experimental.

Cycle II would apply the experimental factor first, then the control.

When applied to the equivalent groups it involves exchanging the factors between different groups cycle-wise.

Cycle I Group A—experimental factor
Group B—control factor
Cycle II Group A—control factor
Group B—experimental factor.

If more than two factors have to be made the subject of study, more than two groups will have to be employed and number of cycles, at least equal to the number of groups employed, have to be observed.

Thus, the rotational method involves the rotation of instructional factors of the experimental and control groups at equal intervals. The measurement of influences is done factor-wise by adding up the results after the introduction of individual factors. Supposing 'X' is the experimental factor and 'Y' the control factor, the rotation group method with Group A and B will take the following form:

Cycle I : A—X → R
B—Y → R_1
Cycle II : A—Y → R_2
B—X → R_3

($R + R_3$) is the result of X
($R_1 + R_2$) is the result of Y
(The difference between ($R + R_3$) ($R_1 + R_2$) is attributable to the difference between X and Y.

More than two groups, mare than two factors and more than two cycles will be handled in the same way. *For example*:

Cycle I : A—X → R
B—Y → R_1
C—Z → R_2
Cycle II : A—Y → R_3
B—Z → R_4
C—X → R_5
Cycle III : A—Z → R_6
B—X → R_7
C—Y → R_8

($R + R_4 + R_7$) is the result of X
($R_1 + R_3 + R_8$) is the result of Y
($R_2 + R_4 + R_6$) is the result of Z
The difference between the three above results are attributable to the differences between X, Y and Z.

The rotation group method is used to secure control of pupil factors when groups cannot be thoroughly equated. It also neutralizes the teacher-variable. In general, it overcomes the chief weaknesses of both the one group and the equivalent group methods. Since in the rotation group design each variable is applied to each group, it is not necessary that the groups be exactly equated. Of the three designs of educational experimentation, this is the most valid but the most complicated too.

It is desirable that the researcher considers the various designs to determine which would be appropriate for his experiments and how he would interpret the results. As explained earlier, the main purpose of experiments is to describe the effect of certain treatments upon some characteristic of a group and to test some hypotheses about it. Therefore, besides designing the experiments it should be thought out as to how the desired effect would be described or measured and how its significance would be tested.

Practical Hints for Experimental Workers

While the experimental method is rapidly gaining popularity as a method of research in education, it is yet not perfected to the point where its results may be considered thoroughly objective and valid. For seeing the best results out of this method it is necessary that:

(a) The experimental researcher be well-trained in the experimental procedure.

(b) The measures to be used be reliable and valid.

(c) The nature and scope of the experimental factor and the dependent variable should be adequately defined.

(d) The non-experimental factors should be discovered and properly controlled.

(e) The findings should be verified experimentally.

(f) The findings should be interpreted intelligently. Plausible explanations should be made for the results

secured giving due consideration to the limitations of the procedure adopted.

(g) The problem in hand be properly analysed and the degree to which experimental conditions can be approached should be calculated to ascertain whether it could not be better attacked from some other angle than the experimental.

In brief the research workers using the experimental method must understand the experimental procedure, recognize the limitations and relative merits of all possible available procedures and work with great care.

10

Historical and Schedule Method

Historical method is specially useful and important for social scientists because it is with its help that they can understand the process of social change on the one hand and growth of present day social institutions and organizations on the other. George Bernad Shaw once said that, "The past is not behind the group but it is within the group." It has very appropriately been said that past contains key to the present. Hans Gerath once pointed out that, "Every model of social structure implies a model of socio-historical change; history consists of changes which social structure undergo." About the place of history in social researcher Abram Kardiner opines that, "The study of all International systems must be generic and therefore historically oriented."

Famous historian Schlesinger once remarked that, "No individual, let alone a social scientist, can wisely ignore the long arm of the past."

New Outlook

In the past history was considered nothing else but recording of past events. Then history did not contain anything else but only deeds and misdeed of the ruling monarchs. Usually, however, whereas the deeds were exaggerated, misdeeds were minimised with the result that even the events narrated were undependable and needed careful scrutiny before acceptance. But now the approach has already changed and since quite a long time past history is being written with a different objective. The history is now not the mere narration of past events and deeds and misdeeds of ruling monarchs but it includes information about social institutions, social organizations, masses and their economic, political, social and cultural conditions. The history records, social systems and phenomenon. In history the role of social system in the life of the people has begun to be depicted. In the present day history prominent place is being assigned to class struggle which is going on between different classes *e.g.*, the capitalists, agriculturists and workers, etc. Our present historians have now come to realise that no event in society can take place without social background and that every event should be studied with that background.

It is, therefore, being accepted that history is very useful source of social research and for the study of present day social problems. It provides material for the study of every social institution and that process of social change and progress can best be appreciated with the help of study of history. Some of the important social scientists who have linked past experiences with present attitudes include W. I. Thomas, A. T. Adorno, Paul Webbin, etc.

Step in Historical Methods

In so far as histroical method for the study of social problems is concerned, there are certain steps involved in that, before a social investigator can usefully use and employ that method. First step is selection of problem. All problems cannot be studied with the help of historical method. Of course, it will have to be seen that only such problems are picked up which need scanning of historical records. No current problem can usefully and purposefully be studied with the help of this method. It can of course provide very useful background study material. Needless to say that before picking up the problem for study the researcher will have to ensure that the problem has social utility and that it is not too expensive.

After the problem has been selected for research and it has been decided that the matter will be collected with the help of historical records, then the question of collecting data will arise. In so far as data collection is concerned, it can be collected with the help of either primary of secondary sources. Primary sources include autobiographies, documents, diaries of the people written by themselves, whereas secondary sources include such published works etc., which do not record the events by the eye witnesses but were recorded at some later stage. In such cases information is collected by the persons concerned from different sources and then recorded in a way which is liked by the person who has collected information.

After the data has been collected problem of generalisation and analysis comes. At this stage what the researcher is required to see is that all available data has been fully collected and that nothing has been left out. If any source material has been left out that can create the problem of tilting the findings either on this side or that side.

Historical Surveys and Historical Studies

Sometimes historical surveys and historical studies are confused with each other and no distinction is made between the two, though in fact such a distinction exists. Whereas historical study is simply chronological account of events, history survey is not that. Out of the whole history, social scientist is concerned only with such events which have some bearing on social institutions, happenings and development. He is interested in knowing how a social institution developed in past and how is struggled to survive. Similarly he will also be interested in knowing the growth of different social institutions as well. His particular interest can be in the original and development of social movements. Then a good social scientist will not satisfy himself with merely the growth of social institutions and movements, but also in knowing the causes of the growth. He will, therefore, be more interested in the 'why' of a historical process rather then its acceptance as a *fait accomplie.* A social scientist will, therefore, be less interested in chronological order and more in casual order of the study. In historical method he will be more interested in the study of processes which led to the formation and modifications of social disorganization.

Sources of Historical Data

From which sources can historical data be collected another problem which needs consideration. These sources are documents, materials of cultural history and personal sources of authentic observers and withnesses. In what way is each source to be tackled will very much depend on the interest of the researcher on the one hand and nature of problem on the other.

Direct use of historical old documents will normally prove more useful and advantageous when :

(a) Events which these documents narrate have not as yet been analysed by the historians.

(b) When a controversial point needs to be settled.

(c) When certain aspects of life in which investigator is interested have not been embodied in the writings of analytical historians.

(d) When these events have not been incorporated in history writings *i.e.*, in history works.

(e) When there is no complete chronology of events.

(f) When there is a missing link in knowledge which needs be connected so that whole event about a social institution or social situation becomes complete.

(g) When the basic idea is to verify certain events directly.

In the words of P. V. Young, "Documents of the present or of the near future will not supply the essential source data necessary for comparable and generalisable similarities." Contemporary documents can, however, prove useful source of information.

Dearth of Reliable Data. One limitations is that one is not sure whether the data used in the work is dependable and reliable or not. This poses still more a serious problem when event and material or data relates to the distant past and cannot be verified from other sources. In such cases one does not know the purpose for which data was collected, 'who collected that', what is the element of subjectivity in the data and so on.

Limitations of Historical Method

Though historical method has its own importance in social research, yet this method has its own limitations as well. Real good results can only be obtained with the help of this method provided these limitations are crossed over and it is ensured that constraints which come by way of these limitations are removed to the extent possible. Some of the important limitations are :

Availability of Records. Even if in certain cases the researcher may be sure that certain facts and datas used in a historical work are authentic and are available in certain records, even then quite often it becomes difficult to lay hand on those records. The records may have been destroyed due to political and other reasons and as such these do not become available to the posterity for consultation and use in research works. In India many valuable old records were destroyed by invaders. The Britishers also destroyed some records which did not suit their political ends.

Not only this, but some records which may be in the possession of an individual, who may have inherited is, may not be willing to part with those.

Many old records are not made available to researchers by the government due to political and other reasons. It is feared that their throwing open can create tensions in society.

Non-Proper Keeping of Records. In every country there are records and records which go on adding themselves with the passage of time. Thses records are usually not kept properly. The result is that the researcher finds it very difficult to trace and locate papers of his concern. In fact, in India one of the serious difficulties is proper preservation, maintenance and upkeeping of records in a proper and right way. This situation obtains in almost all developing countries. This creates serious problem for social science researchers.

Problem of Frame of Conditioning Phenomenon. Next limitation that comes in this regard is that of the problem of taking into the frame of the conditioning phenomena. If that is not done then their importance, both with regard to accurcay and significance gets completely missed. Frame of conditioning phenomena, however, becomes difficult largely because of the time lapse between the situation studied and the analysis presented. The circumstances under which data was collected can only imagined and can neither be repeated nor collected about again, particularly when event is of non-repetitive nature.

No Test or Verification. Under historical method the researcher is supposed to depend on the data which is made available to him either through printed books or with the help of documents. But the question arises whether there is any way of verifying that. The answer is in the negative. Similarly it is really very difficult and rather impossible to repeat the situation and to verify authenticity of data. It is because the event happened in the past, which cannot be brought into existence again. Of course, in social sciences these difficulties arise in the case of every method that is used for data collection but this difficulty is still more serious in the case of this method because data belongs to the remote past.

Problem of Calculation and Measurement of Data. Then another difficulty is that of calculation and measurement of data which is not possible in this method. It becomes very difficult because no researcher can be fully aware of the background in which data was collected. Unless that background is available there can be no proper calculation and measurement of data. It is just possible that in measuring some of the important datas may get omitted. It is equally possible that while measuring some important data may be under estimated whereas less important may be over-estimated or over-stressed.

Problem of Bias. The historians are after all human beings and while recording events they are bound to introduce their biases though their degree may vary. This is particularly true of medieval historians who recorded events to please their masters with complete biases and also with great subjectivity. Thses chronicles were both impressionistic as well as propagandistic. Not only this, but our modern historians have consciously or unconsciously become defenders of a particular principle system or a party. Most of them are as much subjective as the medieval thinkers, though they claim themselves as objective and impartial.

All Happenings cannot be Known. A good historian will of course try to record what he knows. He will try to collect maximum information from all sources. But in a vast country like India, there can be happenings in different parts of the country, including remote villages in far flung areas which may be of much significance, but may not immediately come to the notice of the historians due to communication or any other difficulty. In fact, no historian can claim to know of all the happenings.

No Life Size Writing of History. Each historian has limited space and as such he cannot write everything which he observes or comes to know. That is always impossible. Accordingly each historian records what he considers is the most important for him leaving the rest to its own care. Accordingly no life size history can be written. In the words of P.V. Young, "Of necessity the historians must resort to selection. Description of numerous complex happenings, occurring in rapid succession cannot go on indefinitely until all details are exhausted. The historians find it imperative to omit a mass of detail."

Adequacy of Historical Data. In the the words of P.V. Young, "Historical data may be regarded as adequate and reliable for social research, *(i)* when they are presented as complexes of social forces; *(ii)* when social phenomena meaningfully depict intricate social processes: And *(iii)* when sets of inter-relationship—psychological, economic, educational, political and religious—contribute to a unified whole, a configuration or complex pattern."

Problem of Sampling. History of every period, time, institution and organization is very vast and much deep rooted than *prima facie* it appears. No investigator and researcher can thoroughly examine beliefs, behaviour, patterns, situations and institutions. It is really life-time work and no researcher has either time or resources of studying all or some of these. Accordingly each serious researcher will have to pick up few and that is by way of sampling. When the question of sampling comes, accordingly all problems, difficulties and complexities associated with sampling arise and for any social science researcher these are serious and need careful consideration.

Historical Method in Modern Times

In our modern times historical method is being increasingly used. It is now being realised that every social institution, organization and existing system has some history behind it and in case that background is not properly studied, whole study will be incomplete. Today such important institutions, as family marriage, divorce, caste system, etc., are being studied more seriously with the help of historical method. Efforts are now being made to study their origin, causes of their getting roots in society and also for their strength and weaknesses.

Of course, there are thinkers in social sciences who believe that this method should not be extensively used in social sciences because it is undependable and unreliable one. Much the data contained in historical works is more imaginative and subjective rather than real and objective. They also feel that the myth, fiction and reality in historical documents are so much mixed up that it becomes difficult to separate the two. But even then now this method for studying social problems of present day society is being very much used. One reason for this being that history provides good background for the study of the problem(s) and in a way in finding their solution.

SCHEDULE METHOD

There are two ways in which the response to a questionnaire may be secured. In the first, it may be sent by post to various individuals; and in the second, the researcher may himself present the questionnaire to the individuals whose responses are desired. The first method is called the mailed questionnaire, while the second method is called schedule. In the words of Thomar Carson Macormic, "the schedule is nothing more than a list of questions which it seems necessary to test the hypothesis or hypotheses." A schedule, therefore, is a list of questions formulated and presented with the specific purpose of testing and assumption or hypothesis. *For example*, if social scientist believes on the basis of his general experience that women do not enjoy good status in a joint family, he will so formulate his questions that the actual state of affairs may come to surface in responses to those questions. A sample of qusetions is :

1. Do you often go out of your house?
2. What is the usual purpose of your outside visits?
3. Do you often entertain your friend at home?
4. Do you receive an allowance for personal expenses? etc.

According to W.J. Goode and P.K. Hatt, "Schedule is the name usually applied to a set of questions which are asked and filled by an interviewer in a face to face situation with another." By a schedule, we cannot, however, obtain information about many things at once. It is best suited to the study of a single item thoroughly.

From the foregoing discussion, it is quite clear that in the schedule method, interview occupies a central place and plays a vital role. As a matter of fact success in the use of schedule is largely determined by the ability and tact of the interviewer rather than by the quality of the questions posed. Because the interviewer himself poses the question and notes down the answers all by himself, the quality of questions has not any great significance. The list of questions is merely a formal document intended to maintain uniformity in the questions asked by different persons.

Objects of Schedule

P.V. Young has laid emphasis on the following objects of the schedule. According to her, a researcher "makes the schedule a guide, a means of delimiting, the sense of his enquiry, a memory tickler, a recording device." These may now be discussed point-wise :

1. Delimitation of the Topic. A schedule is always about a definite item of inquiry, its subject is a single and isolated subject-item rather than the subject in general. The interviewer presents questions about one item and notes down answers about it. Therefore schedule delimits and specifies the subject of inquiry.

2. Aids Memory. In an interview the choice of question is left entirely to the interviewer : He may ask any question. In this there is always a chance of some important points being left. Therefore, in the schedule the list of questions is preplanned and noted down formally. The interviewer is always armed with the formal document detailing the questions. Accordingly in the schedule method an interviewer is not dependent upon the memory.

3. Aid to Classification and Analysis. When the interviewer obtains replies to the questions given in the schedule, these replies are classified and analyzed. Many different tables are used in the schedule; and the questions are also of many types. Some need only yes/no answer; other require choosing one of the alternatives given or arranging them in order of preference; still others require certain amount of thinking and can be answered in samll sentences. Therefore, all the varieties of replies are sifted and classified under various heads. This helps in the analysis of the replies.

The above aims of schedule method have been considered by Mrs. Young in the following words : "An observation usually serves several purposes simultaneously :

1. It is a specific memory tickler.
2. It is a standardizing device.
3. It is an objective recording device which makes possible accurate accumulation of large quantities of data.
4. It aids to delimit the scope of the study and to concentrate on the circumscribed elements to the analysis."

Types of Schedules

Schedules are of different types, though the aim of all the schedules is to collect data. These types are :

1. Observation Schedule. This is a type of schedule in which question are put on a specific topic about which investigator wants to collect data and information. The questions are absolutely pointed ones and what the investigator does is that he collects information as well as simultaneously observes what the respondent is saying? If on the basis of his observations he feels necessary, he also puts certain additional questions as well to clarify the position. In this case the respondent can be individual or group of individuals and schedule is filled under certain specific conditions.

2. Institutional Survey Schedule. There are in every society some specialised institutions and agencies. These schedules are used for collecting information about them.

The nature and complexity of the institution decides the size of the schedule. Obviously more complex the working of the institution more bulky will be the size of the schedule. With the help of this schedule it becomes both easy as well as possible to study both traditional as well as immediate problems of an institution.

3. Rating Schedule. In social research rating schedules are used when information is to be collected about attitudes, opinions, preferences and other like elements and their value is to be assessed and value of each is required to be measured. These prove very useful when factors that are responsible for measuring a phenomena are to be measured.

4. Document Schedule. In this schedule whole study is based on certain schedules *e.g.*, studies which deal with the writing of history etc. With the help of these documents certain questions are asked about the life history of a person and on the basis of replies received efforts are made to construct life history. It is felt that more than the required material should be collected so that if need be some material may be kept in the reserve for future use. In this quite a large number of relevant records are consulted. In the schedule of this type those terms are used which frequently occur in the documents otherwise it is felt some confusion may arise.

5. Interview Schedule. Interview schedule is used for testing as well as collecting data and also for the collection of supplementary data. The informant takes the schedule with him and interviews the respondent and fills in the forms. Usually in this method certain standardised questions are asked by the interviewer.

Characteristics of Good Schedule

Every schedule cannot be good one and for a good schedule it is desirable that it should possess certain qualities. These are :

Accurate Communication. From accurate communication we mean that the questions in the schedule should be so worded that there is no gap in what is asked by the investigator and what is understood by the respondent. If the respondent understands exactly what is being asked by the investigator then we can say that there is accurate communication. It is therefore, most desirable that the questions being asked should be very clear and not ambiguous. These should be very short precise so that respondent does not take a very long time in understanding them. The questions should be closely inter-linked with each other and it should appear that whole information is being sought in a rational manner and that one question is following by the other in a natural sequence.

In order to get accurate response it is better that the schedule should be prepared in a scientific way and also in a way that the respondent feels inspired to give correct information. The questions should not be of such a nature that while replying the respondent gets bored. Similarly no informant will like to give reply to a question which injures his feelings. In fact, after such a question has been put to him he will decline to cooperate with the investigator and refuse to respond to remaining part of the schedule and questions contained in that.

The investigator should not put such questions in which there is element of subjectivity because both subjective questions and subjective evaluation are disliked by the people, more particularly when the informant is fully aware that he is under no obligation to answer the questions being put to him by the investigator.

If at all the respondent decides to respond to the questions being put to him, he will be interested in replying to such questions which are directly connected with the sutdy. He may resent replying to such questions with which the study is not directly linked. He may even decline replying such questions and even can become repulsive.

All sorts of questions can, of course, be put in a schedule but what is essential and proper is that only those questions should be put in the schedule which can be analysed and subjected to statistical tests. In case tabulation of questions is not possible, then there in no use in collecting information on such questions.

In order to have some checks and counter-checks as well as to have indepth information, it is better if each question is further sub-divided so that the informant does not feel bore while replying and his faults and falterings can also be checked.

In a schedule idiomatic, technical, ambiguous, indefinite, imaginative and private terms should be avoided bacause it is usually difficult for the investigators to clarify these and much of subjectivity gets introduced in the replies which are recorded. When the same terms are differently understood both by the respondents as well as investigators then the replies will become unreliable and undependable and whole study will become a futile attempt.

No questions should be included and asked which develop a sense of shame in the respondent or on which he is to depend on others for replying or on which he has no information and it is expected of him to go and collect information from others.

While collecting information investigator should always leave an impression that he is enjoying responses and being benefited by the impression being provided by him, no matter whether he is actually enjoying the responses or not.

The investigator should never try to impose himself on the respondent and never forget that the latter is under no obligation to respond to his question. He, therefore, should never behave arrogantly and at no stage suffer from superiority complex.

A good investigator should allow his respondent to respond to questions without any intervention from him. He should intervene when his help is needed or when some stimuli is needed.

FORMATION OF SCHEDULE

As has been pointed out earlier, the difference between a questionnaire and a schedule is due to their structures. Therefore, in order to understand the schedule, it is necessary to know the how of its structure, *i.e.,* what is the method of its formulation. A schedule has two aspects: internal and external. Accordingly, in the formulation of a schedule, both internal and external aspects have to be considered. With regard to the internal aspect, it has to be seen that all the questions included in the schedule should be subservient to the main purpose of the schedule and that there should be included in it no question which does not have direct bearing on the subject matter which is being investigated. To ensure this, the problem or the subject-matter should be very thoroughly studied by referring to the whole gamut of literature connected with it. Thus, the outline of the problem would become transparently clear. One should not be contented even here: but should consult the experts in subject to further sharpen the outlines and gather all the necessary information.

A. The Internal Aspect of the Schedule

1. Sorting Various Aspects. In constructing a schedule, the first step is sorting out of the various aspects of the schedule, for this the problem should be considered from all possible points of view. *For example,* if we wish to study the effects of Hindu Code Bill on the Hindu family, we have first of all to determine the aspects or elements of Hindu family which have been affected by the aforesaid Bill. Moreover, we should distinguish between the elements which have been directly influenced by the Bill from those which have been indirectly influenced.

2. Determination of Essential Information. Having determined the different aspects of a problem, the next point which needs to be determined is the kind of information required on thse aspects. For this purpose, the various aspects may be sub-divided. The sub-division presumes, of course, thorough knowledge of the subject. To illustrate this point by the above-mentioned example of the Hindu Code Bill an investigator whose knowledge of either the clauses of the Bill, or of the complex structure of Hindu family in its historical aspects is deficient can hardly be expected to prepare an efficient schedule about this problem.

3. Test of Reliability. The success of a schedule is to be measured by the fact that it elicits natural responses and that the answers given are not artificial. In order to counteract and forestall the possibility of misleading answers being given, the schedule must be tried on a sample group. If there is some lacuna in the schedule it must be removed and the schedule tried again. This process has to go on till the time all the questions are shown to be easily intelligible and there is no trace of artificiality left in them. If a particular question continues to be confusing inspite of modifications, it should be removed form the schedule.

4. Formation of Questions. After taking decision about the various aspects of the problem, with their respective sub-divisions, to be studied the next step is fromulation of questions to elicit information of each sub-division of each aspect. The distinguishing feature of the question is communicability *i.e.,* they should convey the intended meaning. Therefore, the use of idiomatic, technical, ambiguous indefinite, imaginative, private and inferential terms should be strictly avoided. Unless the words are simple, clear, univocal and unambiguous, they are liable to varying interepretations. And if the respondents understand the questions differently, their responses will not be to one and the same questions but to the different senses of one question. This will make the confusion worse confounded. Besides the fact that questions should not be liable to different interpretations, another important consideration in the formulation of questions is that they should be such as can be easily answered by the respondents themselves, without either external help of sense of shame.

For example, if there is a question : Do you have normal blood pressure, pulse rate and heart beat? Obviously, the question cannot be answered without consulting a doctor. Again if the question is : Do you remain celibate during your wife's absence? The question is too intimate to be answered.

5. Serialization of Questions. In order to obtain well organized information, it is necessary that the questions should be presented to the respondents in a well-ordered serial. It has been experienced in various field studies that the change in the order of questions affects the answers adversely. Therefore, it is of crucial significance that while formulating the questions, these should be so placed in the schedule as to be serially concerned. If any particular question upsets the respondent, its effect is likely to be carried over to later questions.

B. The External Aspect of the Schedule

After taking care of the internal aspect of the schedule, the external aspect must also be attended to. In the external aspect, following elements are considered :

1. The form and size of the schedule,
2. Organization of units and
3. The material used.

The external aspect of the schedule is known as form or structure of the schedule. As has been noted above, if the structure is unattractive the chances of its success are very limited. Therefore, the structure must also be given adequate attention. In this connection, following things are to be considered :

1. Material Used. The paper used for printing should be of high quality, the letters printed on it should stand out visibly and must not be broken, furthermore the ink should not spread. If the paper is rough, the letters printed will be poor in visibility and are liable to be broken due to crumpling of the paper, moreover when the interviewer fills it by ink, the ink may spread. The paper must be both tough and pliable; otherwise, it may break on collapsing. Even if it means more expenses, the paper and printing must be of excellent quality.

2. Form of Schedule. In the determination of form and size of the schedule, a number of things should be taken care of. The schedule should not be unduly long or wide least repeated collapsing and folding affect it adversely. The size of the schedule is, of course, to be determined by the number and length of question, the two following sizes are generally adopted. These are 8½" × 11" and 5" × 8" or 21 cm. × 28 cm. and 18 cm. × 21 cm. Normally printing is done only on one side of the paper in the schedule.

3. Organization of Units. The units of a schedule are comprised of titles, sub-titles and columns. A proper arrangement of these helps in making the schedule well ordered. The questions should be strictly within the context. By taking this precaution the length of the schedule can be kept within reasonable limits.

4. Length of Schedule. As a matter of fact the length of the schedule varies with the nature of the problem, but it should not be so long as to take half an hour or more. Most of the respondents do not want to spend such a long time in filling up the schedule. Therefore, as a rule, the length of schedule should be such as to take less than half an hour in filling it up.

5. Marginal Space. The marginal space on the left should be about 1/2" or 1 cm. and on the right it should be 1/2" or 1/2 cm. This lends attraction to the schedule. Besides, the researcher takes marginal notes in the marginal space. In the absence of margin, the schedule cannot be filled, because punching it will destroy some words and moreover, part of the written matter is concealed.

6. Use of Pictures. It has been found by the researchers that the insertion of appropriate pictures in the schedule increases their present ability and that the respondent takes greater interest in making responses. Therefore, it is desirable to insert suitable pictures, whenever possible. *For example,* if in a schedule the questions pertain to different professions like engineering, law, teaching and medicine, the representative pictures of an engineer, a lawyer, a teacher and a doctor may be inserted at appropriate places.

7. Printing. A printed schedule is definitely more desirable as printing makes it attractive; but if the number of respondents is small, or economy is desired, cyclo-style or type written schedule may be used; but in both cases the schedule must be neat and free from over-writing etc.

OUTLINES OF A SCHEDULE

In a schedule, following three aspects have seen distinct :

1. Prefatory. In this operating part, following data with regard to inquiry and the respondents are sought :

(i) Name of the survey and the surveyor with address.

(ii) Reference number.

(iii) Name of respondent, his address, age, sex, education, profession etc.

(iv) Place of interview.

(v) Time and data of interview.

2. Main Schedule. It includes tiltes sub-titles, columns and the questions.

3. Direction of Field Worker. In this part, the workers who have to present the schedule, hold the interview and collect the data. They are given elaborate instructions regarding the reading and presenting of schedule and the method of the interview. In the absence of these instructions there is a probability of arbitrariness which will surely vitiate the purpose of research. The researchers are given detailed instructions about the use of words in recording the responses. Every other detail is explained in order to ensure uniformity of recording the responses.

❋❋❋

11

Research Design

A research design is a plan of action. It is plan for collecting and analysing, data in an economic efficient and relevant manner. It is blue print and therefore at its best only tentative. Changes in the design are permitted and are dictated by considerations during the operations of the project. In other words, a research design is not highly specific plan to be followed without deviation but rather a series of guide-posts to keep one headed in the right direction. However, research design has been defined by different social scientists in different terms. Miller has defined "Designed research" as "The planned sequence of the entire process involved in conducting a research study." According to Selltiz and others, "Research design is a catalogue of the various phases and facts relating to the formulation of a research effort. It is an arrangement of the essential conditions for collection and analysis of data in a form that aims to combine relevance to research purpose with economy in the procedure."

A few other definitions of Research Design are: 'A research design designates the logical manner in which individuals or other units are compared and analysed, it is the basis of making interpretations from the data.'

'The challenge of a research design is to translate the general scientific model into a practical research operation. Research design will refer to the entire process of planning and carrying out a research study.'

'Research design is the plan, structure and strategy of investigation conceived so to obtain answers to research questions and control variable.' A research design should be based more or less on methodology. It should be made once, the topic and problem for research have been selected and formulated, objectives have been properly oulined, concepts have been properly defined.

Before going into further details let us consider the characteristics and the components of a good research, design and source of the practical difficulties, deficiences and shortcomings in the planning and execution of research projects in the light of the experiences of some researchers are highlighted.

Characteristics of Research Design

In the field of social sciences the designing of a research study is very complex. Every design has its own strengths and weaknesses and at the same time there is no such things as a single correct design. Nevertheless, a good research design should possess the following characteristics:

Objectivity. The objectivity of the procedure (either collection of data or scoring of the responses or both) may be judged by the degree of agreement between the final scores assigned to different individuals by more than one independent observer. The more subjective the observation, recording and evaluation of the responses, the less the different observers agree. It is therefore, any research design should permit the use of measuring instruments which are fairly objective in which every observer or judge seeing a performance arrives precisely. This ensures the objectivity of the collected data which will be used for analysis and findings.

Reliability. It is not easily tested by either by the multiple-form or the split-half technique. The test retest approach is the most effective measure of reliability as it refers to 'consistency' throughout a series of measurements.

Suppose, if a respondent gives a response to a question, he is expected to give the same response to that question whenever he is asked in other form. But if the respondent keeps on changing his responses to the same type of question then the interviewer will be facing a difficulty in considering which one of these responses is genuine. The researcher should frame this question in such a way that the respondent cannot but give only one genuine response. Though there are some methods in determining the reliability of the responses given out by a respondent.

Validity. As in the case of reliability there are a good number of procedures for establishing the validity of test, such as validating the present data against a concurrent criterion or a furture criterion or a theory etc. However, any measuring instrument is said to be valid when it measures what if propose to measure.

Generalization. The next important aspects of a good research design is to ensure that the measuring instruments used in a research investigation yield objective, reliable and valid data and has to answer the 'generalization' of the findings. It will thus, help an investigator in his attempt to generalise the findings, provided he has taken due care in defining the population, selecting the sample and using the appropriate statistical analysis while planning his research design.

Components of Research Design

Research design consists of the following components:

1. Title of the Study—'...should be brief, precise and project the scope in generalised terms.'
2. Review of Previous Studies—'...should be a brief survey of a relevant literature in the subject concerned and presented subjectwise and reviewed critically and pinpoint the stage from where further research is called for.'

3. Definition of Concept or Theoretical Principles involved if any—'...should be defined in general terms and be linked with the study.'
4. Statement of the Problem—'...should be unambiguous, precise and the usage should be clear, simple and concise.'
5. Coverage and Scope of the Study—'...should consider, geographical, temporal and functional dimensions.'
6. Formulation of Hypothesis—'...should be empirical, conceptually clear, specific, close to things observable and related to the body of theory.'
7. Objectives of the Study—'...should explain the main purpose precisely and may be in the form of questions or an explanation to a particular issue.'
8. Methods of Investigation—'...it depends upon the nature of study but researcher should define survey methodology and statistical techniques adopted.'
9. Sampling Design—'...definition of the universe or population, size of the sample and representativeness of the sample should be defined.'
10. Data Collection—'...depends upon the subject matter the unit of enquiry and the scope of the study.'
11. Constructing of Schedule or Questionaire—'...questions should be in a order on a form. Open ended questions are designed to permit a free response. The questions to be asked should be direct bearing on the problem, avoiding the personal questions and multiple meaning'.
12. Analysis of Data—'...to fulfil the objective or hypothesis the researcher should analyse the data subject to the appropriate statistical analysis besides tabulation. Tabulation of results in a meaningful

way is by itself a technique and an art. The data given in the tables must be in self-explanatory form.'

13. Reporting the Findings—'...should be clear, specific, simple and directly relating to the objective of the study. Researeher must report that what has been discovered or innovated to fulfil the need for which the study taken up and to ensure proper directors to other researchers in carrying out of similar researches.'
14. Interpretation of Results—'...researcher should draw inferences based on usual test for significance and relate with previous findings, to a wider field of generalizations, to scientific objectivity and to uncover any additional factors which would not be visualised by the inverstigator earlier.'

Purpose of Research Design

Research design is thus, essential for the whole study and helps in finding out faulterings in anticipation of the starting of the work. There are two basic purposes of a research design namely:

(a) To provide answers to research questions.

(b) To control variance.

In the words of Fred. N. Kerlinger, "Design helps the investigator to obtain answers to the questions of research and also helps him to control the experimental, extraneous and error variance of the particular research problem under study." Since each research problem is prepared with a view to solving some problems therefore the purpose of research design is to control variance. Then another purpose of research design is that the researcher should find answer to research questions validly, objectively, accurately as well as economically. A carefully finalised research design is sure to yield dependable and valid answers to the research questions epitomized by hypothesis. To quote Fred N. Kerlinger again, "Without strong stress on research questions and on use of design to help providing answer to these questions the study of design can degenerate into an interesting but sterile technical exercise."

In a nutshell it can be said that research design tells us what observation to make, how to make and how to analyse the quantitative representation of the observations. A design suggests the direction of observation. It also suggests how many observations to be made, which variables are active and what type of statistical tools should be used. A good design will also help researchers drawing possible conclusions from the statistical analysis.

A research design will always help a researcher in knowing successive stages. A good and properly prepared research design will have logical sequence of steps to be taken one after the other and in that stages will scientifically and logically follow. Thus, it will help in identifying the importance of each step in the whole research scheme. The design will thus, help in making the researcher know as to why he is studying and what type of data will be needed, how his data will be collected *i.e.*, what will be the sources of his data collection. It is important because if the data is not available, it is no use in undertaking research work on that subject. Then design will also help in finding out what total time the study is likely to take and what time each step in the study is likely to consume. Then design will also discuss about the universe of the study *i.e.*, how many cases will be covered in the study and in what manner will these castes be picked up and identified. Then as is well known in research different techniques are used for the collection of material and the design will give an idea as to what techniques will be used and that once the data through different techniques has been collected how will that be analysed. Then how best will, the decisions arrived at, be articulated in a manner that research purpose can be achieved.

In a narrow sense research design refers to the procedures for the collection of data and its analysis. In its broader sense, a research process involves identification and selection of research problem, choice of theoretical framework (conceptual model) for research problem and its relationship with previous researches; formulation of research problem and specification of its objectives, its scope and hypothesis to be tested, design of experiment of enquiry; definition and measurement of variables; sampling procedure; tools and techniques for gathering data; coding, editing and processing of data; analysis of data, selection and use of appropriate statistical procedures for summarising data and for statistical inference, reporting research—description for research process; presentation, discussion and interpretation of data, generalisation of research findings and their limitations and suggestions for further research.

Design Defined. Various definitions of research design have been given by different scholars. Vimal Shah will make us believe that, "The design is the plan of study and as such it is planned in every study, uncontrolled as well as controlled and subjective as well as objective." Russel Lackoff in his publication entitled 'Design in Social Research' has said. "Design is the process of making decisions before a situation arises in which decision has to be carried out. It is a process of deliberate anticipation dictated towards bringing an unexpected situation under control." P.V. Young has said that, "The design results from controlling general scientific model into varied research procedure." According to E.A. Suchaman, "Research design represents a compromise dictated by the many practical considerations that go into social research....A research design is not a highly specific plan to be followed without deviation, but rather a series of guide posts to keep one of the right direction. Fred N. kerlinger has said that, "Research design is the plan, structure and strategy of investigation conceived so as to obtain answer to research questions and control variance." R.L. Achoff has said that, "The idealised research design is concerned with specifying the optimum research procedure that could be followed were there no practical restrictions."

Why Methodologically Research Design?

Now a question arises as to why there should be a methodologically designed research. As already said proper design has its own advantages and as such it is essential that there should be methodologically designed research. It will help the researcher knowing the extent of inaccuracies which his data is likely to have and to check those from getting into the study. Every researcher today is interested in collecting fresh data, no matter whether that is directly to the study or not. A methodologically designed research is most likely to help the researcher in checking this temptation before it is too late. Then again the reseacher will come to know if he has sufficient required tools to carry out his research. If tools and techniques are not available then methodologically designed research will expose this weakness at the very beginning. Such a design will help in establishing how all major studies can be carried with the help of proper research designs. Thus, each special scientist will be contributing his little bit to the cause of research and a process of continuous improvement will thus, set in social research. It is always desirable that a research design before its being put into actual use should be given to other researchers for obtaining their critical views. These should be incorporated where necessary, without any hesitation.

Idealized Research Design

As already pointed out an idealized research design concerns itself with specifying the optimum research procedure that could be followed were there are no practical restrictions. In other words, it concerns itself with an ideal situation because practical restrictions are always there and these are bound to be operative at all times. A question therefore arises as to why to go about a research design which cannot in any way be obtained. Why to bother about procedures which cannot be carried out. But that is not actually so and an ideal research design in any way is not a wishful thinking but quite important to know how good the results would actually be obtained. Ideals are standards by which we can evaluate the practical research conditions and determine their shortcomings. If these shortcomings are clearly understood and their effects are observed on results obtained then the effects of these shortcomings will be minimized. Ideal situations are created and thought of even by natural scientists, though both the natural and social scientists fully well realize that it will be difficult to achieve the ideal. In actual research, though the researcher may try to achieve she ideal, but he will have to work keeping practical difficulties and situations into consideration. Each social science researcher fully well realises that all observations are subjects to errors which creep in the study and that it is impossible to remove observation errors, even if best efforts are made to remove these. Some of the errors may be removed, if many observers observe the same subject and phenomena again and again, which is costly and time consuming process and even then some of the observation errors may remain. It is also possible that all the observers who are put on the job may not have the capacity to observe things to the desired extent and many happenings and events may escape even when the observer is observing in his own way. In fact, there are many problems for creating an idealised situation. Ideals are of course good in their own way, but in social research it is always difficult to create ideal situations.

Inter-Dependence of Designs. In social research of course an ideal research design can be conceived, but what is important is practical rather than an ideal research design. Every practical research design consists of:

1. The Same design
2. Observational design
3. Statistical design

Sampling design of course is one which deals with the method of selecting the subject to be observed in a given study, whereas observational design relates to the conditions under which observations are to be made. Statistical design deals with the questions or how many subjects need be observed and how many are just to be forgotten and how many are to be analysed, whereas operational designs are concerned with specific techniques by which procedures specified in the sampling, statistical and observational are to be carried out. But one thing which ought to be remembered is that none of these designs is independent of the other and that all are interlinked and inter-connected with each other. Thus, decision in one design is bound to influence the other and in many cases these overlap each other as well.

Design Problems in Research Planning

Design problem in research begins as soon as some hypothesis is thought of, but both design and administration of research require decisions by the researcher at every step. The problems of design are not limited to any specific type of method or to any single stage of study. One serious problem in designs which need careful stydy is whether specific hypothesis can be translated into observation phenomena and whether the research method used will produce the kind of data needed to test the hypothesis.

But it is worth remembring that no single research design can sreve the purpose of several research problems. A research design which may be good for one research problem may not be so for another. But every research design should invariably clearly state sources of data collection, types of data to be collected, objectives of the problem under study and availability of time, money and research skills as well as tools of research.

Typologies of Research Designs

Wide varieties of research designs are being used in social sciences and for classifying these several typologies have been used. McGrant (1970), *for example*, has suggested that there are five models of different classes of enquiry namely, controlled experiments, study, survey, investigation and action research. Sellitz and others (1962), have suggested three broad categories of research designs namely, formulative or exploratory studies, descriptive studies and studies testing casual hypothesis. Riley (1983), has suggested a paradigm of alternatives which a researcher will need in planning the type or data to be assembled and the type of procedures to be used in his study. It will include the nature of research case, number of cases, socio-temporal context, primary basis for selecting cases, the time factor, extent of researcher's control over the system under study, basic sources of data, method of gathering data, number of properties used in research, method of handling single properties, method of handling relationships among prophesies and treatment of system properties as unitary and collective. Then another classification which has been given is:

1. Experimental and non-experimental form of controlled enquiry.
2. Descriptive/analytical strategy for analysing data.
3. Field/non-field setting or enquiry.
4. Time dimension or enquiry.
5. Evaluative/non-evaluative objectives of enquiry.
6. Primary and secondary sources of data.

As resecarh design, however, differs depending on research purpose. The purpose of research may broadly be grouped into four categories; namely, Exploratory or Formulative studies, Descriptive studies, Diagnostic studies and Experimental studies. Exploratory or Formulative studies are those which aim at gaining familiarity with a phenomena or which aim at achieving insights into the phenomena or studies which deal with formulation of a more precise research problem or developing a hypothesis. The studies which accurately portray the characteristics of a particular situation or groups or individuals are descriptive studies. Diagnostic studies determine the frequency with which something occurs with something else. Experimental studies aim at testing the hypothesis of a casual relationship between variables. But all these groupings are arbitrary because no study is different from the other. Thus, every classification provides the basis for study. As the knowledge increases with that classification becomes somewhat outdated. Exploratory studies deal with discovery of new ideas and as such these must be flexible. Accuracy is the major consideration in descriptive studies and as such it is essential that in such studies there should be minimum bias and it should be ensured that there is maximum reliability.

Research Design Related Concepts

Some important concepts are frequently used in different types of research designs and as such should be clearly understood, for their proper use. One such term is variable. It is concept which can take on different quantitative values like income, height etc. If one variable depends upon or is a consequence of other variable, it is called dependent variable, but when it is not the consequent of any other variable, it is called independent variable. A variable which can deal with any numerical value within a specific range is called continuous variable. Those variables which are not related to the purpose of study but can effect the dependent variables are called extraneous variables. The factors which minimize the influence or effect of extraneous variables are called control, but when dependent variable are not free from the influence of extraneous variables, the relationship between dependent and extraneous variables is called confounded relationship. Different conditions under which experimental and control groups are put are called treatments and the process of examining the truth of a statistical hypothesis, relating to some research problem is called experiment. The predetermined blocks used for different treatments are called experimental units.

Different Research Designs

Different research designs can be conveniently described if we categorize them as: (1) research design in case of exploratory research studies; (2) research design in case of descriptive and diagnostic research studies and (3) research design in case of hypothesis-testing research studies.

We take up each category separately.

1. Research Design in Case of Exploratory Research Studies. Exploratory research studies are also termed as formulative research studies. The main purpose of such studies is that of formulating a problem for more precise investigation or of developing the working hypotheses from an operational point of view. The major emphasis in such studies is on the discovery of ideas and insights. As such the research design appropriate for such studies must be flexible enough to provide opportunity for considering different aspects of a problem under study. Inbuilt flexibility in research design is needed because the research problem, broadly defined initially, is transformed into one with more precise meaning in exploratory studies, which fact may necessitate changes in the research procedure for gathering relevant data. Generally, the following three methods in the context of research design for such studies are talked about: *(a)* the survey of concerning literature; *(b)* the experience survey and *(c)* the analysis of 'insight-stimulating' examples.

The survey of concerning literature happens to be the most simple and fruitful method of formulating precisely the research problem or developing hypothesis, Hypotheses stated by earlier workers may by reviewed and their usefulness be evaluated as a basis for further research. It may also be considered whether the already stated hypotheses suggest new hypothesis. In this way the researcher should review and build upon the work already done by others, but in cases where hypotheses have not yet been formulated, his task is to review the available material for deriving the relevant hypotheses from it.

Besides, the bibliographical survey of studies, already made in one's area of interest may as well be made by the researcher for precisely formulating the problem. He should also make an attempt to apply concepts and theories developed in defferent research contexts to the area in which he is himself working. Sometimes the works of creative writers also provide a fertile ground for hypothesis-formulation and as such may be looked into by the researcher.

Experience survey means the survey of people who have had practical experience with the problem to be studied. The object of such a survey is to obtain insight into the relationships between variables and new ideas relating to the research problem. For such a survey people who are competent and can contribute new ideas may be carefully selected as respondents to ensure a representation of different types of experience. The respondents so selected may then the interviewed by the investigator. The researcher must prepare an interview schedule for the systematic questioning of informants. But the interview must ensure flexibility in the sense that the respondents should be allowed to raise issues and questions which the investigator has not previously considered. Generally, the experience-collecting interview is likely to be long and may last for few hours. Hence, it is often considered desirable to send a copy of the questions to be discussed to the respondents well in advance. This will also give an opportunity to the respondents for doing some advance thinking over the various issues involved so that, at the time of interview, they may be able to contribute effectively. Thus, an experience survey may enable the researcher to define the problem more concisely and help in the formulation of the research hypothesis.

Analysis of 'insight-stimulating' examples is also a fruitful method for suggesting hypotheses for research. It is particularly suitable in areas where there is little experience to serve as a guide. This method consists of the intensive study of selected instances of the phenomenon in which one is interested. For this purpose the existing records, if any, may be examined, the unstructured interviewing may take place, or some other approach may be adopted. Attitude of the investigator, the intensity of the study and the ability of the researcher to draw together diverse information into a unified interpretation are the main features which make this method an appropriate procedure for evoking insights.

Now, what sort of examples are to be selected and studied? There is no clear cut answer to it. Experience indicates that for particular problems certain types of instances are more appropriate than others. One can mention few examples of 'insight-stimulating' cases such as the reactions of strangers, the reactions of marginal individuals, the study of individuals who are in transition from one stage to another, the reactions of individuals from different social strata and the like. In general, cases that provide sharp contrasts or have striking features are considered relatively more useful while adopting this method of hypotheses formulation.

Thus, in an exploratory or formulative research study which merely leads to insights or hypotheses, whatever method or research design outlined above is adopted, the only thing essential is that it must continue to remain flexible so that many different facts of a problem may be considered as and when they arise and come to the notice of the researcher.

2. Research Design in Case of Descriptive and Diagnostic Research Studies. Descriptive research studies are those studies which are concerned with describing the characteristics of a particular individual, or of a group, whereas diagnostic research studies determine the frequency with which somecthing occurs or its association with something else. The studies concerning whether certain variables are associated are examples of diagnostic research studies. As against this, studies concerned with specific predictions, with narration of facts and characteristics concerning individual, group or situation are all examples of descriptive research studies. Most of the social research comes under this category. Form the point of view of the research design, the descriptive as well as diagnostic studies share common requirements and as such we may group together these two types of research studies. In descriptive as well as in diagnostic studies, the researcher must be able to define clearly, what he wants to measure and must find adequate methods for measuring it along with a clear cut definition of 'population' he wants to study. Since the aim is to obtain complete and accurate information in the said studies, the procedure to be used must be carefully planned. The research design must make enough provision for protection against bias and must maximise reliability, with due concern for the economical completion of the research study. The design in such studies must be rigid and not flexible and must focus attention on the following:

(a) Formulating the objective of the study (what the study is about and why is it being made?)

(b) Reporting the findings.

(c) Collecting the data (where can the required data be found and with what time period should the data be related?)

(d) Selecting the sample (how much material will be needed?)

(e) Processing and analysing the data.

(f) Designing the methods of data collection (what techniques of gathering data will be adopted?)

In a descriptive/diagnostic study the first step is to specify the objectives with sufficient precision to ensure that the data collected are relevant. If this is not done carefully, the study may not provide the desired information.

Then comes the question of selecting the methods by which the data are to be obtained. In other works, techniques for collecting the information must be devised. Several methods (*viz.*, observation, questionnaries, interviewing, examination of records, etc.) with their merits and limitations, are available for the purpose and the researcher may use one or more of these methods. While designing data-collection procedure, adequate safeguards against bias and unreliability must be ensured. Whichever method is selected, questions must be well examined and be made unambiguous; interviewers must be instructed not to express their own opinion; observers must be trained so that they uniformly record a given item of behaviour. It is always desirable to pre-test the data collection instruments before they are finally used for the study purposes. In other words, we can say that "structured instruments" are used in such studies.

In most of the descriptive/diagnostic studies the researcher takes out sample(s) and then wishes to make statements about the population on the basis of the sample analysis or analyses. More often than not, sample has to be designed.

Here, we may only mention that the problem of designing samples should be tackled in such a fashion that the samples may yield accurate information with a minimum amount of research effort. Usually one or more forms of probability sampling, or what is often described as random sampling, are used.

To obtain data free from errors introduced by those responsible for collecting them, it is nccessary to supervise closely the staff of field workers as they collect and record information. Checks may be set-up to ensure that the data collecting staff perform their duty honestly and without prejudice. "As data are collected, they should be examined for completeness, comprehensibility, consistency and reliability."

The data collected must be processed and analyzed. This includes steps like coding the interview replies, observations, etc.; tabulating the data; and performing several statistical computations. To the extent possible, the processing and analysing procedure should be planned in detail before actual work is started. This will prove economical in the sense that the researcher may avoid unnecessary labour such as preparing tables for which he later finds, he has no use or on the other hand, re-doing some tables because he failed to include relevant data. Coding should be done carefully to avoid error in coding and for this purpose the reliability of coders needs to be checked. Similarly, the accuracy of tabulation may be checked by having a sample of the tables re-done. In case of mechanical tabulation the material (*i.e.*, the collected data or information) must be entered on appropriate cards which is usually done by punching holes corresponding to a given code. The accuracy of punching is to be checked and ensured. Finally, statistical computations are needed and as such averages precentages and various coefficients must be worked out. Probability and sampling analysis may as well be used. The appropriate statistical operations, alongwith the use of appropriate tests of significance should be carried out to safeguard the drawing of conclusions concerning the study.

Last of all comes the question of reporting the findings. This is the task of communicating the findings to others and the researcher must do it in an efficient manner. The layout of the report needs to be well planned so that all things relating to the research study may be well presented in simple and effective style.

Thus, the research design in case of descriptive/diagnostic studies is a comparative design throwing light on all points narrated above and must be prepared keeping in view the objective(s) of the study and the resources available. However, it must ensure the minimisation of bias and maximisation of reliability of the evidence collected. The said design can be appropriately referred to as a survey design since it takes into account all the steps involved in a survey concerning a phenomenon to be studied.

3. Research Design in Case of Hypothesis-Testing Research Studies. Hypothesis-testing research studies (generally known as experimental studies) are those where the researcher tests the hypothesis of casual relationships between variables. Such studies require procedures that will not only reduce bias and increase reliability, but will permit drawing inferences about causality. Usually experiments meet this requirement. Hence, when we talk of research design in such studies, we often mean the design of experiments.

Professor R.A. Fisher's name is associated with experimental designs. Beginning of such designs was made by him when he was working at Rothamsted Experimental Station (Centre for Agricultural Research in England). As such the study of experimental designs has its origin in agricultural research. Professor Fisher found that by dividing agricultural fields or plots into different blocks and then by conducting experiments in each of these blocks, whatever information is collected and inferences drawn from them, happens to be more reliable. This fact inspired him to develop certain experimental designs for testing hypotheses concerning scientific investigations. Today, the experimental designs are being used in researches relating to phenomena of several disciplines. Since experimental designs originated in the context of agricultural operations, we still use, though in a technical sense, several terms of agriculture (such as treatment, yield, plot, block etc.), in experimental designs.

Steps in Research Design

However, a further understanding of the components of a design elicit the following steps:

1. Selection and Definition of a Problem. The problem selected for study should be defined clearly in operational terms so that the researcher knows positively what facts he is looking for and what is relevant to the study. Since human behaviour, as an interaction pattern, is the result of various forces it is best to delimit the scope of one's study which reaps ample benefits during the actual course of data collection. Now besides the operational definition of the problem, the problem selected should be practicable in costs of time and money. If the criteria of validity and reliability of results are to be fulfilled, such problems as are unmanageable by the researcher should not be selected for the design.

2. Nature of Study. The research design should be expressed in relation to the nature of study to be undertaken. The choice of the statistical, experimental or comparative type of study should be made at this stage in planning may have relevance to the proposed problem.

3. Sources of Data. Once the problem is selected it is the duty of the researcher to state clearly the various sources of information such as library, personal documents, field work, a particular residential group etc.

4. Object of Study. Whether the design aims at a theoretical understanding or presupposes a "welfare" notion must be explicit at this point. Stating the object of the study aids not only in clarity of the design but also in a sincere response from the respondents.

5. Temporal Context. The geographical limit of the design should also be referred to at this stage that the research related to the hypothesis is applicable to particular social groups only.

6. Social-cultural Context. As one would rightly remember, a research design is always set to a context which has a social and cultural bearing on the individuals. *For example,* in a study of the fertility rate in a people of "backward" class, the context of the so called "backward class of people and the conceptual reference must be made clear. Unless the meaning of the term is clearly defined, there tends to be a large variation in the study because the term backward could have religious, economic and political connotations.

7. Basis of Selection. Now an adequate and representative sample can be selected. The mechanics of drawing a random, stratified, purposive, double cluster or quota sample when followed carefully will produce a scientifically valid sample in an unbiased manner.

8. Dimension. It is physically impossible to analyse the data collected from a large universe. Hence, the selection of an adequate and representative sample is the by word in any research. Depending upon the dimension of the proposed study, such a sample of the large population can be selected to facilitate a practical design.

9. Techniques of Data Collection. Relevant to the study design a suitable technique has to be adopted for the collection of required data. The relative merits of "Observation", "Interview" and "Questionnaire" when studied together will help in the choice of suitable technique.

Forms of Research Design

1. The Classical Design. The classical design of proof can be diagrammatised as follows:

	Before	After	
Experimental Group	X	X^1	After Difference $X_1 - X$
Control Group	X_1	X	Difference $X_1 - X^1$

Concerning the impact of a film on soldier's attitudes, Stouffer aptly remarks, "one of the troubles with using this careful design was that the effectiveness of a single film when thus, measured turned out to be slight. Much more staisfactory, results were obtained when only the after groups were selected. Thus, the soldiers who remembered the film were the ones most affected by it."

2. Successional Experimental Design. Frequently, social researches use only the experimental group.

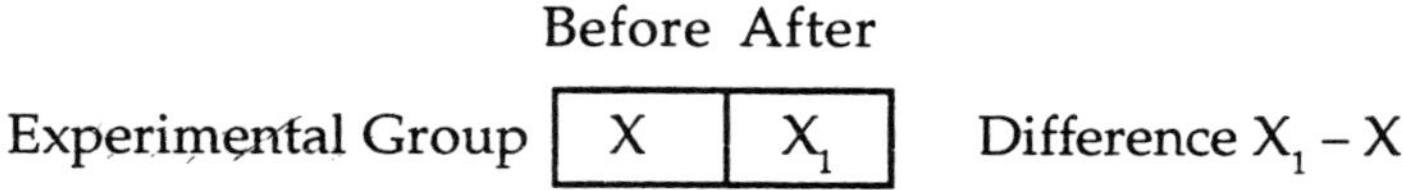

	Before	After	
Experimental Group	X	X_1	Difference $X_1 - X$

In this case the technique would be to have a preliminary observational period to measure 'control' of usual behaviour and thereupon introduce the stimulus.

It may be called a successional experiment. *For example,* the series of relay assembly experiments in the Hawthorne study. The first period was one of intensive observation of the relations of production and behavioural norms. The variables were gradually introduced at intervals. The weakness of this design is that we have no control group comparison.

3. Before and After Measurement. The before and after comparison is adequate for a simple measurement of changes such as panel study.

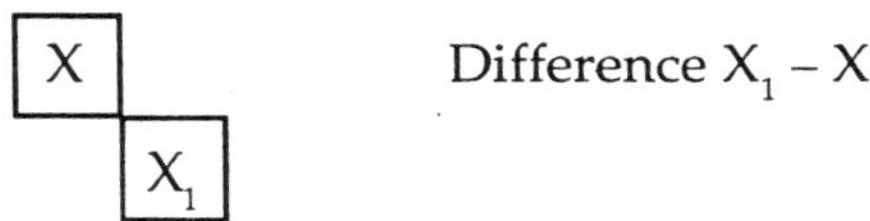

In panel study the after group is an entirely different sample. There are many implied limitations of this design since the samples are entirely different. Stouffer and others used this model for the study of army personnel. Since they could not get the same people over an interval of time, they collected matched samples of men.

4. Comparison of Two After Groups. A very common pattern in social research is to compare two "after" groups in this fashion.

Experimental Group	X	X^1
Control Group	X_1	X^{11}

In this case one tries to assume the before phase. However, one uses statistical techniques to naturalise the variables. This design is frequently used when we are faced with a situation which is already existing and an after situation for two or more groups which differ at least in the important experimental variable.

For example, there are school districts cutting through a slum area. However, here one cannot test the effect of the experimental variable upon the situation.

5. Single All Design. Perhaps an equally common design is the "single all".

Experimental Group | X |

This is actually a report on what exists at the time of the study, *for example,* the young are more literate than old.

Features of a Good Design

A good design is often characterised by adjectives like flexible, appropriate, efficient, economical and so on. Generally, the design which minimises bias and maximises the reliability of the data collected and analysed is considered a good design. The design which gives the smallest experimental error is supposed to be the best design in many investigations. Similarly, a design which yields maximal information and provides an opportunity for considering many different aspects of a problem is considered most appropriate and efficient design in respect of many research problems. Thus, the question of good design is related to the purpose or objective of the research problem and also with the nature of the problem to be studied. A design may be quite suitable in one case, but may be found wanting in one respect or the other in the context of some other research problem. One single design cannot serve the purpose of all types of research problems.

A research design appropriate for a particular research problem, usually involves the consideration of the following factors:

(a) The means of obtaining information.

(b) The objective of the problem to be studied.

(c) The nature of the problem to be studied.

(d) The availability and skills of the researcher and his staff, if any.

(e) The availability of time and money for the research work.

If the research study happens to be an exploratory or a formulative one, wherein the major emphasis is on discovery of ideas and insights, the research design most appropriate must be flexible enough to permit the consideration of many different aspects of a phenomenon. But when the purpose of a study is accurate description of a situation or of an association between variables (or in what are called the descriptive studies), accuracy becomes a major consideration and a research design which minimises bias and maximises the reliability of the evidence collected is considered a good design. Studies involving the testing of a hypothesis of a casual relationship between variables require a design which will permit inferences about casuality in addition to the minimization of bias and maximisation of reliability. But in practice it is the most difficult task to put a particular study in a particular group, for a given research may have in it elements of two or more of the functions of different studies. It is only on the basis of its primary function that a study can be categorized either as an exploratory or descriptive or hypothesis-testing study and accordingly the choice of a research design may be made in case of a paritcular study. Besides, the availability of time, money, skills of the research staff and the means of obtaining the information must be given due weightage while working out the relevant details of the research design such as experimental design, survey design, sample design and the like.

Important Concepts Relating to Research Design

Before describing the different research designs, it will be appropriate to explain the various concepts relating to designs so that these may be better and easily understood.

1. Dependent and Independent Variables. A concept which can take on different quantitative values is called a variable. As such the concepts like weight, height, income are all examples of variables. Qualitative phenomena (or the attributes) are also quanitified on the basis of the presence or absence of the concerning attribute(s). Phenomena which can take on quantitatively different values even in decimal points are called 'continuous variables'. But all variables are not continuous. If they can only be expressed in integer values, they are non-continuous variables or in statistical language 'discrete variables'. Age is an example of continuous variable, but the number of children is an example of non-continuous variable. If one variable depends upon or is a consequence ofthe other variable, it is termed as a dependent variable and the variable that is antecedent to the dependent variable is termed as an independent variable. For instance, if we say that height depends upon age, then height is a dependent variable and age is an independent variable. Further, if in addition to being dependent upon age, height also depends upon the individual's sex, then height is a dependent variable and age and sex are independent variables. Similarly, readymade films and lectures are examples of independent variables, whereas behavioural changes, occurring as a result of the environmental manipulations are examples of dependent variables.

2. Control. One important characteristic of a good research design is to minimise the influence or effect of extraneous variable(s). The technical term 'control' is used when we design the study minimising the effects of extraneous independent variables. In experimental researches, the term 'control' is used to refer to restrain experimental conditions.

3. Extraneous Variables. Independent variables that are not related to the purpose of the study, but may affect the dependent variable are termed as extraneous variables. Suppose the researcher wants to test the hypothesis that there is a relationship between children's gains in social studies achievement and their self-concepts. In this case self-concept is an independent variable and social studies achievement is a dependent variable. Intelligence may as well affect the social studies achievement, but since it is not related to the purpose of the study undertaken by the researcher, it will be termed as an extraneous variable. Whatever effect is noticed on dependent variable as a result of extraneous variable(s) is technically described as an 'experimental error'. A study must always be so designed that the effect upon the dependent variable is attributed entirely to the independent variable(s) and not to some extraneous variable or variables.

4. Research Hypothesis. When a perdiction or a hypothesised relationship is to be tested by scientific methods, it is termed as research hypothesis. The research hypothesis is a predictive statement that relates an independent variable to a dependent variable. Usually a research hypothesis must contain, at least, one independent and one dependent variable. Predictive statements, which are not to be objectively verified or the relationships that the assumed but not to be tested, are not termed research hypotheses.

5. Experimental and Non-experimental Hypothesis-Testing Research. When the purpose of research is to test a research hypothesis, it is termed as hypothesis-testing research. It can be of the experimental design or of the non-experimental design. Research in which the independent variable is manipulated is termed 'experimental hypothesis-testing research' and a research in which an independent variable is not manipulated is called 'non-experimental hypothesis-testing research'. For instance, suppose a researcher wants to study whether intelligence affects reading ability for a group of students and for this purpose he randomly selects 50 students and tests their intelligence and reading ability by calculating the coefficient of correlation between the two sets of scores. This is an example of non-experimental hypothesis-testing research because herein the independent variable, intelligence, is not manipulated. But now suppose that our researcher randomly selects 50 students from a group of students who are to take a course in statistics and then divides them into two groups by randomly assigning 25 to Group A, the usual studies programme and 25 to Group B, the special studies programme. At the end of the course, he administers a test to each group in order to judge the effectiveness of the training programme on the student's performance-level. This is an example of experimental hypothesis-testing research because in this case the independent variable, *viz.*, the type of training programme, is manipulated.

6. Experimental and Control Groups. In an experimental hypothesis-testing research when a group is exposed to usual conditions, it is termed a 'control group', but when the group is exposed to some novel or special condition, it is termed an 'experimental group'. In the above illustration, the Group A can be called a control group and the Group B an experimental group. If both groups A and B are exposed to special studies programmes, then both groups would be termed 'experimental groups' It is possible to design studies which include only experimental groups or studies which include both experimental and control groups.

7. Treatments. The different conditions under which experimental and control groups are put are usually referred to as 'treatments'.

8. Experiment. The process of examining the truth of a statistical hypothesis, relating to some research problem, is known as an experiment. *For example,* we can conduct an experiment to examine the usefulness of a certain newly developed drug. Experiments can be of two types *viz.*, absolute experiment and comparative experiment. If we want to determine the impact of a fertilizer on the yield of a crop, it is a case of absolute experiment; but if we want to determine the impact of one fertilizer as compared to the impact of some other fertilizer, our experiment then will be termed as a comparative experiment. Often, we undertake comparative experiments when we talk of designs of experiments.

9. Experimental Unit(s). The pre-determined plots or the blocks, where different treatments are used, are known as experimental units. Such experimental units must be selected (defined) very carefully.

❋❋❋

12

Data Collection Processing and Presentation

Collection of data is an essential part of a research proposal. Once the purpose of a statistical investigation has been defined, the problem is to collect data which are relevant to that purpose, to analyse these data and to present them in a meaningful manner. We shall, in this chapter, discuss, somewhat sketchily, the methods that are used in gathering and recording data in order to facilitate their analysis and interpretation. Statistical data for research investigations may either by primary or secondary. The former are original observations collected by the researcher or his agents for the first time whereas the latter refer to data that have already been collected by the same or a different agency. Data which are primary at one time point may become secondary at another. Once primary data have been made use of, it looses its original character and becomes secondary.

The nature, purpose and scope of a research study greatly affect the choice of method to be adopted for the collection of research data. Availability of time and finance also affect the choice of method for collecting primary and data. The following methods are usually adopted for the collection of primary data :

(a) Direct personal observation methods.

(b) Indirect oral examination method.

(c) Method of canvassing schedules and questionnaires.

(d) Method of collecting data by local reports.

Direct Personal Observation Method

Many types of data required by the social scientist as evidence in research can be obtained through direct observation. Suppose the researcher is interested in the manner in which mothers rear their infants, or in comparing the quality of housing occupied by different social strata of the population, or in describing religious ceremonies and rituals. To obtain these and many other types of data, he proceed best by observing the appropriate situations. Perhaps the greatest asset of observational techniques is that they make it possible to record behaviour as it occurs. In addition to its independence of a subject's ability to report, observation method is also independent of his willingness to report. There may be occasions when social research meets resistance from the person or group being studied. Although in observation method, we cannot always overcome resistance to research but it is less demanding in case of this method.

Application of this method in the collection of research data necessitates the identification of sources and fields of investigation. This identification is very important to avoid the likelihood of an investigator to go astray and waste time, effort and scarce funds on unwanted data. After the researcher has satisfied himself about the proper identification of the area of operation, he or his appointed agents collect the data personally be meeting the respondents directly. The researcher or investigator should understand fully the characteristics of the area of operation and should identify himself with the respondents for obtaining correct information. He should be a person of keen observation and should possess a number of qualities. He should witty, polite, extremely courteous and intellectually very sharp to elicit correct information from the respondents. The researcher should be quitely adopt in his job and should conduct himself very cautiously paricularly with the those respondents who are largely illiterate and ignorant about statistical investigations. However, there are two important general requirements which must always be met if observations are to furnish dependable information.

The first requirement is that observation should be reliable. The second requirement is that observations should be valid *i.e.,* they should provide a true measure of the characteristic they purport to measure. Carelessness on the part of a researcher may result in the collection of erroneous data and at times errors may be large. Caution is also needed if the questions are such as would touch the sentiments or ask for the secret information of the respondents. Researcher has to look for the most responsible person of the family who cannot only understand him but would also provide him accurate information. Questions should be simple and easy to comprehend and should be posed very politely to the respondent.

This method is more effective in eliciting the information accurately and adequately; the degree of accuracy depending upon the dexterity with which the researcher has conducted himself. The information collected is also original and can be analysed in any desired fashion. However, observation method has its specific limitations. This method of collecting primary data is very costly and time consuming. The scope of this method remains limited by the availability of time and funds. The personal bias of the researcher does great harm to the reliability of the data and it is, therefore, highly essential to have a very dependable investigator who would collect the data without letting his personal bias to effect it. This type of inquiry, while admirable because of additional accuracy due to personal supervision covers too narrow a field to be representative and is also liable to too large an injection of the personal element. The prejudices and desires of the investigator too often, though unconsciously, are woven into the fabric of his conclusions.

Indirect Oral Examination Method

Sometimes, if for some reason, the information cannot be collected directly, an indirect approach is adopted to record the relevant observations. Persons who are supposed to have correct knowledge about the respondents are approached and requested to state the pertinent facts to be required by the researcher. This method is resorted to when the time and funds are limited and an exhaustive direct investigation cannot be taken in hand. A small list of questions is prepared and put to those who are supposed to have an intimate knowledge of research problem and the sources of the pertinent data. Many enquiry commissions conduct indirect oral examinations of the witness to ascetain the relevant facts of the problem. It is desirable that several people be contacted so the cross-checks can be made on the facts and their reliability and desirability increased.

The selection of the persons from whom the information is sought of collected should be made carefully. These persons should be knowledgeable, unbiased, capable of expressing themselves clearly and correctly and should not be influenced by any source to present the data in a wrong fashion. The researcher should carefully use his data and make allowance for all possible errors or inaccuracies.

Method of Canvassing Schedules and Questionnaires

A very commonly used method of collecting research data is through questionnaires and interview schedules and These devices have been used for the collection of personal preferences, social attitude, beliefs, opinions, behaviour patterns, group practices and habits and such other data. The increasing use of questionnaires and schedules is probably due to increased emphasis by social scientists on quantitative measurement of uniformly accumulated data.

Questionnaires

The questionnaires are sent to the concerned persons with the request that the information sought be furnished and the questionnaire return to the concerned office or agency. Questionnaires may also be sent through enumerators to help the respondents to furnish correct information.

Mailed questionnaires method can prove very handy and useful if a wide area of investigation is to be covered and information is required soon. This method as such is least expensive. With a given amount of funds, it is usually possible to cover a wider area and to obtain information from more people by means of questionnaires than by personally interviewing each respondent. Further, the impersonnal nature of a questionnaires, its standarized wording, its standardized order of questions, its standardized instructions for recording responses ensures some uniformity from one measurement situation to another. Another advantage of questionnaires is that respondents may have greater confidence in their anonymity and thus, feel free to express views that fear might be disapprove of or might get them into trouble. Nevertheless this method remains seriously handicapped if the respondents are illiterate and can not porperly fill in the answers. Further, since the method is voluntary in character, the cooperation of the respondents is highly essential. Indifferent respondents either do not care to send back the questionnaires or fill in the answers vaguely and erroneously. This does not serve the purpose of the researcher. The method is, therefore, seldom used in countries where levels of literacy and statistical consciousness are low.

In order to assist the respondents to fill in the correct answers, sometimes, questionnaires are sent through enumerators who are usually trained in this job. The enumerators not only help in explaining the questionnaires and the terms and definitions used therein but also explain the importance of an enquiry to the respondents. As such the importance of correct answers is emphasized and the accuracy of data is greatly increased. The selection of enumerators has, therefore, to be done very carefully. They must be painstaking, patient and polite.

Filling out lengthily questionnaires takes a great deal of time and effort, a favour that few senders have any right to expect of strangers. The unfavourable reaction is intensified when the questionnaire is long, the subject trivial in importance, the items vaguely worded and the form poorly organized. Unless one is dealing with a group of respondents who have a genuine interest in the problem under investigation, who know the sender, or who have some common bond loyalty to a sponsoring institution or organization the rate of returns is frequently disappointing and provides a clumsy basis for generalisation.

Characteristics of a Good Questionnaire

While constructing a good questionnaire the following characteristics may be kept in mind.

1. It deals with a significant topic, one the respondent will recognize as important enough to warrant spending his time on.
2. It is attractive in appearance, neatly arranged and beautifully printed.
3. The questions are objective, with no leading suggestions as to the responses desired.
4. Questions are presented in good psychological order, proceeding from general to specific responses.
5. Directions are clear and complete, important terms are defined, each question deals with a single idea, all questions are worded as simply and as clearly as possible.
6. It is easy to tabulate and interpret.
7. It is as short as possible, only long enough to get the essential data.
8. It seeks only those informations which cannot be obtained from other sources.

Interview Schedules

One of the major drawbacks to the use of questionnaire is that it is appropriate only for subjects with a considerable amount of education. Complicated questionnaires requiring extended written responses can be used with only a very small percentage of the population. Hence, questionnaires are not an appropriate method for large segments of the population. On the other hand, data can be collected by interviewing almost all segments of the population with the help of schedules. Schedule is the name usually applied to a set of questions which are asked and filled in by an interviewer in a face-to-face situation with another person.

Kinds of Schedules

According to uses that are put, the schedules used in the social research can be classified in the following four groups:

1. Observation Schedule. As the name implies, observation schedules are used for recording observations. These offer an opportunity for uniform classification in recording the activities and social situations of persons or groups being observed.

2. Document Schedule. These schedules are used for recording data obtained from documents, case histories and other materials. In order to secure measurable data, the items included on this type of form are limited to those that can be uniformly secured from a large number of case histories or other records.

3. Evaluation Schedule. This type of schedule is mainly used for sociological or psychological research. Such schedules are useful in those cases where the attitude or opinion is to be measured.

4. Interview Schedule. This type of schedule is used for collecting data by interewing the informant. Here, we are more concerned with this type of schedule these contain standard questions that are asked by the interviewer and black tables which are to be filled up after getting information from the respondents.

Merits of Interviews

Surveys conducted by personal interviews have an advantage over surveys conducted by mailed questionnaires in that they usually yield a much better sample of the general population. Many people are willing and able to co-operate in a study when all they have to do is talk. Another advantage of the interview is its greater flexibility. In an interview is the possibility of repeating or rephrasing questions to make sure that they are understood, or of asking further questions in order to clarify the meaning of a response. Its flexibility makes the interview a far superior technique for the exploration of areas, where there is little basis for knowing either what questions to ask or how to formulate them. In addition, the interviewing situation offers a better opportunity than the questionnaire to apprise the validity of reports. In short, the interview method of collecting data is the more appropriate technique for revealing information about complex, emotionally laden subjects or for probing the sentiments that may underline an expressed opinion.

Guidelines for Constructing Questionnaires and Schedules

The questionnaire or interview schedule, serves two major purposes. *First,* it must translate the research objectives into specific questions, the answers to which will provide the data necessary to test the hypothesis or explore the area set by the research objectives. In order to achieve this purpose, each question must convey to the respondent the idea or group of ideas required by the research objectives and each question must obtain a response which can be analysed so that the results, fulfil the research objectives.

In the construction of questionnaires and interview schedules, it is, of course, very important that the verbal stimuli presented by the interviewer or questionnaire be as clear as possible. The appropriate form of question depends on the mode of administration the subject matter, the sample of people to reach and the kind of analysis and interpretation intended. It is very important that the researcher avoids vagueness and ambiguity in the language. The investigator can also promote clarity by avoding long questions and words with double meanings, prefacing unfamiliar or unusually complicated questions with an explanatory paragraph or an illustration; and asking questions in terms of the respondents' own immediate and recent experience rather than in generalities. The use of follow up questions or probes is advisable at many points in the ordinary interview, especially in connection with the free responses. The questionnaire planner also has to decide whether to use a set of several questions rather than a single question on particular points to be covered. Some questions are necessary and often unavoidable in a long interview. These must not only be timely and wisely rational but also must be pharased in terms that show concern to the interviewee's problems. Such blunt questions as, "What is your present income' or "How much do you have in your saving account?" Cause antagonism and withdrawal. In order to secure cooperation, the questions should be indirect and imply concern.

Sequential Order of the Questions

The arrangement or ordering of the questions should receive special attention and be pretested with case. Every effort should be made to have the order appear logical to the respondent. The following points may be kept in mind while formulating questionnaires or schedule:

1. Placing a question early in the questionnaire or schedule that can affect answers to later questions should be prevented wherever possible.
2. The questions placed in the beginning of the questionnaire or schedule should be those easiest to answer.

3. Subject-matter in sequencing of questions is likewise, very important and as far as possible all questions pertaining to one subject should be grouped together.
4. A time sequence shold be observed in the arrangement of questions.

Pre-Testing of Schedules and Questionnaires

Before schedules are used for interviewing the respondents or questionnaires are mailed to the respondents, it is usual to pretest them. 'Pre-testing provides not only a test of the clarity of the questions and of the correctness of interpretation put upon them by the respondent, but also affords the possibility of discovery of new aspects of the problem studies which are not anticipated in the planning stage. In short, pretesting provides a means of detecting mistakes on procedure before the exact heavy penalties in the form of low proportion of returns or of replies lacking in reliability and validity. Pretesting is essentially a trial and error procedure wherein the successful trials are repeated and the errors are avoided when the final questionnaire or schedule is got ready. Through the wider us of pretesting, it may be possible to appease the critics who have so frequently and justly condemned questionnaires or schedules of the past.

Method of Collecting Data by Local Reports

Local correspondents and other localized agencies collect a large volume of information in their own way and many a times data for research studies are compiled from these reports. The data collected as such cannot be held to be as accurate as that collected by other methods and such data are used in those investigations where only rough estimates are required. Though the method is convenient and least expensive, yet it is used only in a few cases.

PROCESSING OF DATA

After collecting the research data they have been processed and analyzed in accordance with the outline laid down for the purpose at the time of developing the research plan. This is essential for a scientific study and for ensuring that we have all relevant data for making contemplated comparisons and analysis. Technically speaking, processing implies editing, coding, classification and tabulation of collected data so that they are amenable to analysis. The term analysis refers to the computation of certain measures alongwith searching for patterns of relationship that exist among data-groups. Thus, "in the process of analysis, relationships or differences supporting or conflicting with orginal or new hypotheses should be subjected to statistical tests of significance to determine with what validity data can be said to indicate any conclusions". But there are persons (Selltiz, Jahoda and others) who do not like to make difference between processing and analysis. They opine that analysis of data in a general way involves a number of closely related operations which are performed with the purpose of summarising the collected data and organising these in such a manner that they answer the research question(s).

Processing Operations

With this brief introduction concerning the concepts of processing and analysis, we can now proceed with the explanation of all the processing operations.

1. Editing. Editing of data is a process of examining the collected raw data (specially in surveys) to detect errors and omissions and to correct these when possible. As a matter of fact, editing involves a careful scrutiny of the completed questionnaires and/or schedules. Editing is done to assure that the data are accurate, consistent with other facts gathered, uniformly entered, as complete as possible and have been well arranged to facilitate coding and tabulation.

With regard to points or stages at which editing should be done, one can talk of field editing and central editing. Field editing consists in the review of the reporting forms by the investigator for completing (translating or rewriting) what the latter has written in abbreviated and/or in illegible form at the time of recording the respondents' responses. This type of editing is necessary in view of the fact that individual writing styles often can be difficult for others to decipher. This sort of editing should be done as soon as possible after the interview, preferably on the very day or on the next day. While doing field editing, the investigator must restrain himself and must not correct errors of omission by simply using what the informant would have said if the question had been asked.

Central editing should take place when all forms or schedules have been completed and returned to the office. This type of editing implies that all forms should get a thorough editing by a single editor in a small study and by a term of editors in case of a large inquiry. Editor(s) may correct the obvious errors such as an entry in the wrong place, entry recorded in months when it should have been recorded in weeks and the like. In case of inappropriate or missing replies, the editor can sometimes determine the proper answer by reviewing the other information in the schedule. At times, the respondent can be contacted for clarification. The editor must strike out the answer if the same is inappropriate and he has no basis for determining the correct answer or the response. In such a case an editing entry of 'no answer' is called for all the wrong replies, which are quite obvious, must be dropped from the final results, especially in the context of mail surveys.

Editors must keep in view several points while performing their work:

(a) They should be familiar with instructions given to the interviewers and coders as well as with the editing instructions supplied to them for the purpose.

(b) They must make entries (if any) on the form in some distinctive colour and that too in a standardised form.

(*c*) While crossing out an original entry for one reason or another, they should just draw a single line on it so that the same may remain legible.

(*d*) Editor's initials and the date of editing should be placed on each completed from or schedule.

(*e*) They should initial all answers which they change or supply.

2. Coding. Coding refers to the process of assigning numerals or other symbols to answers so that responses can be into a limited number of categories or classes. Such classes should be appropriate to the research problem under consideration. They must also possess the characteristic of exhaustiveness (*i.e.,* there must be a class for every data item) and also that of mutual exclusivity which means that a specific answer can be placed in one and only one cell in a given category set. Another rule to be observed is that of undimensionality by which is meant that every class is defined in terms of only one concept.

Coding is necessary for efficient analysis and through it the several replies may be reduced to a small number of classes which contain the critical information required for analysis . Coding decisions should usually be taken at the designing stage of the questionnaire. This makes it possible to precode the questionnaire choices and which in turn is helpful for computer tabulation as one can stright forward key punch from the original questionnaires. But in case of hand coding some standard method may be used. One such standard method is to code in there margin with a coloured pencil. The other method can be to transcribe the data from the questionnaire to a coding sheet.

3. Classification. Most research studies result in a large volume of raw data which must be reduced into homogeneous groups if we are to get meaningful relationships. This fact necessitates classification of data which happens to be the process of arranging data in groups or classes on the basis of common characteristics. Data having a common characteristic are placed in one class and in this way the entire data get divided into a number of groups or classes. Classification can be one of the following two types, depending upon the nature of the phenomenon involved:

(a) Classification According to Attributes. As stated above, data are classified on the basis of common characteristics which can either be descriptive (such as literacy, sex, honesty, etc.) or numerical (such as weight, height, income etc.). Descriptive characteristics refer to qualitative phenomenon which cannot be measured quantitatively; only their presence or absence in a individual item can be noticed. Data obtained this way on the basis of certain attributes are known as statistics of attributes and their classification is said to be classification according to attributes.

Such classification can be simple classification or manifold classification. In simple classification we consider only one attribute and divide the universe into two classes—one class consisting of items possessing the given attribute and the other class consisting of items which do not possess the given attribute. But in manifold classification we consider two or more attributes simultaneously and divide the data into a number of classes (total number of classes of final order is given by 2^n, where n = number of attributes considered)." Whenever data are classified according to attributes, the researcher must see that the attributes are defined in such a manner that there is least possibility of any doubt/ambiguity concerning the said attributes.

(b) Classification According to Class-Intervals. Unlike descriptive characteristics, the numerical characteristics refer to quantitative phenomenon which can be measured through some statistical units. Data relating to income, production, age, weight, etc., come under this category. Such data are known as statistics of variables and are classified on the basis of class intervals. For instance, persons whose incomes, say, are within ₹ 2001 to ₹ 4000 can form one group, those whose incomes are within ₹ 4001 to ₹ 6000 can form another group and so on. In this way the entire data may be divided into a number of groups or classes or what are usually called, 'class intervals.' Each group or class-interval, thus, has an upper limit as well as a lower limit which are known as class limits. The difference between the two class limits is known as class magnitude. We may have classes with equal class magnitudes or with unequal class magnitudes. The number of items which fall in a given class is known as the frequency of the given class. All the classes or groups, with their respective frequencies taken together and put in the form of a table, are described as group frequency distribution or simply frequency distribution. Classification according to class intervals usually involves the following three main problems:

(i) How many classes should be there? What should be their magnitudes?

There can be no specific answer with regard to the number of classes. The decision about this class for skill and experience of the researcher. However, the objective should be to display the data in such a way as to make it meaningful for the analyst. Typically, we may have 5 to 15 classes. With regard to the second part of the question, we can say that, to the extent possible, class-intervals should be of equal magnitudes, but in some cases unequal magnitudes may result in better classification. Hence, the researcher's objective judgement plays an important part in this connection. Multiples of 2, 5 and 10 generally prefered while determing class magnitudes. Some statisticians adopt the following formula, suggested by H.A. Sturges, determining the size of class interval:

$$i = R / (1 + 3.3 \log N)$$

where i = size of class interval;

R = Range (*i.e.,* difference between the values of the largest item and smallest item among the given items);

N = Number of items to be grouped.

It should also be kept in mind that in case one or two or very few items have very high or very low values, one may use what are known as open-ended intervals in the overall frequency distribution. Such intervals may be expressed like under ₹ 500 or ₹ 10001 and over. Such intervals are generally not desirable, but often cannot be avoided. The researcher must always remain conscious of this fact while deciding the issue of the total number of class intervals in which the data are to be classified.

(ii) How to choose class limits?

While choosing class limits, the researcher must take into consideration the criterion that the mid-point (generally worked out first by taking the sum of the upper limit and the lower limit of a class and then divide this sum by (2) of a class-interval and the actual average of items of that class interval should remain as close to each other as possible. Consistent with this, the class limits should be located at multiples of 2, 5, 10, 20, 100 and such other figures. Class limits may generally be stated in any of the following forms:

Exclusive Type Class Intervals. They are usually stated as follows:

10 – 20

20 – 30

30 – 40

40 – 50

The above intervals should be read as under:

10 and under 20

20 and under 30

30 and under 40

40 and under 50

Thus, under the exclusive type class intervals, the items whose values are equal to the upper limit of a class are grouped in the next higher class. *For example,* an item whose value is exactly 30 would be put in 30–40 class interval and not in 20–30 class interval. In simple words, we can say that under exclusive type class intervals, the upper limit of a class interval is excluded and items with values less than the upper limit (but not less than the lower limit) are put in the given class interval.

Inclusive Type Class Intervals. They are usually stated as follows:

11 – 20

21 – 30

31 – 40

41 – 50

In inclusive type class intervals the upper limit of a class interval is also included in the concerning class interval. Thus, an item whose value is 20 will be put in 11 – 20 class interval. The stated upper limit of the class interval 11 – 20 is 20 but the real limit is 20,99999 and as such 11 – 20 class interval really means 11 and under 21.

When the phenomenon under consideration happens to be a discrete one (*i.e.,* can be measured and stated only in integers), then we should adopt inclusive type classification. But when the phenomenon happens to be a continuous one capable of being measured in fractions as well, we can use exclusive type class intervals.

(iii) How to determine the frequency of each class?

This can be done either by tally sheets or by mechanical aids. Under the technique of tally sheet, the class-groups are written on a sheet of paper (commonly known as the tally sheet) and for each item a stroke (usually a small vertical line) is marked against the class group in which it falls. The general practice is that after every four small vertical lines in a class group, the fifth line for the item falling in the same group, is indicated as horizontal line through the said four lines and the resulting flower (𝍸) represents five items. All this facilitates the counting of items in each one of the class groups. An illustrative tally sheet can be shown as under:

An Illustrative Tally sheet for Determining the number of 70 Families in Different Income Groups

Income groups (Rupees)	*Tally mark*	*Number of families or (Class frequency)*
Below 400	𝍸 𝍸 |||	13
401 – 800	𝍸 𝍸 𝍸 𝍸	20
801 – 1200	𝍸 𝍸 ||	12
1201 – 1600	𝍸 𝍸 |||	18
1601 and above	𝍸 ||	7
Total		70

Alternatively, class frequencies can be determined, specially in case of large inquiries and surveys, by mechanical aids *i.e.,* with the help of machines *viz.,* sorting machines that are availabe for the purpose. Some machines are hand operated, whereas others work with electricity. There are machines which can sort out cards at a speed of something like 25000 cards per hour. This method is fast but expensive.

4. Tabulation. When a mass of data has been assembled, it becomes necessary for the researcher to arrange the same in some kind of concise and logical order. This procedure is referred to as tabulation. Thus, tabulation is the process of summarising raw data and displaying the same in compact form (*i.e.*, in the form of statistical tables) for further analysis. In a broader sense, tabulation is an oderly arrangement of data in columns and rows.

Tabulation is essential because of the following reasons:

1. It conserves space and reduces explanatory and descriptive statement to a minimum.
2. It facilitats the process of comparison.
3. It facilitates the summation of items and the detection of errors and omissions.
4. It provides a basis for various statistical computations.

Tabulation can be done by hand or by mechanical or electronic devices. The choice depends on the size and type of study, cost considerations, time pressures and the availability of tabulating machines or computers. In relatively large inquiries, we may use mechanical or computer tabulation. If other factors are favourable and necessary facilities are available. Hand tabulation is usually preferred in case of small inquiries where the number of questionnaires is small and they are of relatively short length. Hand tabulation may be done using the direct tally, the list and tally or the card sort and count methods. When there are simple codes, it is feasible to tally directly from the questionnaire. Under this method, the codes are written on a sheet of peper, called tally sheet and for each response a stroke is marked against the code in which it falls. Usually after every four strokes against a particular code, the fifth response is indicated by drawing a diagonal or horizontal line through the strokes. These groups of five are easy to count and the data are sorted against each code conveniently. In the listing method, the code responses may be transcribed into a large worksheet, allowing a line for each questionnaire. This way a large number of questionnaires can be listed on one work sheet, tallies are then made for each question. The card sorting method is the most flexible hand tabulation. In this method the data are recorded on special cards of convenient size and shape with a series of holes. Each hole stands for a code and when cards are stacked, a needle passes through particular hole representing a particular code. These cards are then separated and counted. In this way frequencies of various codes can be found out by the repetition of this technique. We can as well use the mechanical devices or the computer facility for tabulation purpose in case we want quick results, our budget permits their use and we have a large volume of straight forward tabulation involving a number of cross-breaks.

Tabulation may also be classified as simple and complex tabulation. The former type of tabulation gives information about one or more groups of independent question, whereas the latter type of tabulation shows the division of data in two or more categories and as such is designed to give information concerning one or more sets of inter-related questions. Simple tabulation generally results in one-way tables which supply answers to questions about one characteristic of data only. As against this, complex tabulation usually results in two-way tables (which give information about two interrelated characteristics of data), three-way tables (giving information about three interrelated characteristics of data) or still higher order tables, also known as manifold tables, which supply information about several interrelated characteristics of data. Two-way tables, three-way tables or manifold tables are all examples of what is sometimes described as cross tabulation.

Generally Accepted Principles of Tabulation. Such principles of tabulation particularly of constructing statistical table, can be briefly stated as follows:

1. Every table should have a clear, concise and adequate title so as to make the table intelligible without reference to the text and this title should always be placed just above the body of the table.

2. The units of measurement under each heading or sub-heading must always be indicated.
3. Source or sources from where the data in the table have been obtained must be indicated just below the table.
4. The column headings (captions) and the row headings (stubs) of the table should be clear and brief.
5. Every table should be given a distinct number to facilitate easy reference.
6. Usually the columns are separated from one another by lines which make the table more readable and attractive. Lines are always drawn at the top and bottom of the table and below the captions.
7. The columns may be numbered to facilitate reference.
8. There should be thick lines to separate the data under one class from the data under another class and the lines separating the sub-divisions of the classes should be comparatively thin lines.
9. Explanatory footnotes, if any, concerning the table should be placed directly beneath the table, along with the reference symbols used in the table.
10. It is generally considered better to approximate figures before tabulation as the same would reduce unnecessary details in the table itself.
11. Those columns whose data are to be compared should be kept side by side. Similarly, percentages and/or averages must also be kept close to the data.
12. It is important that all column figures be properly aligned. Decimal points and (+) or (–) signs should be in perfect alignment.
13. In order to emphasie the relative significance of certain categories, different kinds of type, spacing and indentations may be used.

14. Abbreviations should be avoided to the extent possible and ditto marks should not be used in the table.
15. Miscelleneous and exceptional items, if any, should be usually placed in the last row of the table.
16. Table should be made as logical, clear, accurate and as simple as possible. If the data happen to be very large, they should not be crowded in a single table for that would make the table unwieldy and inconvenient.
17. The arrangement of the categories in a table may be chronological, geographical, alphabetical or according to magnitude to facilitate comparison. Above all, the table must suit the needs and requirements of an investigation.
18. Total of rows should normally be placed in the extreme right column and that of columns should be placed at the bottom.

PRESENTATION OF DATA

Whereas it is essential that whole data should be properly presented, in a way that it is acceptable to the society and is clearly understandable by the clientele for whom it is meant. Target group should be the main consideration of the investigator in the presentation of data. The data can be presented in several forms and ways, but obviously most appealing will be one which puts least strain on the readers and tempts them to read what the researcher wants them to go through.

Descriptive Presentation. Data collected can be presented in several forms. One such form is descriptive presentation. In such a presentation a very important role is played by the language used. It is expected of the researcher that he should use only simple and clear language which can be easily understood. Though usually it is claimed that such a language should be non-technical, yet in actual practice many technical terms are likely to get introduced. But even otherwise, for the sake of simple and understandable language, basic character of the study should in no way be sacrificed. It should not be forgotten that such a description is not to be read by only those who are technically qualified or research minded but also by those who are interested in the study of the problem and as such flow of the language should be carefully maintained.

Graphic Presentation. Then another way of presentation of data is that of presenting that with the help of graphs, charts, maps, etc. The aim of such a presentation again is to present the way that it is easy to understood. In graphic presentations, maps, pictrographs, charts, pictures, diagrams, etc., are used. Graphic presentation becomes useful when relationship of two or more variables is to be studied. Similarly these are useful in time series and frequency distribution. Cause and effort relationships can also be studied with the help of graphs.

Diagrams. In some cases data can be presented with the help of diagrams as well. Such presentation does away with dry figures and makes that more attractive. These help the readers in understanding conclusions without mental thumbing or reading of dry statements. Since the people usually avoid calculations and these do not come of diagrams, therefore, readers feel like looking of at diagrams. With their help it becomes easy to understand the problems and these can also be easily remembered. Diagrams can be of one, two or multi-dimensions. Similarly, these can be in vertical and horizontal lines and bars, which may also be further sub-divided. Diagrams can also be in square, rectangle or circular form. These can also be in cube, block or cylindrical form. These are no rigid rules for constructing diagrams but at the same time it is essential that only such diagrams should be picked which give correct and not misleading idea about the data being represented. The another point which needs consideration is that only attractive diagrams should be selected *i.e.,* the diagram should be neither too big nor too small but only of resonable size. These should be appealing to eyes of those, for whom presentation of data is meant. Each diagram should bear complete title and the reader should be in a position to understand it without any outside assistance. Where necessary suitable colours should be used and all words and figures should be clearly readable. While preparing diagrams cost factors should be taken into account and very costly diagrams should not be prepared.

Tabular Presentation. Data can also be presented with the help of tables as well. Tables make the readers easily understand the whole data. These also reduce the data in a readable form without serious strains and mass of data can become easy and presentable. But the tables have their own problems. There is a lot of data which cannot be presented in the form of tables. Similarly a vast data, which is presented in the from of tables makes the whole system more complex and complicated, rather than making that simple and easily understandable.

Pictures and Maps. In some cases use of maps and charts becomes unavoidable in the presentation of data. Their use is increasing because with their help relative values increase and comparisons become easy. In this case it is essential that size of pictures and maps should be attractive and appealing. But main difficulty with these is that it is not possible for every researcher to draw attractive and beautiful pictures and as such services of artists become unavoidable. But pictures have proved their utility and worth in the areas and among the people who are not literate or are not research minded. Their use among literary and educated persons has not found much favour. Some researchers feel that use of pictures in a research work lowers down its values and makes the whole work cheap.

As regards maps their use is not common with social researchers but all the more these are used by those who are deveoted the regional studies, distribution of areas, mines and minerals, etc. Battle-field, locations of the theatres and strategic points can easily be presented with the help of maps. But difficulty with the maps is that every researcher cannot prepare these and even if one can prepare, to exactly located and find out places shown in the map is not an easy affair.

Difficulties in Presentation of Data

Each method for the presentation of data has its own limitations. Descriptive method of presentation for serious research is of course quite common, but its greatest limitation is that of the language. In this method, it is very essential that language should have proper flow and should be such that it can be easily understood and followed. Usually, it is difficult to find researchers who have command over the language and can present report in a flawless language. But pictorial representation in spite of its advantages is disliked for serious studies and it is believed that such a representation is only proper for low literacy areas. In fact, no serious attention is paid to charts maps and pictures and labour put in the preparation of maps and charts is simply wasted. Then another difficulty is that unless maps and diagrams are very carefully prepared, there is every danger that the researcher may frustrate his own efforts and instead of giving a very correct picture he may give either partially or fully wrong picture and results may become misleading. Still another limitation is that all these aids can only be supplementary to the data and help in their presentation and thus, cannot be used as original instrument for the collection, verification and finding out reliability of data.

Though there are several problems in the presentation of data with the form of aids, yet in social research all the aids have come to stay in varying degree and are being increasingly used. Social researchers use these in their final reports and are being liked in many quarters by large number of readers as well.

CLASSIFICATION OF DATA

Let us first of all understand as to what is mean by classification. As is known data, by whatever means and methods that may be collected, is always jumbled on *i.e.*, just a heap of papers and no inferences can be drawn from it. If any inferences or conclusions are required to be drawn from that, for that it is very essential that it should be properly classified. It is classification which makes the whole jumbled data useful and usable. It is only after classification that tabulation and generalisation becomes possible. Thus, classification is important stepping stone towards even a report writing process. It will therefore be right to say that through classification haphazard and complex and un-intelligible mass of data can be converted into understandable form and made worth using. In fact, all schedules and questionnaires which are used in the collection of data, take classification system into consideration *i.e.,* whether classification of data will or will not be possible. In brief it can be said that classification is nothing else but putting the data into different classes, in a way that whole data becomes understandable and a complex problem becomes easily understandable. Classification can be on different basis, but the whole idea is to arrange the collected data in a scientific way, putting material relating to each similar category or almost similar matter at one place.

Objectives of Classification

Classification of collected data is not only essential but it is unavoidable, if it is desired that it should be put to any use. Without such a classification whole data will remain jumbled, complex and un-understandable bundle of papers. Thus, the main object of classification is to arrange the data in some scientific manner. Then there are several other objects of the classification of data. One important object can be that points of similarities and dissimilarities, which are otherwise not clear in the data, should be clearly brought out. In this way data can be grouped into two groups, one having similarity and the other dissimilarity. In this way with the help of classification different characteristics of data can also become clear *e.g.,* if a researcher has collected data about educational standards of the people of a locality, with the help of classification we can find out the % age of students who could go up to primary, middle, secondary and higher education levels and also the category of students falling in each broad category *i.e.*, poor, middle and rich to which they belong. It also becomes possible to find out the purpose for which they got education.

The data is also classified with the object of making comparisons. Such comparison can be between two countries, areas and societies *e.g.*, with the help of classification it becomes easy to find out, as to what is % age of educated persons in two areas or among the people belonging to the same community but living in different areas and localities and so on. Then classification can also be made with the object of finding out what is relevant and what is irrelevant data for the purposes of study. Thus, when the information needed for the study has been placed under different boxes, the material which has not found a place in any box can be classified as 'irrelevant' and thus, can be considered of secondary importance for the present and for that particular study. Thus, when classification has made it clear as to which data is relevant and which is irrelevant, then the labour wasted in studying irrelevant data is saved and can be channelised in the study or relevant data.

Advantage of Classification

The objectives of the classification of data make its utility quite clear and understandable. It can be said that utility of classification is that it makes the data understandable and socially useful and usable. It gives an idea about the points of similarities and dissimilarities on the one hand and what is relevant and irrelevant on the other. It helps in saving human labour and energy by not wasting time, in finding out what is considered less useful for the present study. With the help of classification comparisons become possible. Not only this, but it is after classification that generalization and anaysis of the whole data in a scientific way can become possible. In fact, it can be said that the most important advantage of classification is that mass of jumbled data becomes readable and the whole complex becomes simple and also clearly understandable.

Classification and its Characteristics

A good classification obviously is one, which gives a clear picture of what is desired to be presented. In case that is not done or with the help of that classification that does not become possible, it can be said that classification is not good or that it does not represent essential qualities and characteristics of good classification. The essential of a good classification is that it should give idea about what is similar and what is dissimilar in the data. Similarily it should be clearly pointed out as to what is relevant and what is irrelevant in the study as a whole. It is, of course, accepted that when we deal with human beings there can never be absolute similarity. It is because behaviours, attitudes, habits and situations are bound to differ from individual to individual and place to place. But since the people have been picked up for study and made a part of one universe of study, it is in itself evident that there is some basic similarity in them.

A good classification should clearly spell out the principles on which classification has been made. Unless those principles are clear, it shall not be possible to understand the whole process of classification and that it itself will become a jumble. Thus, out of one jumble *i.e.,* data, another jumble *i.e.,* classification will emerge. In fact, each term used in the classification should be very clear and understandable *e.g.,* when we talk of the 'poor', 'rich', literate etc., the classifier should clearly spell out as to who has been placed under the category of 'poor', 'rich' or literate and so on.

A good classification should also ensure that whatever definition of terms is given once, that should be strictly adhered to, so that there are least variations. Obviously when there are no basic variations, there is stability which is most essential for a good classification. If a classification is instable that is bound to be non-dependable and non reliable which is neither good for analysis non for generalization of the material, nor for the research work as a whole. But at the same time some scope for adjustability should also be kept in view. As is well known that during the course of data collection and analysis and also when classification process is going on, some new situations and developments may take place.

An important characteristic and consideration for classification is that it should be adequate. In other words, what is meant is that the classes and categories in which data is being classified. The fear being that should not be too few. That after classification has been done, nothing may come out of that and whole data still may remain jumbled. Similarly the classes and categories should also not be too many. The danger again being that it may become more or less unmanageable to control and a situation of confusion may arise. The fear also being that in the process focus of the study may get lost. It is, therefore, essential that categories in which data is being classified, should neither be too few nor too many.

Types of Classification

After discussing basis of classification we now come to the types of classification. Such a classification can be on the basis of attributes and variable etc. Each one is briefly discussed as under:

1. Classification According to Attributes. Classification by attributes is also known as qualitative classification. In this classification all data is classified on the basis of certain attributes and characteristics. This classification on the basis of attributes can be simple as well as manifold. As regards simple classification data is classified under two heads *i.e.*, that which has similar characteristics is placed under one head. Similarly the data that is not similar or has no similar characteristic is placed under another group. Obviously the data placed in one group in bound to be quite different from the one placed under another group *e.g.*, in one group highly educated persons are placed, in the other illiterate or less educated will be placed or for that matter if in one group righ and elite of the society are placed in the other, the poor and the down-trodden will find place.

As against simple classification is complex or manifold classification. In this classification the basis is not one characteristic but many characteristics. The data will be placed in different boxes, on the basis of each characteristic. Thus, in the classification there are not two but many groups *e.g.*, in this type of classification, if literacy is to be studied, the people will have to be classified firstly on the basis of sex (male and female), then class will come into picture *i.e.*, (rich, middle, poor); thereafter will come the level of education (primary, middle, secondary and higher). It can also be on the basis of medium of instruction (Hindi, English, mother tongue) or on the nature of educational institution (Public School, Government School, Private School) etc. Thus, manifold aspects of the same problem can be studied with the help of manifold classification of data system, according to attributes.

2. Classification According to Variables. Classification can also be according to variables as well. Data according to variables can be on the basis of frequency distribution and such variables as height, weight, age and production can be found out with its help. In this method, datails classified under various categories and each category is than called 'class interval' and limit under which that is kept is called 'class limit'. Since this type of classification is not possible with the help of classification by attributes, therefore, method of classification by variable is adopted. Related to this classification which makes classification of statistical data possible, is what is known as statistical series. When classification according to variables is presented in a tabulated form that is known as 'statistical series', which again are of different categories. When series have individual units in ascending or decsending order, then we call these as arrays *e.g.*, the unit is a family and we are to find out the present income of ten families in ascending or descending order. This will be presented as follows:

Sl. No.	*Income of the family as a whole per month (Ascending order)*	*Sl. No.*	*Income of the family as a whole, per month (Descending order)*
	₹		₹
1.	100/-	7.	290/-
2.	120/-	6.	250/-
3.	150/-	5.	190/-
4.	180/-	4.	180/-
5.	190/-	3.	150/-
6.	250/-	2.	120/-
7.	290/-	1.	100/-

Then there are discreate series in which measurement of size is represented through one unit. Such a Table has only two columns namely, one which contains the size of measurement and second represents no. of cases upon which that size is applicable example:

Sl. No.	*Income of the family ₹ per month*	*Number of families which come within this income*
1.	100/-	10
2.	120/-	8
3.	150/-	11
4.	180/-	7
5.	190/-	9
6.	250/-	5
7.	290/-	6

Thereafter comes what is known as 'Continuous series'. In these series measurement is in the form of a group and there is continuity in flow instead of independent integers. Two limits of each class are known as upper and lower limits and the numbeı of subjects is called frequency *e.g.,*:

Sl. No.	*Monthly income of families of an area between ₹*	*No. of families*
1.	0 – 100	90
2.	101 – 150	80
3.	151 – 200	70
4.	201 – 250	60
5.	251 – 300	50
6.	301 – 400	40
7.	351 – 400	30
8.	401 and above	20

Thereafter come 'Time Series' or periodical classification, in which data is arranged according to time sequence *e.g.*, can be population of an area at different intervals. The main consideration is that time is divided into various groups and data is then accordingly arranged.

Data can also be classified on the basis of space and when that is done it is called 'Spatial Classification' and basis of such a classification can be a district, region or a State and when data has been collected at various places, it can also be compared as well *e.g.*, Industrial Production of two States in India can be compared by covering the same period.

Category Set. Now we come to what is known as 'category set'. In cases where universe of study is very wide and it is not possible to cover the whole universe some sampling method is adopted and in order to make the information collected usable and readable, it is essential that it should be put into different classes or categories. There can be very limited categories *e.g.*, when a question is 'Do you feel that our present system of examination should continue, the answer can be 'Yes', 'No', 'No Comments', 'No reply' and thus, the information can be put into four categories. But there can be questions to which reply can be in several ways *e.g.*, the question can be 'Do you feel that the performance of present Government, is statisfactory' and the reply can be:

(i) Yes, extremely satisfactory.

(ii) It has not come up to my satisfaction.

(iii) It is satisfactory only in political field.

(iv) It is satisfactory only in economic field.

(v) I am simply satisfied.

(vi) It is absolutely disappointing.

(vii) It have no comments to offer.

(viii) It is satisfactory only in foreign affairs.

(ix) I am not bothered about that.

(x) I have no interest in politics.

In this way, it is very essential that a researcher, before putting question to the respondent, must have an eye on the classification *i.e.*, whether it will be easy or possible to classify the information collected. A sound classification, with less variations, is likely to produce better results. When entire information can be classified under certain categories and nothing is beyond that, such categories combined together, form what is known as 'category set'.

Discrete and Continuous Series. Usually a confusion arises about the difference between discrete and continuous series. According to same there is no difference between the two and that the one can be used for the other. But that is not so. A discrete series is one in which measurement is expressed in the form of a single data or number, but when it is expressed in time group, it is called continous series. In this regard it is essential to understand some such terms as 'Integers' and 'Measurement'. When the size moves forward by certain immediate values, it is called 'integer'. In other words, when values of any two items can be measured in whole numbers, that would be called 'integers' *e.g.*, number of workers in a factory can be 15, 20, 25, or 30 but it cannot be 15.75 or 20.50 or 30.25 and so on. Certain values, however, advance in continuous manner and the difference can be meausred in degrees between the two units *e.g.*, differences in age of workers working in a factory may not be essentially in terms of years, but may be in months and days but age advancement is a continuous flow and the difference can be displayed by continuous series.

Class Intervals. Continuous series can be possible only, when class intervals are determined, but that is not an easy task. It is because this effects both the classes to be formed and nature and frequency of distribution and thereafter only that mode, median etc., are determined. In determining class intervals following factors need be taken into consideration:

First important factor that needs consideration is that the classes should be so arranged that there should be no material departure from even distribution of cases within each class. It becomes necessary because in all subsequent interpretations mid value of each class is taken into account and that represents the value of all cases only within that class. Then another consideration is that number of classes should be so determined that both arbitrary and regular sequences of frequency can be secured. Then next factor which needs taking into consideration is that all class intervals should be equal. Usually what happens is that in the last placed class there are only few frequencies and measurement is quite large. This should be avoided, because otherwise many difficulties are created in proper tabulation. Difference between the highest and the lowest should be avoided to the extent possible.

While classifying interval total range of measurement should also be taken into consideration. In case the range is large, the size of the class interval is also bound to be large and *vice-versa*. It is always better, if classes with zero frequency are shown separately along with the other classes. This will help in getting more and better correct results. It is expedient if multiple of 5 or 10 are taken as class intervals, but there is no hard and fast rule in this regard.

***

13

Data Analysis of Central Tendency

The following are the five measures of central tendency or measures of location which are commonly used in practice.

(A) Arithmetic mean or simple Mean

(B) Geometric Mean

(C) Harmonic Mean

(D) Median

(E) Mode

ARITHMETIC MEAN

The most popular and widely used measure of representing the entire data by one value is what most laymen all an 'average' and what the statisticians call the arithmetic mean. Its value is obtained by adding together all the items and by dividing this total by the number of items. Arithmetic mean may either by simple arithmetic mean, or weighted arithmetic mean.

1. Simple Arithmetic Mean. It can be obtained by using direct method, short-cut method, step deviation method and summation method.

(*a*) ***Direct Method.*** The process of computing mean in case of individual observations (*i.e.*, where frequencies are not given) is very simple. Add together the various value of the variable and divide the total by the number of items. Symbolically—

$$\overline{X}^* = \frac{X_1 + X_2 + X_3 ... + X_n}{N} \text{ or } \overline{X} = \frac{\Sigma X}{N}$$

Here $\overline{X}$ = Arithmetic Mean, ΣX = Sum of all the values of the variable X, *i.e.*, $X_1, X_2, X_3, ... X_n$: N = Number of observations.

Steps. The formula involves two steps in calculating mean:

(i) Add together all the values of the variable X and obtain the total, *i.e.*, ΣX.

(ii) Divide this total by the number of the observations, *i.e.*, N.

(b) Short-cut Method. The arithmetic mean can be calculated by using, what is known as an arbitary origin. When deviations are taken from an arbitrary origin, the formula for calculating arithmetic mean is:

$$\overline{X} = A^* + \frac{\Sigma d}{N}$$

Where A is the assumed mean and d is the deviation of items from assumed mean, *i.e.*, d = (X–A*). (A* – Assumed Mean)

Steps.

(i) Take an assumed mean.

(ii) Take the deviations of items for the assumed mean and denote these deviations by d.

(iii) Obtain the sum of these deviations, *i.e.*, Σd.

(iv) Apply the formula : $\overline{X} = A + \frac{\Sigma d}{N}$

(c) Step-Deviation Method. The short-cut mehod may be simplified if all classes in a frequency disribution are of the same size, the deviations (dx) from the assumed average have the common factor.

The formula will now stand modified as follows.

$$X = A + \frac{\Sigma fdx'}{N}$$

Where $dx' = dx/i$

i = Common factor

$\Sigma fdx'$ = Total of the products of each class frequency with the steps deviation of the respective class.

N = Total frequency

X = Arithmetic mean

(d) Summation Method of Calculating Arithmetic Mean. In a continuous frequency distribution with class intervals of equal width, arithmetic average can be calculated by summation method also. The following steps are involved in computing arithmetic mean by this method.

(i) The frequencies of the distribution are made cumulative.

(ii) The total of cumulative frequencies (Σcf) is divided by Σf to obtain 'F'.

(iii) The mid-value of the last class-interval is calculated.

(iv) The arithmetic mean is obtained by applying the following formula.

$$\overline{X} = M - (F - 1).\, i$$

where i is the magnitude of class-intervals.

Such a method of calculating average is suitable for mechanical calculation subject of course to the condition than the class intervals are equal.

Appropriate Method. The answer will be the same if average mean is calculated by any methods mentioned above. Generally short-cut or step deviation methods are used. If numbers of class intervals are large and frequencies are very high, then the use of step-deviation method is good. On the other hand if class intervals are equal and simple or difference in different class intervals is very small, then short-cut method should be used. The direct method can be used in case of large differences in the class intervals.

CHARLIER'S CHECK

Charlier's Check is used to test the value of arithmetic mean calculated by short cut or step deviation method. For this, the following procedure is adopted:

(1) We add i in every deviation or step deviation get (dx+1)

(2) To find out $\Sigma[f(dx + 1)]$, we multiply dx + 1 to frequency and then following equations will be used.

(i) Σ fdx = Σ (f (dx + 1) – Σf in short cut method,

(ii) Σ fdx' = Σ [f (dx' + 1) – Σf in step deviation method.

It both sides are equal in above mentioned equations, then our calculations are correct otherwise calculations are incorrect.

Example. Calculate the mean for the following frequency distribution.

Mark :	0-10	10-20	20-30	30-40	40-50	50-60	60-70
Number of Students :	6	5	8	15	7	6	3

Solution.

COMPUTATION OF A.M. BY STEP DEVIATION METHOD

Marks (X)	*Mid-value* (f)	*No. of students*	$d = \frac{X-35}{10}$	*fd*
0-10	5	6	–3	–18
10-20	15	5	–2	–10
20-30	25	8	–1	–8
30-40	35	15	0	0
40-50	45	7	1	7
50-60	55	6	2	12
60-70	65	3	3	9
	$\Sigma f = 50$		$\Sigma fd = -8$	

A = 35 i (class interval) = 10

$$\bar{X} = A + \frac{\Sigma fd}{N} \times i$$

$$= 35 + \frac{-8}{50} \times 10$$

$$= 35 - 1.6$$

$$= 33.4 \text{ Marks.}$$

Example. Calculate the arithmetic mean and test Charlier's check for the following frequency distribution.

Class interval	*Frequency*
1-5	3
6-10	17
11-15	20
16-20	8
21-25	2

Solution.

ARITHMETIC MEAN (SHORT-CUT METHOD) AND CHARLIER CHECK

Class Interval	*Middle Value (MV or x)*	*Fre- quency (f)*	*Deviation From A (dx)*	*Total Deviation (fdx)*	*[fx (dx + 1)] (dx+1)*	*f+(dx+1)*
1-5	3	3	–10	–30	–9	–27
6-10	8	17	–5	–85	–4	–68
11-15	13	20	0	0	1	+20
16-20	18	8	+5	+40	+6	+48
21-25	23	2	+10	+20	+11	+22
		Total 50 N = Σf		+60–115 = –55 Σfdx		+90–95 = –5 [S{f(dx+1)}]

Arithmetic Mean—

$$\overline{X} = A \pm \frac{\Sigma fdx}{N} = 13 \pm \frac{-55}{50} = 13 - 1.1$$

Charlier' Check. If both sides of equation are equal then calculation will be correct.

$$\Sigma fdx = \Sigma[f(dx+1) - \Sigma f$$

$$-55 = -5 - 50$$

$$-55 = -55$$

Hence, there is no mistake in calculation.

Example. Calculate arithmetic average of the following data by using summation method.

Marks	*Number of Students*
1-10	2
11-20	4
21-30	6

31-40	3
41-50	3
51-60	2

Solution.

Marks	*Frequency*	*Cumulative Frequency*
	(f)	(cf)
1-10	2	2
11-20	4	6
21-30	6	12
31-40	3	15
41-50	3	18
51-60	2	20
	N or $\Sigma f = 20$	$\Sigma cf = 73$

Mean value of largest marks interval

$$M = \frac{51+60}{2} = 5.55$$

Class interval $\quad i = 10$

$$F = \frac{\Sigma cf}{N} = \frac{73}{20} = 3.65$$

On using formula

$$\begin{aligned} \overline{X} &= M - i\,(F-1) \\ &= 55.5 - 10\,(3.65 - 1) \\ &= 55.5 - 10 \times 2.65 \\ &= 55.5 - 26.5 = 29.0 \text{ marks} \end{aligned}$$

$$\overline{X} = 29.0 \text{ marks}$$

Combined Arithmetic Mean. If we know the sizes and means of two component series, then we can find the mean of the resultant series obtained on combing the given series.

If n_1 and n_2 are the sizes. and $\overline{X}_1$, $\overline{X}_3$ are the respective means of two series then the mean $\overline{X}$ of the combined series of size $n_1 + n_2$ is given by :

$$\overline{X} = \frac{n_1\overline{X}_1 + n_2\overline{X}_2}{n_1 + n_2}$$

The above result can be generalised to the case of more than two series. If we have k series with respective sizes n_1, n_2...., n_k and means $\overline{X}_1, \overline{X}_2......\overline{X}_k$ respectively, then the mean $\overline{X}$ of the combined series of size $n_1 + n_2$ ....$+n_k$ is given by:

$$\overline{X} = \frac{n_1\overline{X}_1 + n_2\overline{X}_2 + ... + n_2\overline{X}_n}{n_1 + n_2 + ... + n_n}$$

Correction Incorrect Value. It sometimes happens that due to an oversight or mistake in copying, certain wrong items are taken while calculating mean. The problem is how to find out the correct mean. The process is very simple. From incorrect ΣX deduct wrong items and add correct items and then divide the correct ΣX by the number of observations. The result, so obtained will give the value of correct mean.

Example. Mean of 100 observations is found to be 40. If at the time of computation two items are wrongly taken as 30 and 27 instead of 3 and 2. Find correct mean.

Solution.

$$\overline{X} = \frac{\Sigma X}{N} \text{ or } \Sigma X = N\overline{X}$$

Here $\overline{X} = 40, N = 1000$

$\therefore$ $\Sigma X = 100 \times 40 = 4000$

Less incorrect items = $\frac{57}{3943}$

Add correct items = 75

Correct total $= 4018$

Correct mean $= \frac{4018}{100} = 40.18$

Merits of Arithmetic Mean

In the light of the properies laid down by Prof. Yule for an ideal measure of central tendency, arithmetic mean possesses the following merits :

1. It is based on all the observations.
2. It is rigidly defined.
3. It is easy to calculate and understand.
4. It is suitable for further mathematical treatment. The mean of the combined series is given by (5-8) or (5.8 a). Moreover, it possesses many important mathematical properties (Properties 1 to 4 as discussed earlier) because of which it has very wide applications in statistical theory.
5. Of all the averages, arithmetic mean is affected least by flucuations of sampling. This property is explained by saying that arithmetic mean is a *stable* average.

Demerits of Arithmetic Mean

1. The strongest drawback of arithmetic mean is that it is very much affected by extreme observations. Two or three very large values of the variable may unduly affect the value of the arithmetic mean. Let us consider an industrial complex which houses the workers and some big officials like general manager, chief engineer, architect etc. The average salary of the workers (skilled and unskilled) is, say, Rupees 5,000 per months. If the salaries of the few big bosses (who draw very high salaries) are also included, the average wage per worker comes out to be ₹ 8000, say. Thus, if we say that the average salary of the workers in the factory is ₹ 8000 p.m. it gives a very good impression and one is tempted to think that the workers are well

paid and their standard of living is good. But the real picture is entirely different. Thus, in the case of extreme observations, the arithmetic mean gives a distorted picture and is no longer representative of the distribution and quite often leads to very misleading conclusions. Thus, while dealing with extreme observations, arithemtic mean should be used with caution.

2. Arithmetic mean can not be used in the case of open end classes such as less than 10, more than 70 etc., since for such classes we cannot determine the mid-value X of the class intervals unless *(i)* we estimate the end intervals or *(ii)* we are given the total value of the variable in the open end classes. In such cases mode or median (discussed latter) may be used.
3. Arithmetic mean cannot be used if we are dealing with qualitative characteristics which can not be measured quantitatively such as intelligence, honesty, beauty etc. In such cases median (discussed later) is the only average to be used.
4. Arithmetic mean can not be obtained if a single observation is missing or lost or is illegible unless we drop it out and compute the arithmetic mean of the remaining values.
5. It cannot be determined by inspection nor can it be located graphically.
6. Arithmetic mean may not be one of the values which the variable actually takes and is termed as a fictitious average. Sometimes, it may give meaningless results.
7. In extremely asymmetrical (skewed) distribution, usually arithmetic mean is not representative of the distribution and hence, is not a suitable measure of location.
8. Arithmetic mean may lead to wrong conclusions if the details of the data from which it is obtained are

not available. In this connection it is worthwhile to quote the words of H. Secrist :

"If an average it taken as a substitute for the details, then the arithmetic mean, in spite of the simplicity and case of calculation, has little to recommand when series are non homegoneous."

The following example will illustrate this view point.

Let us consider the following marks obtained by two students A and B in three tests, *viz.*, terminal test, half yearly examination and annual examination respectively.

Marks in :	I Test	II Test	III Test	Average marks
A	65%	70%	75%	70%
B	75%	70%	65%	70%

The average marks obtained by each of the two students at the end of year are 70%. If we are given the average marks alone we conclude that the level of intelligence of both the students at the end of the year is same. This is a fallacious conclusion since we find from the data that student. A has improved consistently while student B has deteriorated consistently.

Weighted Arithmetic Mean

In the calculation of simple arithmetic mean each item of the series is considered equally important but there may be cases where all items may not have equal importance and some of them may be comparatively more important than others. This face should not be overlooked altogether in the calculation of arithmetic mean. We should take into account the relative importance of the different items from which arithmetic mean is being calculated. The weighted arithmetic mean gives different weightage depending on their importance to all the items of a series.

Weighted arithmetic mean may be defined as the mean whose component items are being multiplied by certain values known as 'weights' and the aggregate of the multiplied results are being devided by the total sum of their 'weights' instead of the sum of the items. If $X_1, X_2, ... X_n$ be the values of a variable X with respective weights of $W_1, W_2, ... W_n$ assigned to them, each weight indicating the relative importance given to each of the values in the context of the total weights assigned. The formula for computing weighted arithmetic mean is :

$$\text{Direct Method : } \overline{X}_w = \frac{W_1W_1 + W_2X_2 + ...W_nX_n}{W_1 + W_2 + ...W_n +} = \frac{\Sigma_{wx}}{\Sigma_w}$$

$$\text{Short-cut Method } \overline{X}_w = Aw + \frac{\Sigma wdx}{\Sigma w}$$

Where Aw = Assumed (weighted) mean.

Σwdx = Sum of the product of the deviation from the assumed mean (AW) multiplied by the respective weights.

When to Use Weighted Arithmetic Mean

(a) When the importance of all the items in a series is not equal. In many cases, all the items may not be of equal importance. If it is so, a simple arithmetic mean would give us misleading conclusions.

(b) Where there is a change either in the proportion of values of items or in the proportion of their frequencies.

(c) When the classes of the some group contain widely varying frequencies.

(d) When ratios, percentages or rates are being averages.

(e) When it is desired to calculate the average of series from the average of its component part.

Example. Obtain the Crude Accident Rate (CAR) and the Standardised Accident Rate (SAR) of the workers in a local factory from the following table:

Category of workers	*Local Factory* *No. of workers*	*No. of workers involved in accident*	*Standard Factory* *No. of workers*
Skilled	500	10	300
Semi-skilled	1,200	36	1,000
Unskilled	800	32	700
Total	2,400	78	2,000

Solution.

CALCULATIONS FOR C.A.R. AND S.A.R.

Category of workers	*Standard Factory No. of workers (w)*	*Local Factory* *No. of workers*	*No. of workers involved in accident*	*Accident rate per 1,000 (x)*	*Specific wX*
Skilled	300	500	10	20	6,000
Semi-skilled	1,000	1,200	36	30	30,000
Unskilled	700	800	32	40	28,000
Total	2,000	2,500	78	90	64,000

Crude accident rate of local factory:

$$\text{C.A.R.} = \frac{\text{Total number of workers involved in accident}}{\text{Total number of workers in the factory}} \times 1,000$$

$$= \frac{78}{2,500} \times 1,000 = 31.2$$

Standardised accident rate of local factory:

$$\text{S.A.R.} = \frac{\Sigma wx}{\Sigma w}$$

where X = specific accident rate of each category of workers

w = weight, *i.e.*, the number of workers of each category in the standard factory

$$= \frac{64,000}{2,000} = 32$$

Example. Comment on the performance of the students of the three universities given below using simple and weighted averages :

University Course of Study	*Bombay*		*Calcutta*		*Madras*	
	Pass %	*No. of Students (in hundreds)*	*Pass %*	*No.of Students (in hundreds)*	*Pass %*	*No. of Students (in hundreds)*
M.A.	71	3	82	2	81	2
M. Com.	83	4	76	3	76	3.5
B.A.	73	5	73	6	74	4.5
B.Com.	74	2	76	7	58	2
B.Sc.	65	3	65	3	70	7
M.Sc.	66	3	60	7	73	2

Solution.

CALCULATION OF SIMPLE AND WEIGHTED ARITHMETIC MEANS

University Course of Study	*Bombay*			*Calcutta*			*Madras*		
	Pass %	*No. of Students (in hundreds)*		*Pass %*	*No.of Students (in hundreds)*		*Pass %*	*No. of Students (in hundreds)*	
	X	W	WX	X	W	WX	X	W	WX
M.A.	71	3	213	82	2	164	81	2.0	162
M. Com.	83	4	332	76	3	228	76	3.5	266
B.A.	73	5	365	73	6	438	74	4.5	333
B.Com.	74	2	148	76	7	532	58	2.0	116
B.Sc.	65	3	195	65	3	195	70	7.0	490
M.Sc.	66	3	198	60	7	420	73	2.0	146
	ΣX =432	ΣW =20	ΣWX =1,451	ΣX =432	ΣW =28	ΣWX =1,977	ΣX =432	ΣW =21	ΣWX =1.513

SIMPLE AND WEIGHTED ARITHMETIC MEAN

Bombay $\bar{X} = \frac{\Sigma X}{N} = \frac{432}{6} = 72; \bar{X}w = \frac{\Sigma WX}{\Sigma W} = \frac{1,451}{20} = 72.55$

Calcutta $\bar{X} = \frac{\Sigma X}{N} = \frac{432}{6} = 72; \bar{X}w = \frac{\Sigma WX}{\Sigma W} = \frac{1,977}{28} = 70.61$

Madras $\bar{X} = \frac{\Sigma X}{N} = \frac{432}{6} = 72; \bar{X}w = \frac{\Sigma WX}{\Sigma W} = \frac{1,513}{21} = 72.05$

The arithmetic mean is the same for all the three universities, *i.e.*, 72 and hence, it may be concluded that the performance of students is alike. But this will be a wrong conclusion because what we should compare here is the weighted arithmetic mean. On comparing the weighted arithmetic means we find that for Bombay the mean value is the highest and hence, we can say that in Bombay University the performance of students is best. Here we have taken actual weight.

Note. An important problems that arises using weighted mean is regarding selection of weights. Weights may be either actual or arbitrary, *i.e.*, estimated. Needless to say, if actual weights are available, nothing like this. However, in the absence of actual weights, arbitrary or imaginary weights may be used. The use of arbitrary weights may lead to some error, but it is better than no weights at all. In practice, it is found that if weights are logically assigned keeping the phenomena view, the error involved will be so small that it can be easily overlooked.

GEOMETRIC MEAN

Geometric mean is the nth root of the product of *n* items of a series. Thus, if the geometric mean of 3 and 27 is to be calculated it would be equal to the square root of the product of these figures *i.e.*, $\sqrt{3 \times 27} = 9$. Similary the geometric mean of 20, 36 and 45 would be the cube root of the product of these three figure would be 30.

$$
\begin{aligned}
\text{G.M.} &= \sqrt[3]{30 \times 36 \times 45} \\
&= \sqrt[3]{2700} \\
&= \sqrt[3]{27 \times 100} \\
&= \sqrt[3]{3 \times 3 \times 3 \times 10 \times 10 \times 10} \\
&= 3 \times 10 = 30
\end{aligned}
$$

Symbolically G.M. = $\sqrt[n]{X_{1.}X_{2.}X_{3}...X_{n}}$ where G.M. stands for the geometric mean, N for the number of items and x for the values of the variable.

Ungrouped Data. The geometric mean for ungrouped data can be expressed as follows:

Geometric Mean (G.M.)

$$= \sqrt[n]{\text{The product of N values}} = \sqrt[n]{X_{1,}X_{2},...X_{n}}$$

When the number of observations exceeds two, the computations becomes difficult and these are simplified through the use of logarithms. The above formula be written as

$$\log \text{G.M.} = \frac{1}{N} \log (X_1, X_2, ..., X_n)$$

$$= \frac{1}{N} [\log X_1 + \log X_2 + ... + \log X_n] = \frac{1}{N} \Sigma \log X$$

$$\therefore \qquad \text{G.M.} = \text{Antilog}\left(\frac{1}{N}\Sigma \log X\right)$$

i.e., the logarithm or simple/weighted G.M. is equal to simple/weighted A.M. of the logarithms of observation. The antilog of A.M., so found gives G.M.

Produces

(*i*) Convert the given values of the variable X into logarithms and take the total of all logs so obtained.

(*ii*) Divide Σ log X by N and take the anti log of the quotient so obtained.

Discrete Series

$$\text{G.M.} = \text{Antilog}\left(\frac{\Sigma f \log x}{N}\right)$$

Steps

(*i*) find the logarithms of the variable x.

(*ii*) Multiply these logarithms with the respective frequencies and obtain the total Σf long x.

(*iii*) Divide Σ f log x by the total frequency and take the antilog of the values so obtained.

Continuous Series

$$\text{G.M.} = \text{Antilog}\left(\frac{\Sigma f \log m}{N}\right)$$

Steps

(*i*) Find out the mid points of the clases and take their logarithms.

(*ii*) Multiply these logarithms with the respective frequencies of each class and obtain the total Σf log m.

(*iii*) Deivde the total obtain in step (ii) by the total frequency and take the antilog of the value so obtained.

Weighted Geometric Mean

The formula for calculating weighted Geometric Mean is :

$$\text{G.M.w} = \text{A.L.}\left[\frac{(\log X_1 \times W_1) + (\log X_2 \times W_2) + \ldots + (\log X_n \times W_n}{W_1 + W_2 + W_3 + \ldots W_n}\right]$$

$$= \text{A.L.}\left[\frac{\Sigma(\log X \times W)}{\Sigma W}\right]$$

Symbolically, $\text{G.M.w} = \sqrt{X_1^{w_1} \times X_2^{w_2} \times \ldots\ldots \times X_n^{w_n}}$

Uses of Geometric Mean

Geometric mean is specially useful in the following cases :

1. The geometric mean is used to find the average per cent increase in sales, production, population or other economic or business series. *For example,* from 1986 to 1988 prices increased by 5%, 10% and 18% respectively. The average annual increase is not 11% $\left(\frac{5+10+18}{3}=11\right)$ as given by the arithmetic average but 10.9% as obtained by the geometric mean.
2. Geometric mean is theoretically considered to be the best average in the construction of index numbers. It satisfies the time reversal test and gives equal weight to equal ratio of change.

Calculation of Rate of Increase. Geometric mean is most frequently used in the determination of average per cent of change particularly population growth, compound interest, per centage change in prices etc. The average annual per cent increase may be computed by applying the formula.

$$Pn = Po\ (1 + r)^n$$

Where Po = The value at the begining of the period;

pn = The value at the end of the period n;

r = Rate of change;

n = Length of time period

Merits of Geometric Mean

1. The geometric mean is rigidly defined, it is the nth root of the product of n number of items.
2. It is based on all items. A geometric mean, when substituted for individual items, will yield the same product, *e.g.,*

$$9 \times 4 = 36 = 6 \times 6$$

3. Geometric mean has a bias towards lower values. It is unlike arithmetic mean which has bias for higher values. The geometric mean is then appropriate for certain skewed or asymmetrical distributions. It is

particularly useful when a given phenomenon has a limit for lower value but no such limit for upper value but no such limit for upper value. Take the case of price which cannot fall below zero but has no upper limit.

4. It is very suitable for averaging ratios, rates and percentages. In case of the averaging of two rates wherein one doubts from 100 to 200 and the other half from 100 to 50, the geometric mean will be 100 in both situations. The arithmetic mean will be 100 for the earlier but 125 for the latter showing a bias for higher values. Therefore, an average of change is properly represented by geometric mean.
5. With the use of geometric mean change in the reverse does not distort results. It is because of the use of geometric mean in Fisher's Ideal Formula for calculation of index numbers that it stand the test of time and factor reversal tests.
6. Geometric Mean of two or more groups known as the Geometric Mean of the composite group can be determined. Therefore, it can be treated algebraically.
6. Unlike A.M., G.M. is not affected much by the presence of extremely small or large observations.

Demerits of Geometric Mean

1. It is difficult to calculate particularly when the items are very large or when there is a frequency distribution.
2. The bias for lower values may not suit in some cases where disparities have to be brought out as in the case of incomes, levels of living, etc.
3. It brings out the property of the ratio of change and not the absolute difference of change as the case in arithmetic mean.

4. It cannot be used when the values are negative or if any of the observations is zero.
5. The G.M. may not be the actual value of the series.

Example. The geometric mean of 10 observations on a certain variable was calculated as 16.2. It was later discovered that one of the observations was wrongly recorded as 12.9; in fact it was 21.9. Apply appropriate correction and calculate the correct geometric mean.

Solution. Geometric mean G of *n* observations is given by :

$$G = (X_1\, X_2 \ldots. X_n)^{1/n} \quad \Rightarrow \quad G^n = X_1\, X_2 \ldots X_n \qquad \ldots(*)$$

Thus, the product of the numbers is given by:

$$X_1 X_2 \ldots X_n = G^n = (16.2)^{10} \quad [\text{Given } n = 10, G = 16.2] \ldots(**)$$

If the wrong observation 12.9 is replaced by the correct value 21.9 then the corrected value of the product of 10 numbers is obtained on dividing the expression in (**) by wrong observation and multiplying the correct observation. Thus,

$$\text{Corrected product } (X_1 X_2 \ldots X_n) = \frac{(16.2)^{10} \times 21.9}{12.9}$$

Hence, corrected value of the geometric mean G', (say),

is given by :

$$G' = \left[\frac{(16.2)^{10} \times 21.9}{12.9}\right]^{1/10}$$

$$\log G' = \frac{1}{10}\left[\log (16.2)^{10} + \log 2.19 - \log 12.9\right]$$

$$= \frac{1}{10}\left[10 \log 16.2 + \log 21.9 - \log 12.9\right]$$

$$= \frac{1}{10}\left[10 \times 1.2095 + 1.3404 - 1.1106\right]$$

$$= \frac{1}{10}[12.0950 + 1.3404 - 1.1106]$$

$$= \frac{1}{10}[13.4354 - 1.1106] = \frac{12.3248}{10} = 1.2325$$

$$G' = \text{Antilog } (1.2325) = 17.08$$

Example. The weighted geometric mean of the four numbers 8, 25, 19 and 28 is 22.15. If the weights of the first three numbers are 3, 5, 7 respectively, find the weight (positive integer) of the fourth number.

Solution. Let the weight of the fourth number be w.

COMPUTATION OF WEIGHTED GEOMETRIC MEAN

X	*log X*	W	*W log X*
8	0.9031	3	2.7093
25	1.3979	5	6.9895
19	1.2788	7	8.9516
28	1.4472	W	1.4472w
Total		15+W	18.6504 + 1.4472w

The weighted geometric mean G is given by:

$$\log G = \frac{\Sigma W \log X}{SW} \Rightarrow \log (22.15) = \frac{18.6504 + 1.4472w}{15 + w}$$

$$\Rightarrow \quad (15 + w) \times 1.3454 = 18.6504 + 1.4472w$$

$$\Rightarrow 15 \times 1.3454 + 1.3454w = 18.6504 + 1.4472w$$

$$\Rightarrow \quad 20.1810 + 1.345w = 18.6504 + 1.4472w$$

$$\Rightarrow \quad 1.4472w - 1.3454w = 20.1810 - 18.6554$$

$$\Rightarrow \quad 0.1018w = 1.5306$$

$$w = 1.5306 \div 0.1018 = 15 \text{ approx.}$$

Example. Calculate geometric mean from the following data :

125 1462 38 7 0.22 0.08 12.75 0.5

Solution.

CALCULATION OF GEOMETRIC MEAN

X	*Log X*
125	2,0969
1462	3.1650
38	1.5798
7	0.8451
0.22	.3424
0.08	.9031
12.75	1.1055
0.5	.6990
	Σ log X = 10.768

$$\text{G.M.} = \text{A.L.}\left(\frac{\Sigma \log X}{N}\right) = \text{A.L.}\left(\frac{10.7368}{8}\right)$$

$$= \text{A.L. } (1.8421) = 6.952.$$

HARMONIC MEAN

If X_1, X_2,...., X_n is a given set of n observations, then their harmonic mean, abbreviated as H.M. or simply H is given by :

$$H = \frac{1}{\frac{1}{n}\left[\frac{1}{X_1}+\frac{1}{X_2}+\ldots+\frac{1}{X_n}\right]} = \frac{1}{\frac{1}{n}\Sigma\left(\frac{1}{X}\right)} = \frac{n}{\Sigma\left(\frac{1}{X}\right)}$$

In other words Harmonic Mean is the reciprocal of the arithmetic mean of the reciprocals of the given observations.

$$\frac{1}{H} = \frac{1}{N}\left[\frac{f_1}{X_1}+\frac{f_1}{X_2}+\ldots+\frac{f_n}{X_n}\right] = \frac{1}{N}\Sigma(f/X)$$

$$\Rightarrow \qquad H = \frac{N}{\Sigma(f/X)}$$

where N = Σf, is the total frequency, X is the value of the variable or the mid-value of the class (in case of grouped or continuous frequency distribution) and f is the corresponding frequency of X.

Weighted Harmonic Mean

Instead of fixed (constant) distance being travelled with varying speed (c.f. Remark 2 Example 5.55) let us now suppose that different distances are travelled with corresponding different speeds. In that case what is going to be the average speed?

Let us suppose that distances $s_1, s_2, ..., s_n$, are travelled with speed $v_1, v_2, ..., v_n$ per unit of time. If $t_1, t_2, ... t_n$ are the respective times taken to cover these distances then we have :

$$t = \frac{s_1}{v_1},\ t_2 = \frac{s_2}{v_2}, ..., t_n = \frac{s_n}{v_n}$$

$$\therefore \text{ Average speed} = \frac{\text{Total distance travelled}}{\text{Total time taken}}$$

$$= \frac{s_1 + s_2 + ... + s_n}{t_1 + t_2 + ... + t_n}$$

$$= \frac{s_1 + s_2 + ... + s_n}{\left[\frac{s_1}{v_1} + \frac{s_2}{v_2} + ... + \frac{s_n}{v_n}\right]}$$

$$= \frac{\Sigma s}{\sum\left(\frac{s}{v}\right)} = \frac{1}{\left(\frac{1}{\Sigma s}\right)\sum(s/v)}$$

which is the weighted harmonic mean of the speeds, the corresponding weights being their distances covered.

Merits of Harmonic Mean

1. Harmonic mean is rigidly defined.
2. It is based on all the observations.
3. It is suitable for further mathematical treatment.

If H_1 and H_2 are the harmonic means of two series of sizes N_1 and N_2 respectively, then harmonic mean H of the combined series of size $N_1 + N_2$ is given by :

$$\frac{1}{H} = \frac{1}{N_1 + N_2}\left[\frac{N_1}{H_1} + \frac{N_2}{H_2}\right]$$

4. It is not affected very much by fluctuations of sampling.
5. It is particularly useful in averaging special types of rates and ratios where time factors is variable and the act being performed remains constant.
6. Since the reciprocals of the values of the variable are involved, it gives greater weightage to smaller observations and as such as not very much affected by one or two big observations.

Demerits of Harmonic Mean

1. It is not easy to understand and calculate.
2. It iş not a representative figure of the distribution unless the phenomenon requires greater weightage to be given to smaller items. As such, it is hardly used in business problems.
3. Its value cannot be obtained if any one of the observations is zero.

Uses. As has been pointed out in merit (vi) above, harmonic mean is specially useful in averaging rates and ratios where time factor is variable and the Act being performed *e.g.*, distance is constant. The following examples will clarify the point.

Example. You make a trip which entails travelling 900 kms. by train in an average speed of 60 km. p.h. 3000 kms. by boat at an average of 35 km p.h., 400 km.s by plane at 350 km. p.h. and finally, 15 kms by taxi at 25 km. p.h. What is your average speed for the entire hence.

Solution. Since different distance are covered with varying speeds, the required average speed is given by the weighted harmonic mean of the speeds (in km. p.h.) 60,25,350 and 25 the corresponding weights being the distances covered (in kms) *viz.*, 900, 3000, 400 and 15 respectively.

COMPUTATION OF WEIGHTED HARMONIC MEAN

X	W	W/X
60	900	15
25	3000	120
350	400	1.43
25	15	0.60
	ΣW = 4315	Σ(W/X) = 137.05

$$\therefore \quad \text{Average Speed} = \frac{\Sigma W}{\Sigma(W/X)} = \frac{4315}{137.03}$$

$$= 31.49 \text{ km. p.h.}$$

Example. The following table gives the weights of 31 persons in a sample enquiry. Calculate the mean weight using *(i)* Geomeric mean and *(ii)* Harmonic mean.

Weight (Ibs) :	130	135	140	145	146	148	149	150	157
No. of person :	3	4	6	6	3	5	2	1	1

Solution.

COMPUTATION OF G.M. AND H.M.

Weight (Ibs) (X)	*No. of persons (f)*	*log X*	*flog X*	$\frac{1}{X}$	$\frac{f}{X}$
130	3	2.1139	6.3417	0.00769	0.02307
135	4	2.1303	8.5212	0.00741	0.02964
140	6	2.1461	12.8766	0.00714	0.04284
145	6	2.1614	12.9684	0.00690	0.04140

146	3	2.1644	6.4932	0.00685	0.02055
148	5	2.1703	10.8515	0.00676	0.03380
149	2	2.1732	4.3464	0.00671	0.01342
150	1	2.1761	2.1761	0.00667	0.00667
157	1	2.1959	2.1959	0.00637	0.00637
	$\Sigma f = N$ = 31		$\Sigma f \log X$ = 66.7710		$\Sigma (f/X)$ = 0.21776

$$\text{G.M.} = \text{Antilog}\left(\frac{1}{N}\Sigma f \log X\right)$$

$$= \text{Antilog}\left(\frac{66.7710}{31}\right)$$

$$= \text{Antilog}\ (2.1539) = 142.5$$

$$\text{H.M.} = \frac{N}{\Sigma(f/X)} = \frac{31}{0.21776} = 142.36$$

Hence, the mean weight of 31 persons using *(i)* geometric mean is 142.5 Ibs and *(ii)* harmonic mean is 142.36 Ibs.

Relationship among the Averages

In any distribution when the original items differ in size the value of A.M. G.M. and H.M. would also differ and will be in the following :

$$\text{A.M.} \geq \text{G.M.} \geq \text{H.M.}$$

i.e., arithmetic mean is greater than geometric mean and geometric mean is greater than harmoric mean. The equality signs hold only if all the numbers $X_1, X_2, ... X_n$ are identical.

Proof. Prove that if a and b are two positive numbers their A.M. ≥ G.M. ≥ H.M.

Solution. Let a and b be two positive quantities such that a 1 b.

Then A.M. and H.M. of these two quantities are

$$\bar{X} = \frac{a+b}{2};\ \text{G.M.} = \sqrt{a \times b};\ \text{H.M.} = \frac{2}{\frac{1}{a}+\frac{1}{b}} = \frac{2ab}{a+b}$$

We have to prove that A.M. > H.M. Let us first prove that A.M. > G.M. or $\frac{a+b}{2} > \sqrt{a+b}$.

$$\frac{a+b}{2}\sqrt{a+b};\ a+b>\sqrt{ab}.$$

$$a + b - 2\sqrt{ab} > 0. \qquad [\text{Since } a + b - 2\ \sqrt{ab} = \left(\sqrt{a} - \sqrt{b}\right)^2\ ]$$

$$\left(\sqrt{a} - \sqrt{b}\right)^2 > 0.$$

But the square of any real quantity is positive. Hence, $\left(\sqrt{a} - \sqrt{b}\right)^2$ will be positive. Hence, $\frac{a+b}{2} > \sqrt{ab}$

Let us now prove that G.M. > H.M.

or $$\sqrt{ab} > \frac{2ab}{a+b} 1 > \frac{\sqrt{ab}}{a+b} \text{ or } a + b > 2\sqrt{ab}.$$

This has already been proved above. Hence, G.M. > H.M.

Since we have shown that A.M. > G.M. and G.M. > H.M. It is automatically proved that A.M. > G.M. > H.M.

If a and b are equal in that case A.M. = G.M. = H.M. Thus, A.M. > G.M. > H.M.

MEDIAN

The median by definion refers to the middle value in a distribution. Median splits the observation into two halves.

As the name itself suggests median is the value of the middle item of a series arranged in ascending or descending order of magnitude. Median divides the series in two equal parts one part containing values less than the median value and the other part containing values more than the median value. L.R. Conner defines median as, "that value of the variable which divides the group into two equal parts, on part comprising all values greater and the other, all values less than median. Secrist has given the following definition of median "median of a series is the value of the item actual or estimated when a series is arranged in order of magnitude which divides the distribution into two parts."

The calculation of median involves two baic steps *viz.*, *(1)* The location of the middle item and *(2)* finding out its value.

Discrete Series

The middle item in series of individual observations and also in a discrete series in $\left(\frac{n+1}{2}\right)^{th}$ item,, where n is the total number of observation.

Once the middle item is located its value has to be found out. In a series of individual observations, if the total number of item is an odd figure, the value of the middle item is the median value. If the number of items is even the median value is the average of the two items in the centre of the distribution.

The various steps in the computations of median in discrete series are as follows:

1. Arrange the values in ascending or descending order of magnitude.
2. Find out the cumulative frequencies.
3. Find out the middle item by the formula $\left(\frac{N+1}{2}\right)^{th}$
4. Now find out the value of item. It can be found by first locating the cumulative frequency which is equal to $\left(\frac{N+1}{2}\right)$ or next higher to it and then determining

the value corresponding to it. This will be the value of the median.

In a continuous frequency distribution the value of the median would be in a class-interval. To get a precise value of the median we assume that the frequency of the median class is uniformaly spread over the whole class-interval. On this assumption the value of the median can be located by the following formula.

$$M = l_1 = \frac{l_2 - l_1}{f_1} \ (M–C)$$

where M = The value of the Median

l_1 and l_2 = The lover and the upper limit of the class in which median lie

f_1 = The frequency of the median class

m = The middle number whose value is median (N/2)

c = The cumulative frequency of the class preceeding the median class.

The above formula has been written in a slightly different from by some authors. According to their nominclature.

$$\text{Median} = L + \frac{N/2 - cf}{f} \times i$$

where L is the lower limit of the median class, N/2 = the middle number, c.f. = the cumulative frequency of the class preceeding the median class, f = the frequency of the median class and i = the magnitude of the median class interval.

The two formula are the same and would give the same result.

Formula No. 2.

There is another formula for calculating median when instead of the lower limit of the median class we take its upper limit. The formula is as follows.

$$M = l_2 - \frac{l_2 - l_1}{f_1}(m - c)$$

This formula should be used only when the class-intervals are in descending order and the frequencies have been cumulated from top to bottom.

Merits of Median

1. It is especially useful in case of open-end classes since only the position and not the values of items must be known. The median is also recommended if the distribution has unequal classes, since it is easier to compute than the mean.
2. Extreme values do not affect the median as strongly as they do the mean. *For example,* the median of 10, 20, 30, 40 and 150 would be 30 whereas the mean 50. Hence, very often when extreme values are present in a set of observations, the median is a more satisfactory measure of the central tendency than the mean.
3. In markedly skewed distributions such as income distributions or price distributions where the arithmetic mean would be distored by extreme values, the median is especially useful. Consequently, the median income for some purposes be regarded as a more representative figure, for half the income earners must be receiving at least the median income. One can say as many receive the median income and as many do not.
4. It is the most appropriate average in dealing with qualities data, *i.e.,* where ranks are given or there are other type of items that are not counted or measured but are scored.
5. The value of median can be determined graphically whereas the value of mean cannot be graphically ascertained.

6. Perhaps the greatest advanage of median is, however, the fact that the median actually does indicate what many people incorrectly believe the arithmetic mean indicates. The median indicates the value of the middle items in the distribution. This is a clear-cut meaning and makes the median a measure that can be easily explained.

Limitations of Median

1. For calculating median it is necesary to arrange the data; other averages do not need any arrangement.
2. The value of median is affected more by sampling fluctuations than the value of the arithmetic mean.
3. Since it is a positional average, is value is not determined by each and every observations.
4. It is erratic if the number of item is small.
5. The median, in some cases, cannot be computed exactly as the mean. When the number of items included in a series of data is even, the median is determined approximately as the mid-point of the two middle items.
6. It is not capable of algebraic treatment. *For example,* median cannot be used for determined the combined median of two or more groups as is possible in case of mean. Similarly, the median wage of a skewed distribution times the number of workers will not give the total payroll. Because of this limitation the median is much less popular as compared to the arithmetic mean.

The median is useful for distributions containing open-end intervals since these intervals do not enter its computation. Also since the median is affected by the number rather than the size of items, it is frequently used instead of the mean as a measure of central tendency in cases where such values are likely to distort the mean.

Related Positional Measures. Quartile, Percentile etc.

Besides median, there are other measure which divide a series into equal parts. Important amongst these are quartiles, deciles and percentiles, Quartiles are those values of he variate which divide the total frequency into four equal are those value of the variate which divide the total frequency into four equal parts, deciles divide the total frequency into 10 equal parts. The quartiles are denoted by symbol Q, deciles by D and percentiles by P. The subscripts 1, 2 3, etc., beneath Q, D, etc., would refer to the particular value that we want to compute. Thus, Q_1 would denote first quartile, Q_2 second quartile, D_1 first decile, D_6 6th decile, P_1 first percentile and P_{10} 10th percentile etc.

Computation of Quartiles, Percentiles etc. The procedure for computing quartiles, deciles, etc., is the same as the median. While computing these values in Individual and discret series we add 1 to N whereas in continuous series we do not add.

Quartile's

Individual and discrete series:

$$Q_1 = \text{Size of } \left(\frac{N+1}{4}\right)^{th} \text{ item}$$

$$Q_2 = \text{Size of } 3\left(\frac{N+1}{4}\right)^{th} \text{ item}$$

Continuous series

$$Q_1 = \left(\frac{N}{4}\right)^{th} \qquad Q_1 = l_1 + \frac{i}{f}(q_1 - c)$$

$$Q_3 = \text{Size of } 3\left(\frac{N}{4}\right)^{th} \qquad Q_3 = l_3 + \frac{i}{f}(q_3 - c)$$

Quintile. If we divide any series in five equal parts, then there will be four quintile Q_{n1}, Q_{n2}, Q_{n3}, Q_{n4}. The formula for the calculation will be:

Individual and Discrete Series

$$Q_{n3'} = \text{Size of } \left(\frac{N+1}{5}\right)^{th} \text{ item}$$

$$Q_{n3'} = \text{Size of } 4\left(\frac{N+1}{5}\right)^{th} \text{ item}$$

Continuous Series

$$Q_{n1} = \text{Size of } \left(\frac{N}{5}\right)^{th} \text{ item} \qquad Q_{n1} = l_1 + \frac{i}{f}(q_{n1} - c)$$

$$Q_{n4} = \text{Size of } 4\left(\frac{N}{5}\right)^{th} \text{ item} \qquad Q_{n1} = l_4 + \frac{i}{f}(q_{n4} - c)$$

Octile. If we divide any series in eight equal parts, then it will have 7 octiles like O_1, O_2, O_3, O_4, O_5, O_6, O_7. The formula or calculation will be

Individual and Discrete Series

$$Q_1 = \text{Size of } \left(\frac{N+1}{8}\right)^{th} \text{ item}$$

$$Q_7 = \text{Size of } 7\left(\frac{N+1}{8}\right)^{th} \text{ item}$$

Continuous Series

$$O_1 = \text{Size of } \left(\frac{N}{8}\right)^{th} \text{ item;} \qquad O_1 = 1 + \frac{i}{f}(o_1 - c)$$

$$O_7 = \text{Size of } \left(\frac{N}{8}\right)^{th} \text{ item;} \qquad O_7 = 1_1 + \frac{i}{f}(o_7 - c)$$

Decile. If we divide any series in 10 equal parts then it will have 9 decile like, D_1, D_2, D_3, D_4, D_5, D_6, D_7, D_8, D_n. The forumula for calculation will be

Individual and Discrete Series

$$D_1 = \text{Size of } \left(\frac{N+1}{10}\right)^{th} \text{ item;}$$

$$D_1 = \text{Size of } 9\left(\frac{N+1}{10}\right)^{th} \text{ item}$$

$$D_1 = \text{Size of } \left(\frac{N}{10}\right)^{th} \text{ item}; \qquad D_1 = 1_1 + \frac{i}{f}(d_1 - c)$$

$$D_9 = \text{Size of } 9\left(\frac{N}{10}\right)^{th} \text{ item}; \qquad D_9 = 1_1 + \frac{i}{f}(d_9 - c)$$

Percentile. If we divide any series in 100 equal parts. Then it will have 99 percentile like, P_1, P_2, P_{99}. The formula for calculation will be

Individual and Discrete Series

$$P_1 = \text{Size of } \left(\frac{N+1}{100}\right)^{th} \text{ item};$$

$$P_{99} = \text{Size of } 99\left(\frac{N+1}{100}\right)^{th} \text{ item};$$

$$P_1 = \text{Size of } \left(\frac{N}{100}\right)^{th} \text{ item}; \qquad P_1 = 1_1 + \frac{i}{f}(p_1 - c)$$

$$P_{99} = \text{Size of } 99\left(\frac{N}{100}\right)^{th} \text{ item}; \qquad P_1 = 1_1 + \frac{i}{f}(p_{99} - c)$$

Example. Calculate the median, quartiles. 6th decide and 70th percentile from the following data.

Marks	*No. of students*	*Marks*	*No. of students*
Lass than 80	100	Less than 40	32
Lass than 70	90	Less than 30	20
Lass than 60	80	Less than 20	13
Lass than 50	60	Less than 10	5

Solution. We are given 'less than' cumulative frequency distribution. We shall first convert it into a grouped frequency distribution. Since 'marks' is a discrete random variable taking only integral values, the classes are 0-9, 10-19,...., 70-79. Further, since the formula for median, quartiles and percentiles are based on continuous frequncy distribution, we convert the distribution into exclusive type classes with class boundaries below 9.5, 9.5-19.5,.... 69.5-79.5 as given in the following table.

COMPUTATIONS FOR MEDIAN, QUARTILES AND PERCENTILES

Class	*Frequency (f)*	*Less than c.f.*	*Class Boundaries*
0-9	5	5	Below 9.5
10-19	13 – 5 = 8	13	9.5-19.5
20-29	20 – 13 = 7	20	19.5-29.5
30-39	32 – 20 = 12	32	29.5-39.5
40-49	60 – 32 = 28	60	39.5-49.5
50-59	80 – 60 = 20	80	49.5-59.5
60-69	90 – 80 = 10	90	59.5-69.5
70-79	13 – 5 = 8	100 = N	69.5-79.5

Median. $\frac{N}{2}\left(\frac{100}{2}\right) = 50.$ The c.f. just geater than 50 is 60. Hence, the corresponding class 39.5-49.5 is the median class.

$$\therefore \text{ Median} = 39.5 + \frac{10}{28}(50 - 32) = 39.5 + \frac{10 \times 18}{28}$$

$$= 39.50 + 6.43 = 45.93$$

Hence, median marks are 45.93

Quartiles. $\frac{N}{4} = \frac{100}{4} = 25$ and $\frac{3N}{4} = \frac{3 \times 100}{4} = 75.$ The c.f. just greater than N/4 is 32. Hence, the corresponding class 29.5 –39.5 contains Q_1 which is given by:

$$Q_1 = 29.5 + \frac{10}{12}(25 - 20) = 29.5 + \frac{10 \times 5}{12}$$

$$= 29.50 + 4.17 = 33.67$$

The c.f. just greater than 3N/4 = 75 is 80. Hence, the corresponding class 49.5 – 59.5 contains Q_3 which is given by :

$$Q_3 = 49.5 + \frac{10}{20}(75-60) = 49.5 + \frac{10\times 5}{12}$$

$$= 49.50 + 7.5 = 57.0$$

6th Decide. $\frac{6N}{10} = \frac{6\times 100}{10} = 60$. The c.f. just greater than 60 is 80. Hence, the corresponding class 49.5 – 59.5 contains D_6 which is given by :

$$D_6 = 49.5 + \frac{10}{20}(60-60) = 49.5$$

70th Percentile. $\frac{70N}{100} = \frac{70\times 100}{100} = 70$. The c.f. just greater than 70 is 80. Hence, the corresponding class 49.5 – 59.5 contains P_{70} which is given by :

$$P_{70} = 1 + \frac{i}{f}\left(\frac{70N}{100} - C\right)$$

$$= 49.5 + \frac{10}{20}(70-60)$$

$$= 49.5 + \frac{10\times 10}{20}$$

$$= 49.5 + 5$$

$$= 54.5$$

Example. Find the missing frequency from the following distribution of sales of shops, given that the median sale of shops is ₹ 2,400.

Sale in hundred ₹ :	0-10	10-20	20-30	30-40	40-50
No. of Shaps :	5	25	—	18	7

Solution. Let the missing frequency be 'a'

CALCULATIONS FOR MEDIAN

Sales in hundred Rs.	*No. of Shops (f)*	*Cumulative Frequency (c.f.)*
0-10	5	5
10-20	25	30
20-30	a	30+a
30-40	18	48+a
40-50	7	55+a

Since median sales is ₹ 2,400 (24 hundred), ₹ 20-30 is the median class. Using median formula

$$Md = l + \frac{i}{f}\left(\frac{N}{2} - C\right),$$

we get
$$24 = 20 + \frac{10}{a}\left(\frac{55+a}{2} - 30\right)$$

$\Rightarrow$
$$4 = \frac{10}{a}\left(\frac{55+a-60}{2}\right) = \frac{5(a-5)}{a}$$

$\Rightarrow$
$$4a = 5a - 25$$
$$a = 25$$

Hence, the missing frequency is 25.

MODE

The word mode is derived from the french word (la mode) which mean fashion or the most popular phenomenon. Mode, thus, is the most popular item of a series around which there is the highest frequency density. When we speak of the 'average student, average collar size, average size of show,' we are referring to mode. When we say that on an average a student spends ₹ 300 per month. It is the value of mode. it is the most typical or fashionable value of the series.

Mode is the most common item of a series. Generally it is the value which occurs the largest number of times in a series. In the words of Croxton and Cowden "the mode of a distribution is the value of the point around which the items tend to be most heavily concentrated."

Computation of Mode

It appears from the definitions given above that it must be very easy to calculate the mode of a series. In fact is not always so. The most satisfactory method of calculating mode is that of "curve fitting" which is an extremely different process. In ordinary practice, however, mode is estimated by easier methods which are comparatively very much less accurate than the method of curve fitting. These methods are no doubt very simply and easy. The methods of locating mode are the following:

Individual Series. There are three methods of locating mode:

(i) ***Inspection Method.*** By observing the series, we come to know the value repeated most and it is mode.

(ii) ***Converting Individuals Series into Discrete Series.*** Under this methods the values are placed in ascending order with their frequencies. The value occurs most, is called mode value.

(iii) ***On the Basis of Median and Arithmetic Mean.*** The model value can be calculated by using following formula if the values for median and arithmetic mean are known to us.

$$Z = 3m - 2\overline{X}$$

This formula is based on this assumption that distribution is asymmetrical. In this distribution

$$\left(\overline{X} - z\right) = 3\left(\overline{X} - m\right)$$

Discrete Series. There are two methods to find out the modal values.

(i) ***Inspectation Method.*** In discrete series mode can be located merely by inspectation as the value having

the highest frequency would generally to be modal value.

(ii) Grouping Method. In discrete series if the items concentrate at more than one value, attempts are mode to find out the point of maximum concentration with the help of grouping method. In this method values are first arranged is ascending order and the frequencies against each value are written down. These frequencies are then added in two's and the totals are written in lines between the values added.

Frequncies can be added in two's in two ways:

(i) By adding frequencies of item numbers 1 and 2, 3 and 4, 5 and 6 and so on.

(ii) By adding frequencies of item mumbers 2 and 3, 4 and 5, 6 and 7 and so on. After this the frequencies are added in three's. This can be done is three ways:

(a) By adding frequencies of items numbers 1, 2 and 3, 4, 5 and 6, 7, 8 and 9 and so on.

(b) By adding frequencies of item numbers 3, 4 and 5, 6, 7 and 8, 9 and 10 and so on.

(c) By adding the frequencies of item numbers 3, 4 and 5, 6, 7 and 8, 9, 10 and 11 and so on.

If necessary frequencies can be added in four's and five's also. After this the size of items containing the maximum frequencies are noted down and the item which has the maximum frequencies the largest number of items is called the mode.

Continuous Series. In a continous series the determination of mode involves two steps, First by the process of grouping the class in which there is maximum concentration has to be located. After this the value of mode is interpolated by the use of a formula. The exact value of mode in the modal class interval can be obtained by using the formula given below :

$$z = l_1 + \frac{f_1 - f_0}{zf_1 - f_0 - f_2} \times i$$

where z = mode

l_1 = lower limits of modal class

f_1 = frequency of model class

f_0 = frequency of the class preceding the modal class

f_2 = frequency of the class succeeding the model class

i = size of the class interval of modal class.

Example. Calculate mode from the following data :

Marks	*No. of Students*	*Marks*	*No. of Students*
Below 10	4	Below 60	86
Below 20	6	Below 70	96
Below 30	24	Below 80	99
Below 40	46	Below 90	100
Below 50	67		

Solution. Since we are given the cumulative frequency distribution of marks, first we shall convert it into the frequency distribution as given below:

Marks	*Frequency (f)*
0-10	4
10-20	6 − 4 = 2
20-30	24 − 6 = 18
30-40	46 − 24 = 22
40-50	67 − 46 = 21
50-60	86 − 67 = 19
60-70	96 − 86 = 10
70-80	99 − 96 = 3
80-90	100 − 99 = 1

Further, since the frequencies first decrease, then increase and again decrease, the distribution is irregular and hence, the modal class is located by the method of grouping as explained in the table given below :

GROUPING TABLE

X	*Frequencies* (1)	(2)	(3)	(4)	(5)	(6)
0-10	4	6		24		
10-20	2		20		42	
20-30	18	40				61
30-40	22		43	62		
40-50	21	40			50	
50-60	19		29			10
60-70	10	13		14		
70-80	3		4			
80-90	1					

For computing modal class, we prepare another table as given below :

ANALYSIS TABLE

Column No. of above Table (I)	*Maximum frequency* (II)	*Class (es) corresponding to maximum frequency in (II)* (III)				
(1)	22		30-40			
(2)	40	20-30	30-40	40-50	50-60	
(3)	43		30-40	40-50		
(4)	62		30-40	40-50	50-60	
(5)	50			40-50	50-60	60-70
(6)	61	20-30	30-40	40-50		
Frequency of the Variable (X)		2	5	5	3	1

In the above table there are two classes *viz.*, 30-40 and 40-50 which are repeated maximum number (5) of times and as much we cannot decide about the modal class. Thus, even the method of grouping fails to give the modal class.

We say that in the above example mode is ill-defined and we locate it by the empirical formula :

$$Mo = 3Md - 2M$$

COMPUTATIONS OF ARITHMETIC MEAN AND MEDIAN

Marks	*Mid-value (X)*	*Frequency (f)*	*Less than c.f.*	$d = \frac{X-45}{10}$	*fd*
0-10	5	4	4	–4	–16
10-20	15	2	6	–3	–6
20-30	25	18	24	–2	–36
30-40	35	22	46	–1	–22
40-50	45	21	67	0	0
50-60	55	19	86	1	19
60-70	65	10	96	2	20
70-80	75	3	99	3	9
80-90	85	1	100	4	4
		$\Sigma f = 100$			$\Sigma fd = -28$

$$\text{Mean} = A + \frac{\Sigma fd}{N} \times i = 45 + \frac{10 \times (-28)}{1000} = 45 - 2.8 = 42.2$$

Here $\frac{N}{2} = \frac{100}{2} = 50$. Since *c.f.* just greater than 50 is 67, the corresponding class 40-50 is the median class.

Hence,

$$Md = 40 + \frac{10}{21}\left(\frac{100}{2} - 46\right) = 40 + \frac{10 \times 4}{21} = 40 + 1.9 = 41.9$$

Substituting in we get :

Mode = 3 × 41.9 – 2 × 42.2 = 125.7 – 84.4 = 41.3

Merits of Mode

The main merits of mode are :

1. Like median, the mode is not unduly affected by extreme values. Even if the high values are very high and the low values are very low we choose the most frequent value of the data to the modal value; *for example,* the mode of 10, 2, 5, 10, 5, 60, 5, 10, 60, is 10 as this value, *i.e.,* 10 has occurred most often in the data set.
2. By definition mode is the most typical or representative value of a distribution. Hence, when we talk of model wage, modal size of shoe or modal size of family it is this average the we refer to. The mode is a measure which actually does indicate what many people incorrectly believe the arithmetic mean indicates. The mode is the most frequently occuring value. If the modal wage in a factory is ₹ 916 then more workers receive ₹ 916 than any other wage. This is what many believe the 'average' wage always indicates, but actually such a meaning is indicated only if the average used is the mode.
3. It can be used describe qualititative phenomenon. *For example,* if we want to compare the consumer preferences for different tyeps of products say, soap, toothpaste, etc., or different media of advertising we should complete the modal preferences expressed by different groups of people.
4. Its value can be determined in open-end distributions without ascertaining the class limits.
5. The value of mode can also be determined graphically whereas the value of mean cannot be graphically ascertained.

Limitations of Mode

The important limitations of this average are:

1. The value of mode cannot always be determined. In some cases we may have a bimodal series.
2. It is not a rigid defined measure. There are several formula for calculating the mode, all of which usually give somewhat different answers. In fact, mode is the most unstable average and its value is difficult to determine.
3. It is not capable of algebraic manipulations. *For example,* from the modes of two sets of data we cannot calculate the overaall mode of the combine data. Similarly, the modal wage times the number of workers will not give the total payroll-except, of course, when the distribution is normal and then the mean, median and mode are all equal.
4. The value of mode is not based on each and, every item of the series.
5. While dealing with quantitative data, the disadvantages of the mode outweight its good features and hence, it is seldom used.

The mode is employed when the most typical value of a distribution is desired. It is the most meaningful measure of central tendency in case of highly skewed or non-normal distributions, as it provides the best indication of the point of maximum concentration.

Relationship among Mean, Median and Mode. A distribution in which the values of mean, median and mode coincide, (*i.e.,* Me = $\overline{X}$ = Mo) is known as a sysmmetrical distribution. Conversely stated, when the values of mean, median and mode are not equal the distribution is known as asymmetrical or skewed. In moderately skewed or asymmetrical distributions a very important relationship exists among mean, median and mode. In such distributions the distance between the mean and the median is about one-third the distance between the mean and the mode as will be clear from the diagram given below.

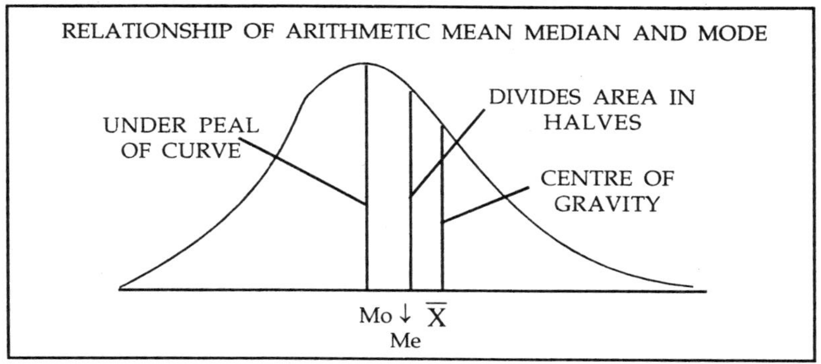

Karl Pearson has expressed this relationship as follows:

$$\text{Mode} = \text{Mean} - 3\,[\text{Mean} - \text{Median}]$$

$$\text{Mode} = 3\,\text{Median} - 2\,\text{Mean}$$

and $$\text{Median} = \text{Mode} + \frac{2}{3}\,[\text{Mean} - \text{Mode}]$$

If we know any of the two values out of the three, we can find out the third from these relationship. The following example will illustrate this point.

WHICH AVERAGE TO USE

It must be clearly understood that no one average can be regarded as best or all circumstances. The following considerations influence the selection of an appropriate average.

1. The purpose which the average is designed to serve.
2. Would the average be used for further computations?
3. The typical value required in the particular problem. Within the framework of descriptive statistics the mean requirement is to know what each average means and then select one that fulfils the purpose in hand. Is a composite average of all absolute or relative values needed (arithmetic mean or geometric mean), or is middle value wanted (median), or the most common value (mode)?

On occassions, it may even be advisable to work out more than one average and present them, although, to be sure, this procedure creates an added burden for the reader as well as for the statistician. But the added burden is preferable to the use of single average that may be an incomplete description. To use it also is like looking through a key hole, the part of the room you can see cannot give a full idea of the whole room.

Arithmetic Mean. In the following cases arithmetic mean should not be used:

1. When the distribution is unevenly spread, concentration being smaller or large at irregular points.
2. When there are very large and very small items, arithmetic mean would be seriously misleading on account of undue influene from extreme items.
3. In hightly skewed distributions.
4. In distributions with opened intervals.
5. The arithmetic mean should not be used to average ratios and rates of change. In such cases the geometric mean is more suitable.

Leaving aside the above specific cases where either median, mode, geometric mean or harmonic mean is more appropriate, in other cases we should apply as a rule of thumb the arithmetic mean—the most popular and widely used average in practice.

Geometric Mean. Geometric mean is useful in averaging ratio and percentages and in computing average rates of increase or decrease. It is particularly important in Economics and Business Statistcs' in index number construction.

Harmonic Mean. Harmonic mean is useful in problems in which values of a variable are compared with a constant quantity of another variable, *i.e.*, rates, time, distance covered within certain time and quantities purchased or sold per unit, etc.

Median. The median is generally the best average in opened grouped distributions, especially where if plotted as a frequency curve one gets a J or reverse J curve; *for example,* in case of price distribution or income distribution. In such cases very high or very low values would cause the mean to be higher of lower than the most "common" values. In such instances, the median or middle value of the series may be a more representative figure to use in describing the mass of data.

Mode. Generally speaking, the need of mode lies in the fact that it can be used to describe qualitative data. The mode can be used in problems involving the expression of preferences where quantitative measurements are not possible. Thus, the preferred type of package design among a number of alternative designs would be the modal design. If we want to compare consumer preferences for different kinds of products, or different kinds of advertising, we can compare the modal preferences expressed by different groups of people but we cannot calculate the median or mean. Mode is particularly useful average for discrete series, *e.g.,* number of people wearing a given size of shoe, or number of children per household, etc. The mode is best suited where there is an outstandingly large frequency.

Limitations of Average

1. Since an average is a single value representing a group of values, it must be properly interpreted; otherwise, there is every possibility of a story. A person had to cross the river from one bank to another. He was not aware of the depth of the river, so he enquired of another man who told him that the average depth of water is 5' 6". The mean was 5' 8" and he thought that he can very easily cross the river because at all time he would be above the level of water. So he started. In the beginning the level of water was very low but as he reached the middle, the water was 20 ft. deep and he lost his life. The man was drowned because he had a misconception

that average depth means uniform depth throughout. But it is not so. An average represents a group of values and lies somewhere in between the two extremes, *i.e.*, the largest and the smallest items of the series.

2. At times the average may given a very absurd result. *For example*, if we are calculating size of a family we may get a value 4' 8". But this is impossible as a person cannot be a fractions. However, we should remember that it is an average value representing the entire group.

3. An average may give us a value that does not exist in the data. *For example*, the arithmetic mean of 100, 300, 250, 50, 100 is $\frac{800}{5}$ = 160 a value that does not exist in the data.

4. Measures of central value fail to give an idea about the formation of the series. Two or more series may have the same central value but may differ widely in composition. *For example*, observe the following two series.

Series A	*Series B*
140	400
180	400
190	20
210	78
180	2
Total 900	900
X = 180	180

5. We must remember that an average is a measure of central tendency. Hence, unless the data show a clear single concentration of observations, an averge may not be meaningful at all. This evidently precludes the use of any average to typify a bimodal, A U-shaped or a J-shaped distribution.

❋❋❋

14

Chi-Square Test

The various tests of significance such as t, F and Z are based on the assumption that the samples were drawn from normally distributed populations, or more accurately that the sample means were normally distributed. Since the testing procedure requires assumption about type of population or parameters, *i.e.,* population values, these tests are known as 'parametric tests'.

There are many situations in which it is not possible to make any rigid assumption about the distribution of the population from which samples are being drawn. This limitation has led to the development of a group of alternative techniques known as non-parametric tests are used, no assumption about the parameters of the population or populations from which we draw our samples is made. Chi-square test of indepen-dence and goodness of fit is a prominent example of the use of non-parametric tests. Here, we shall limit our discussion to Chi-square test.

The χ^2 test is one of the simplest and most widely used non-parametric tests in statistical work. The symbol χ^2 is the Greek letter Chi. The χ^2 test was first used by Karl Pearson in the year 1890. The quantity χ^2 describes the magnitude of the discrepancy between theory and observation. It is defined as :

$$\chi^2 = \sum \frac{(O - E)^2}{E}$$

where O refers to the observed frequencies and E refers to the expected frequencies.

Steps. The determine the value of χ^2, the steps required are:

1. Calculate the expected frequencies. In general the expected frequency for any cell can be calculated from the following equation:

$$E = \frac{RT \times CT}{N}$$

E = Expected frequency

RT = The row total for the row containing the cell

CT = The column total for the column containing the cell

N = The total number of observations

2. Take the difference between observed and expected frequencies and obtain the squares of these differences, *i.e.*, obtain the values of $(O - E)^2$.
3. Divide the values of $(O - E)^2$ obtained in step (2) by the respective expected frequency and obtain the total $\Sigma[O - E)^2/E]$. This gives the value of χ^2 which can range from zero to infinity. If χ^2 is zero it means that the observed and expected frequencies completely coincide. The greater the discrepancy between the observed and expected frequencies, the greater shall be the value of χ^2.

The calculated value of χ^2 is compared wih the table value of χ^2 for given degree of freedom at a certain specified level of significance. It at the stated level (generally 5% level is selected), the calculated value of χ^2 is more than the table value of χ^2, the difference between theory and observation of considered to be significant, *i.e.*, it could not have arisen due to fluctuation of simple sampling. If, on the other hand, the calculated value of χ^2 is less than the table value, the difference between theory of observation is not considered as significant, *i.e.*, it is regarded as due to fluctuations of simple sampling and hence ignored.

It should be noted that the value of χ^2 is always positive and its upper limit is infinity. Also since χ^2 is derived from observation, it is a statistic and not a parameter (there is no parameter corresponding to it). The χ^2 test is, therefore termed non-parametric. It is one of the great advantage of this test that it involves no assumption about the form of the original distribution from which the observations come.

There is a χ^2 distribution for every number of degree of freedom. The following diagram is constructed to show various χ^2 distribution curves corresponding to the number of degree of freedom 2, 5 and 10. The Y sacle represents the relative height of any point on each curve.

The height, like an ordinate of a normal curve, may be computed by a formula $Y = \frac{1}{[(v/2)-]} 2^{-v/2} (X^2)^{1/2(v-2)} e - \chi^2/2$

The horizontal scale represents the values of χ^2.

Chi-Square Distributions for d.f. 1,3,5 and 10

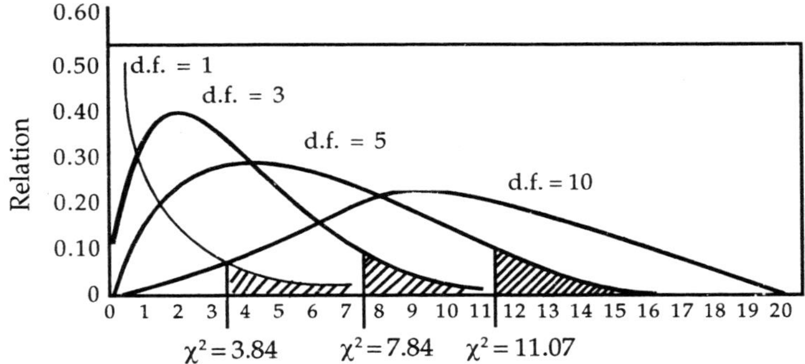

Some important properties of the χ^2 distribution curves are as follow :

1. For n>1, as χ^2 increase, p (χ^2) decreases rapidly and finally tends to zero as χ^2 approaches infinity. Thus,

for n>1, the χ^2 probability curve is positively skewed towards the higher values of χ^2.

2. The mode of each distribution is equal v–2 on the χ^2 scale when v is equal to or larger than 2. *For example,* the maximum height of y for the curve with v = 5 is at the point where $\chi^2 = 3$ (or 5 – 2 = 3).
3. The total area under each curve is 1 or 100%. The median of a χ^2 distribution divides the area into two equal parts, each part being 0.50 or 50%.
4. The curve shows a fairly fast approach to symmetry as the number of degree of freedom increases.
5. The mean of χ^2 distribution is equal to the number of degrees of freedom.
6. The smallest possible value of Chi-square is zero and the largest value is infinite.

χ^2 TEST

The chi-square, denoted by the GreeK letter χ^2, is frequently used in testing of hypothesis concerning the difference between a set of observed frequencies of a sample and a corresponding set of expected or theoetical frequencies. In other words, a test statistics which measures the discrepancy between observed or actual frequencies O_1, O_2,......O_n and their corresponding expected frequencies E_1, E_2,.....E_n is called the chi-square (χ^2) statistics.

We obtain X^2 using the formula :

$$\chi^2 = \sum \frac{(O_i - E_i)^2}{E_i} = \left[\frac{(O_1 - E_1)}{E_1} + \frac{(O_2 - E_2)^2}{E_2} + \ldots\ldots + \frac{(O_n - E_n)^2}{E_n} \right]$$

i.e., we square the difference between the observed and expected frequencies and then divide the result by the expected frequencies, the chi-square (χ^2) statistics is the sum of the quotients of all the cells or categories.

CHARACTERSTICS OF χ^2 -TEST

1. This test is based on frequencies on events as against the Z and the t-tests based on parametres like the mean and standard deviation.
2. This is applied for drawing inferences only and therefore can be used for testing hypothesis and is not useful for estimation as the Z or the t-tests are.
3. Although chi-square distribution is continuous, it is applied to discrete variables whose frequencies can be counted and tabulated with or without grouping.
4. This possesses additive property so that when χ^2 and χ_2^2 are independent and have a chi-square distribution with n_1 and n_2 degrees of freedom χ_1^2 + χ_2^2 will also be distribution as a chi-square distribution with $n_1 + n_2$ degrees of freedom.
5. Whereas some earlier distribution could be used for testing the significance of the difference between single expected and observed proportion or percentage (as in the case of Binomial distribution) this can be used or testing the difference between the entire set or expected and observed frequencies.
6. This distribution is similar to t-distribution where the critical values vary with the degrees of freedom. For every increase in the number of the degrees of freedom there is a new χ^2 distribution.
7. Whereas Z or t distribution cannot be used there are several characteristics involved in this distribution, which can be applied to a complete contingency table with several classes. It is therefore a general-purpose test and is very useful in research work.

Assumptions

1. The application of χ^2 test assume that the observations recorded an collected on a random basis. This is the condition for other sampling test also.

2. The events for which the test is used are mutually exclusive. This condition is the same as for the Binomial distribution.
3. That the outcome of each observation is independent of the previous outcome.
4. The frequency of each cell should not be less that 5. Since the chi-square distribution is a continuous distribution, it cannot maintain its characteristics of continuity if cell frequency is less than 5. The pooling is resorted to when such frequencies are less than 5.
5. The total number of observations should be large, say, more than 50.
6. The data should be expressed in original units for convenience of comparison and not in percentage or ratios.

DEGREES OF FREEDOM (V)

As was true for t-test there is a whole family of chi-square distributions based on the degree of freedom involved. The chi-square also depends on the number of degrees of freedom (v). Now, when the observed frequencies can be listed along one dimension (row or column) there are k – 1 degrees of freedom, where k is the number of categories of obseved frequencies.

But for a contingency tabel with r number of rows and c number of columns the degrees of freedom are :

$$v = (r-1)\ (c-1)$$

Therefore, for a 2×2 table the number of degrees of freedom will be

$$v = (2-1)\ (2-1) = 1 \text{ Only}$$

In case of contingency table with 3 row and 3 columns it will be

$$v = (3-1\ (3-1) = 4$$

Significance of Testing

The χ^2-test is used in the following ways:

1. To indicate the null hypothesis and alternate hypothesis.
2. To list the observed frequencies resulting from a given investigation.
3. To calculate the expected frequencies which would have applied if the investigated data had followed a given theoretical distribution which we assume to apply to the situation in hand.
4. To calculate the difference between the observed frequency and the corresponding expected frequency for each class or group in the series and express the square of the difference as a fraction of the expected frequency concerned.
5. To add together all the fractions obtained from step 4.
6. Ascertain the appropriate χ^2 value from the χ^2 table, which is reproduced in the Appendix at the end of the book. As in the case of t-distribution table, the χ^2 table comprises of columns headed with symbols $\chi_{0.05}$ for 5% level and $\chi_{0.01}$ for the 1% level to denote the relevant significance levels while the rows refer to the number of degrees of freedom. It may be noticed in the tabel that chi-square values increase with increase in the degree of freedom and reduction in the degree of reliance.

   It should be obvious from the above diagram that all χ^2 tests are one-tailed significance test.
7. The result of our χ^2 -test is significant if the figure obtained from step 5 exceeds the appropriate table value of χ^2 for the given degrees of freedom at a certain level of significance, which means that in such a case the null hypothesis is rejected.

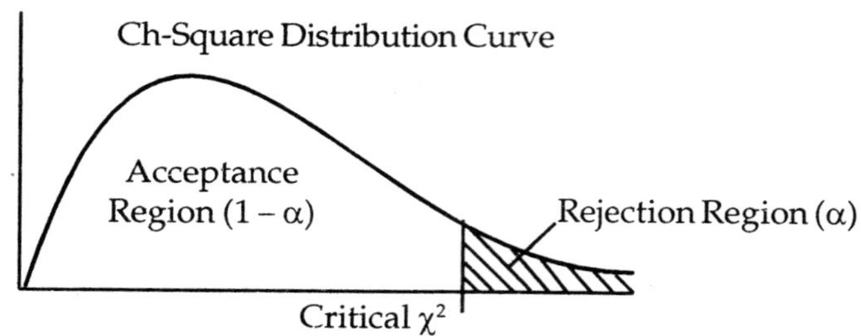

The chi-square test is used broadly for purposes listed below in the chart.

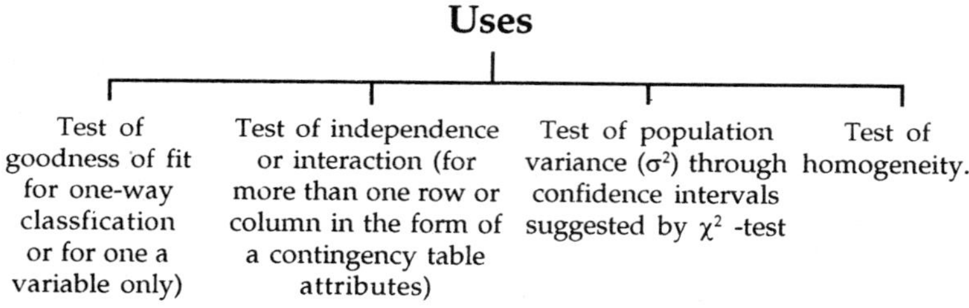

TEST OF GOODNESS OF FIT

Under the test of goodness of fit we try to find out how far observed values of given phenomenon are significantly difference from the expected values. This is done by comparing the desired values of χ^2 from the formula given earlier with the table value of χ^2 for the required degrees of freedom depending on the number of observations and a reliance level of .50 (normally) unless otherwise stated.

In this there is only one variable and therefore only one row or column and the degree of freedom are k–1 only.

The term 'Goodness of Fit' is also used for comparison of observed sample distribution with expected probability distribution such as the Binomial, Poison, Normal, Etc. The chi-square statistic can be used to judge the divergence between the observed and expected frequencies, *i.e.,* the curve of expected frequencies is superimposed on the curve of the observed frequencies and the chi-square statistic determines whether the fit is good or not.

TEST OF INDEPENDENCE

For more than two rows and columns we have a contingency table in which the classification is on the basis of more than two attributes simultaneously rather than only one or two. The observed frequencies are indicated in various cells of the table for respective rows and columns.

Suppose we designate the two attributes by A and B; A has r mutually exclusive and collectively exhaustive categories $A_1, A_2, ... A_r$ while B has categories denoted by $B_1, B_2, ...B_c$. To conducted the test, a random sample of size n drawn from the population is classified simultaneously with expect to these categories and observed frequencies are presented in a cross-classfied contingency table in the following form :

A \ *B*	B_1	B_2 B_i	–	B_c	*Row Totals*
A_1	O_{11}	$O_{12}......O_{1j}$	...	O_{1c}	O_{10}
A_2	O_{21}	$O_{22}......O_{2j}$	...	O_{2c}	O_{20}
:	:	:..........:	:	:	:
A_i	O_{i1}	$O_{i2}......O_{ij}$	...	O_{1c}	O_{i0}
:	:	:......:	:	:	:
A_r	O_{r1}	$O_{r2}......O_{rj}$	...	O_{rc}	O_{r0}
Column Totals	O_{01}	$O_{02}......O_{0j}$	...	O_{0c}	n

In this table

O_{ij} = Frequency of occurrence, r of the class (A_i, B_j) out of n observations

and O_{ij} = Total of ith row, *i.e.*, the frequency of A_i irrespective of B classification.

O_{j0} = Total of ith column, *i.e.*, the frequency of B_j irrespective of classification.

The frequency in these cells are called cell frequencies and the totals of the frequencies in each of the rows and columns are termed marginal frequencies.

The null hypothesis of interest is that A and B classifications are independent, *i.e.*, there is no association or relationship between the two characteristics or attributes, A and B.

Expected cell frequencies are computed according to the rules of probability : "If two events are statistically independent, their joint probability is the product of two marginal probabilities. "Thus, the general formula for obtaining expected cell frequencies is

$$E_{ij} = \frac{O_{io} \times O_{oj}}{N}$$

i.e. Expected (i, j)th cell frequency

$$= \frac{(\text{ith row total}) \times (\text{jth column total})}{\text{Grand Total}}$$

The test statistic compares the expected and observed cell frequenciesm

$$\chi^2 = \sum_{i=j}^{r} \sum_{j=1}^{c} \frac{(O_{ij} - E_{ij})^2}{E_{ij}} \text{ or simply } \sum \frac{(O-E)^2}{E}$$

where k = rs, the number of cells in the contingency table.

The distribution of the statistic follows the chi-square distribution with v = (r–1) (c–1) degrees of freedom. Looking at any row in a contingency table, we note that when (r–1) of the values are determined, the rth value is automatically fixed. Likewise for the columns, for any column, the eth value is fixed once the (c–1) value have been determined. Hence, there are only (r–1) (c–1) values that may be determined freely and therefore (r–1) (c–1) are the degrees of freedom.

As before, in order to test the hypothesis of independence, the calculated value of χ^2 is compared with the table value for given degrees of freedom at a certain level of significance. If the calculated value of χ^2 is greater than the table value, the hypothesis in independence is rejected, otherwise not.

PRECAUTION IN THE USE OF χ^2 -TEST

The following precautions should be taken while using the χ^2 -test.

1. Frequencies are not small. Normally no frequency should be less that 10 but generally χ^2 -test is used if no frequency is less than 5. If the frequency is less than 5 it should be pooled with the neighbouring frequency. Yates Corrections way also be used.

2. Frequency of non-occurrence should never be omitted.

If we know the number of cases which have been cured by 4 different medicines, we should not use the χ^2-test unless we know the numbers not be applied to a frequency distribution of the following type.

Medicine	:	A	B	C	D	Total
Number Cured	:	12	20	15	28	75

Here, we do not know the frequency of non-occurrance or the people who were not cured by these medicines.

3. χ^2-test should not be used if we do not have the original data. *For example,* if we have only proportions, percentages or rate χ^2-test should not be used. We should have actual frequencies.

4. Is repeated measurements are made on the same units χ^2-test should not be used. If we have obtained the marks of 10 students before and after coaching, we should not use χ^2-test to find out the coaching have done any good. In such cases the difference of means should be tested. In case of attributes of opinion of the same set of person is obtained about the quality of 2 commodities, χ^2-test should not be used to find out if their opinion differs about the quality of the two items. The tables which we will get in such case would not be contingency tables as the same person would be counted twice. Thus, the following is not a contingency table and is unsuitable for the calculation of χ^2.

	Very good	*Good*	*Poor*	*Total*
Quality of Item A	100	200	50	350
Quality of item B	200	60	90	350

5. Care should be taken that *(a)* the degrees freedom are correctly found out *(b)* the critical value of χ^2 are correctly used *(c)* the hypothesis is properly set and tested *(d)* the sum of observed and expected frequencies in various sub-totals and in the grand total are the same and *(e)* the expected values have been calculated on a rational basis.

✸✸✸

Index

G

H

I

J

L

M

N

O

P

Q

R

S

T

Other Books on

TEXT BOOKS

1. Philosophical & Sociological Foundations of Education **(New)** 225/-
2. Research Methods in Education **(New)** 225/-
3. Psychology of Learning & Human Development **(New)** 225/-
4. Safety and Disaster Management **(New)** 225/-
5. A New Approach to Teacher Education in the Emerging Indian Society **(New)** 225/-
6. Measurement & Evaluation in Psychology and Education**(New)** 225/-
7. Special Education **(New)** 225/-
8. Principles of Office Management **(New)** 195/-
9. History of Ancient India **(New)** 395/-
10. Methodology of Educational Research **(New)** 225/-
11. Environmental Education **(New)** 195/-
12. Experimental Psychology **(New)** 195/-
13. Teaching of Home Science **(New)** 195/-
14. Select World Constitutions **(New)** 395/-
15. Educational Thought and Practice **(New)** 195/-
16. Guidance and Counselling A Manual **(New)** 175/-
17. School Organization and Administration **(New)** 195/-
18. Developmental Psychology **(New)** 195/-
19. Social Work Theory and Practice **(New)** 225/-
20. Modern Education for New Generation 175/-
21. Advanced Educational Technology 175/-
22. Comparative Education 175/-
23. Introduction to Educational Research 175/-
24. Computer Education 175/-
25. Teaching of Chemistry 175/-
26. Teaching of Physics 175/-
27. Handbook of Journalism & Mass Media 225/-
28. Advanced Educational Psychology 175/-
29. Educational Administration & Origanisation Management 195/-
30. Social Psychology 225/-
31. Teaching of Commerce 175/-
32. Educational Development & Technology 175/-
33. Disaster Management 195/-
34. Information Technology 195/-
35. Human Resource Development 195/-
36. Mass Media Communication Theory & Practice 225/-
37. Adult Education 195/-
38. General Psychology 175/-
39. Distance Education in India 175/-
40. Teacher Education 175/-
41. Educational Philosophy 175/-
42. Science Teaching in Schools 175/-
43. Indian National Congress **(New)** 450/-
44. Indian Polity **(Revised Edition)** 295/-

45. New Comparative Government **(Revised Edition)** 295/-
Advanced Study in the History of Modern India
46. (Volume-1: 1707-1813) 225/-
47. (Volume-2: 1813-1920) 325/-
48. (Volume-3: 1920-1947) 175/-
49. Handbook of Nutrition & Dietetics 250/-
50. Development of Education in India 195/-
51. A Text Book of Environmental Studies 195/-
52. Teaching of History 175/-
53. Administrative Thinkers 195/-
54. Research Methodology 175/-
55. Curriculum Development 195/-
56. Teaching of Science 175/-
57. Teaching of Mathematics 175/-
58. Principles of Educational & Vocational Guidance 195/-
59. Child Psychology 175/-
60. Abnormal Psychology 175/-
61. Indian Education in Emerging Society 195/-
62. Human Resource Management 175/-
63. Higher Education and Global Challenges 175/-
64. Teaching of Geography 175/-
65. Teaching of Social Studies 175/-
66. Teaching of English 175/-
67. Education for All The Indian Saga 175/-
68. Value Education in Global Perspective 195/-
69. Teacher Training 175/-
70. Public Administration 175/-
71. Public Relations & Integrated Communications 195/-
72. Educational Psychology 175/-
73. Introduction to Educational Technology 175/-
74. Textbook of Food and Nutrition 175/-